# THE SWEEP OF PROBABILITY

# THE
# SWEEP OF PROBABILITY

George N. Schlesinger

UNIVERSITY OF NOTRE DAME PRESS
NOTRE DAME                    LONDON

*Library of Congress Cataloging-in-Publication Data*

Schlesinger, George N.
    The sweep of probability / George N. Schlesinger.
        p.   cm.
    Includes bibliographical references and index.
    ISBN 0-268-01738-7
    1. Probabilities.   I. Title.
BC141.S24   1990
160—dc20                                                                  90-70848
                                                                          CIP

# CONTENTS

INTRODUCTION

  1. The Amplitude of Elementary
     Probability Theory      1
  2. The Basic Theorems      2
  3. The Principle of Indifference      5
  4. The Constructive Role of Criticism      15

Part One

I.   CONDITIONAL PROBABILITY AND DEPENDENCE

  1. Statistical Dependence      19
  2. Base Rates      25
  3. Correlations and Indicative Conditionals      29

II.   THE USEFULNESS OF THE RULE OF ELIMINATION

  1. Alternative Ways of Elimination      36
  2. 'Nothing Is Probable Unless Something
     Is Certain'?      39
  3. Concrete Examples Where Probability
     Keeps Eroding      42
  4. The Status of Knowledge Claims in General      44
  5. The Issue of Combined Evidence      46

III.   COMPARING CREDIBILITIES

  1. The Positive Instance Criterion
     of Confirmation      51
  2. The Special Consequence Condition      55

3. Comparing Posterior to Prior Credibility 58
4. Which of the Two Criteria of Confirmation
Is Preferable? 59
5. Comparing the Confirmation of Different
Hypotheses 63
6. Justified Belief 65
7. A Rational Justification of Total Skepticism 67

IV. PROBABILITY AND INDUCTION

1. Bayes's Theorem and Induction 73
2. Proving the Impossibility of Inductive
Probability 76
3. Using the Elementary Theorems of Probability
in Justifying Induction 79
4. Establishing Prior Probabilities by Analogical
Arguments 82
5. Laplace's Rule of Succession 84
6. The "New" Problem of Induction 87

Part Two

V. EXTRAORDINARY PHENOMENA AND CONFIRMATION

1. The Credibility of Extraordinary Stories 95
2. Is the "Extraordinary" What Is More Probable
on an Alternative Hypothesis? 99
3. Improbable Events and Improbable Kinds
of Events 103
4. Some Notable Scientific Examples 104
5. What, in General, Calls for a Scientific
Explanation? 109
6. Revising Nicod's Criteria 111
7. The Bayesian Approach 113

VI. FORESIGHT AND HINDSIGHT

1. Two Kinds of Evidence 117
2. Attempts to Prove that Accommodation and
Prediction Have Precisely the Same Effect 119

3. An Attempt to Demonstrate the Utter
   Worthlessness of Accommodation    123
4. The Irrelevance of the Time at Which a
   Hypothesis Is Advanced    125
5. The Importance of Being Fit to Serve as an
   Instrument for Prediction    126
6. The Condition of Sustained Maximum
   Adequacy    127
7. An Illustration from Mathematical Sequences    129
8. Legitimate Hypotheses Are Likely To Be
   Proposed at an Early Stage    132
9. An Attempt To Meet the History of Science
   Halfway    133
10. What Exactly Is an Ad Hoc Hypothesis?    136
11. Right Hypotheses Based on Wrong
    Assumptions    140

VII. COMBINED EVIDENCE

1. Hypotheses That Do Not Imply Their
   Evidence    145
2. The Case of the Timid Witness    148
3. Diseases and Their Origin    149
4. The Case of the Witness Who Has a Grudge
   Against the Defendant    152
5. An Informal Discussion of the Relationship
   Between One of the Premises and Our
   Conclusion    154
6. The Formal Derivation of the Conclusion    155
7. The Case of the Bribed Witness    158
8. Diagnostic Evidence That Reinforce Each
   Other    159

VIII. RELEVANCE

1. Prospective Evidence    163
2. The Traditional Definition of the Relevance
   of Prospective Evidence    164
3. A New Definition    166
4. An Amended New Definition    170

5. The Need for Independent Ways of Investigating the Evidence and the Hypothesis     171
6. The Different Senses of Relevance     173
7. Probablistic Explanatory Relevance     175
8. Catchall Explanations     179

IX.   INDIFFERENCE

1. Interpretation and Evaluation     181
2. Does the Principle Lead to the Wrong Results?     188
3. An Objection from Bernoulli's Theorem     191
4. The Principle of Indifference and Empiricism     195
5. A Fundamental Principle of Inductive Reasoning     199

X.   DEONTIC LOGIC

1. The Furthermost Reach of Elementary Probability     203
2. The Bridge Between the Logic of Probabilistically Justified Belief and That of Moral Obligations     206
3. The Application of Criterion $(\delta)$     207
4. Disjunctive Obligations     212
5. Disjunctive Permissions     214

XI.   PROBABILITY AND METAPHYSICS

1. Skepticism about the External World     217
2. The Argument from Design     220
3. The Anthropic Principle     222

Index     227

# INTRODUCTION

## 1. The Amplitude of Elementary
## Probability Theory

In some areas of thought an enormous amount of work is required to produce relatively small results. Topology provides a number of startling examples of theorems that appear rather obvious yet are based on exceedingly complex proofs or have altogether defied all attempts to prove them. The famous four-color problem proposed by Moebius in the beginning of the nineteenth century is a case in point. If a country is subdivided into states and districts of any number and shape, four different colors seem always sufficient to color a map of this country in a way that no two states with a common boundary have the same color. Although everyone who has tried diagramming even the most intricate kinds of subdivision has convinced himself that four colors will always suffice, a successful proof that this must be so was not provided until recently, a proof that took over 150 pages to expound.

There are however some rather rare instances, such as elementary probability theory, where to our gratification we find the opposite to be true. The present subject belongs to one of those rare intellectual ventures where the returns are disproportionately high to the initial investment; where so surprisingly much can be done with so little.

Not many writings in the philosophy of science conform to Dr. Johnson's noble sentiment that "The only end of writing is to enable the reader better to enjoy life, or better to endure it." Still, this work may well prove that elementary probability reasoning is among the few fields in the domain of mathematics to yield a goodly amount of satisfaction at the cost of a minimum degree of endurance.

While the book does not of course exhaust all the many philosophical applications of rudimentary probability theory, it does, I trust, provide an indication of its wide range and multifarious relevance.

In Part One the emphasis is on illustrating the uses of a few elementary theorems such as Bayes's Theorem and the Rule of Elimination. In Part Two, discussions of philosophical ideas in which such theorems play a considerable role predominate. Chapters 5, 6, and 9 might strike the reader as somewhat unusual since in the first two of these chapters a single distinction—namely, the distinction between what is merely improbable and what is also extraordinary and thus astonishing—and in the last, a single comparison—namely, the comparison of an aspect of the logic of (highly probable and thus) justified belief to an aspect of deontic logic—are claimed to accomplish a remarkably great amount of work. Such claims often have the tendency to generate the suspicion that they are too extravagant to be true. A balancing factor should be the considerable appeal to common sense which nearly all the results asserted to follow from these meager premises make.

This work is mainly devoted to the study of the wide-ranging relevance of simple probabilistic reasoning and thus little is going to be said about the various interpretations of probability on which philosophers usually focus most of their attention.

One exception is the treatment of the classical interpretation according to which probability means the ratio between the number of favorable events to the total number of equipossible events, an interpretation that has in the past been subjected to a great amount of criticism and has lately found virtually no supporters. While I do not wish to claim it to be *the* correct interpretation, I shall attempt to show that most of the major attacks on it are unjust and many stem from a basic misunderstanding of what the classical theory of probability is about.

Many a reader likes to roam freely and does not wish the author dictating to him what topics to read about and in what order to read about them. Anyone who wishes to take a random walk among the pages of this book will be able to do so; he may perhaps fail to see how some major themes are developed over successive chapters, but is not likely thereby to create for himself any difficulties in following the individual arguments.

## 2. The Basic Theorems

As indicated earlier a tiny amount of mathematical formalism will take us a very long way in probability. Technical material that can be mastered in a matter of minutes puts at our disposal a machinery with which to solve myriad practical problems as well as to tackle a vast variety of philosophically significant issues. I propose to begin by developing the meager formalism beyond which nothing is required for the reader to be able to follow fully every argument, even though none of the chapters repeat merely what is familiar and can be found elsewhere. The primary objective in this section is not rigor but ease of presentation.

In Figure 1 we see a board divided into six congruent rectangles. Two of these are $A$-rectangles and four $B$-rectangles. One of these overlaps, thus there is one $AB$-rectangle. Suppose a dart is thrown blindly at the board, so that it is equally likely to hit any point on it. What is the probability that it if hits the board it hits an $A$-square? It appears clear to our intuitions that since 1/3 of the area of the board is covered by $A$-squares, the probability is 1/3. On the other hand, in view of the fact that four among the board's six squares are $B$-squares, if it is given that the dart lands somewhere on the board, we should want to assign a probability of 2/3 to its landing on a $B$-square. Thus if

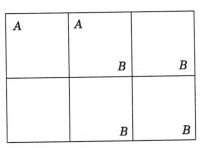

Figure 1

$r =$ The dart hits the board,
$a =$ The dart hits an $A$-square,
$b =$ The dart hits an $B$-square,

then $P(a/r) = 1/3$ (i.e., the probability of $a$, *given* that $r$, equals 1/3) and $P(b/r) = 2/3$. (Note that the /-sign stands for division when inserted between numbers, but when separating two sentences such as $b$ and $r$ it denotes 'given that'.)

Suppose it is known that the dart landed on a $B$-square; what is the probability that it also landed on an $A$-square? Since one quarter of the $B$-area is also and $A$-area, we should say that $P(a/r \& b) = P(a/b) = 1/4$. By examining Figure 1, we can easily check that $P(b/a) = 1/2$, while $P(a \& b/r) = 1/6$. Figure 1 is also useful for illustrating what is called the Conjunctive Axiom:

$$P(a \& b/r) = P(a/r) \cdot P(b/a \& r) = P(b/r) \cdot P(a/b \& r)$$
$$1/6 \quad = \quad 1/3 \times 1/2 \quad = \quad 2/3 \times 1/4.$$

To spell out the first equation: *given* $r$, the probability of both $a$ and $b$ being true is the prior probability of $a$ multiplied by the probability of $b$ on the assumption that $a$ is true. The second equation follows from interchanging $a$ and $b$. Dividing both sides of the second equation by $P(b/a \& r)$ we obtain an expression that is perhaps used more often than any other and is called Bayes's Theorem:

$$P(b/a \,\&\, r) = \frac{P(b/r) \cdot P(a/b \,\&\, r)}{P(a \,\&\, r)}.$$

A simpler representation is possible on assuming the truth of $r$ throughout:

$$P(b/a) = \frac{P(b) \cdot P(a/b)}{P(a)}.$$

Another axiom is the Disjunctive Axiom:

$$P(a \lor b) = P(a) + P(b) - P(a \,\&\, b)$$

('$\lor$' is the sign for disjunction). If we look once more at Figure 1 we see that what we are after is the sum of the areas of the $A$-squares and the $B$-squares, divided by the area of the whole board. In order to obtain this we have to subtract the area where $a$ and $b$ overlap since otherwise we would count those squares twice.

When we are confronted with two incompatible statements $x$ and $y$ (that is, when $x$ and $y$ cannot be true together), and thus where $x \,\&\, y$ is definitely false, $P(x \,\&\, y) = 0$, and the Disjunctive Axiom abbreviates to:

$$P(x \lor y) = P(x) + P(y).$$

It is a basic law of logic, called the Law of Excluded Middle, that every proposition is either true or false. That is, regardless what the proposition $x$ may be, it is absolutely certain that either $x$ or $\sim x$ holds, that is, $P(x \lor \sim x/k) = 1$. Since $x$ and $\sim x$ are clearly incompatible, the Disjunctive Axiom gives us:

$$P(x \lor \sim x/k) = P(x/k) + P(\sim x/k)$$

and therefore,

$$P(x/k) + P(\sim x/k) = 1.$$

Finally, we derive another useful expression called the Rule of Elimination. As we know, $a$ is logically equivalent to $(a \,\&\, b \lor a \,\&\, \sim b)$. (The $A$-squares are made up of $A \,\&\, B$-squares, plus $A \,\&\, \sim B$-squares.) Thus the Rule of Elimination is simply:

$$P(a) = P(a \,\&\, b) + P(a \,\&\, \sim b)$$

i.e.,

$$P(a) = P(b) \cdot P(a/b) + P(\sim b \cdot P(a/\sim b) \dots\dots\dots\dots\dots\text{(RE)}$$

(RE) is useful whenever the value of $P(a)$ is not directly available; in such cases we may eliminate $P(a)$ by replacing it by the right hand side of (RE). Often (RE) is employed in combination with Bayes's Theorem. Thus instead of

$$\Pr(b/a) = \frac{P(b) \cdot P(a/b)}{P(a)}$$

we write

$$P(b/a) = \frac{P(b) \cdot P(a/b)}{P(b) \cdot P(a/b) + P(\sim b) \cdot P(a/\sim b)}.$$

### 3. The Principle of Indifference

œ

It is essential to realize that none of the theorems we have considered, nor indeed any theorem that may be derived from them, can do more than yield new expressions by applying them to expressions we already have. Thus these theorems are of no use unless there exists some method for discovering the values of certain basic probabilities from which new ones may be generated with the help of the theorems listed in the previous section. In this connection a certain principle, (usually associated with the name of Laplace and which James Bernoulli called the Principle of Non-Sufficient Reason, but is better known by the name Keynes gave it), the Principle of Indifference, has played a central role. Keynes has described the principle in the following way:

> if there is no *known* reason for predicating of our subject one rather than another of several alternatives, then "relatively to such knowledge the assertion of each of those alternatives have an equal probability."[1]

This is a highly controversial principle. On the one hand, there are those who have claimed that the Principle of Indifference is in constant use and is the very cornerstone of the entire theory of probability, without which not a single result could be established. On the other hand, a far greater number of contemporary philosophers have expressed the opinion that it is an a priori principle, whose employment is contrary to the tenets of empiricism. C. I. Lewis, for example, has gone as far as to denounce it as "that bete noire of clear thinking," and more recently H. Kyburg

---

[1] J. M. Keynes, *A Treatise on Probability* (London, 1921), p. 420.

has called it "the most notorious principle in the whole history of probability."

Later in the book a whole chapter is going to be devoted to this vital and widely misunderstood principle. In these introductory remarks I merely wish to draw attention to certain precautions that are necessary in handling this principle which is too easily misapplied.

*Example I*

Suppose we have twenty marbles entirely indistiguishable from one another except with respect to their color: six are red and twelve are green. We have also two perfectly similar urns, $a$ and $b$ : $a$ contains two of the red and ten of the green marbles, and $b$ contains four of the red and two of the green marbles. We pick a marble at random from one of the urns, having no clue whether it is $a$ or $b$. What is the probability that its color is red? Let

> $A =$ The marble was drawn from urn $a$;
> $\sim A =$ The marble was drawn from urn $b$;
> $R =$ The marble is red.

Substituting into equation (RE):

$$P(R) = P(A) \cdot P(R/A) + P(\sim A) \cdot P(R/\sim A)$$
$$= 1/2 \times 1/6 + 1/2 \times 2/3$$
$$= 1/12 + 4/12 = 5/12.$$

Some might find this result puzzling. The marbles have been said to be indistinguishable and therefore if the Principle of Indifference were always applicable, then each marble should have precisely the same chance of being selected. There are only six red marbles whereas there are precisely twice as many green marbles. Surely then the probability of drawing a red marble should be $4/12$ only and not $5/12$?

On a closer look, however, we should realize that it is not really true that there is no significant difference between the red and the green marbles. They may all be identical with respect to weight, smoothness, size, and shape, yet they are not symmetrically arranged between the urns (which they would be if each urn contained three red and six green marbles). On the stipulation that each urn is equally likely to be chosen the specific distribution of the marbles offers the red ones a higher chance to be selected than they would otherwise have.

Let me cite briefly a more conspicuous example, in the context of which I do not believe anyone for a moment would fail to see that the complete identity of all the physical properties discernible upon handling the marbles exemplifying them does not make them indifferent with respect to their chances of being picked. Suppose all the red marbles and no green ones are in $A$, and all the green marbles and no red ones are in $B$. Obviously in this case we do not need to know at all the number of either kind of marbles; whether there are ten times more or ten times less red than green marbles makes absolutely no difference. As long as we are given that neither urn is more likely to be selected than the other, the Principle of Indifference instructs us to ascribe equal probability to a red or to a green marble being selected.

*Example II*

The following interesting problem was presented almost a hundred years ago by F. Galton who published it in *Nature*, (1894). I do not believe it has yet lost its instructiveness. Galton raises the question: If three coins are tossed, what is the probability that they all come down alike, i.e., all three are either heads or tails? There is a fairly persuasive argument to show that the probability is $1/2$. It is unquestionably true that it is not possible for three coins, which have two sides only, to all come down differently. Thus we are absolutely certain that two of the coins are either both heads (HH), or both tails (TT). In the first case all we need is that the third throw be H, the probability of which is $1/2$, and in the second case that the third throw be T, which is also $1/2$. In either case the probability that all three come alike is $1/2$.

This result, however, cannot be correct. Clearly, when we are tossing two coins only, then since there are four equiprobable outcomes, i.e., HH, HT, TH, TT, the probability that they both come down on the same side is no more than $1/2$. As it is not a certainty that the third coin should then also come down on the same side, the probability in the case of three coins must be less than $1/2$. Where then did the first argument go wrong?

The answer is: through the misapplication of the Principle of Indifference. We have erroneously assumed that given that two of the coins have come down, say HH, the remaining coin is as likely to show heads as tails. This assumption must clearly be distinguished from the correct assumption that the throws of each fair coin should be treated alike. Thus had we been confronted by the question, "given that throw #1 and #2 were heads what is the probability that #3 is also?" the answer would of course have been $1/2$. But the question relevant to our topic was: Given a set of three throws and that two of its members were heads, what is the probability that the remaining throw (which may of course chronologically be the first, second, or the last throw) is also heads? There are four equiprobable sets of three throws in which at least two members are heads: HHH, HHT, HTH, THH. Only the first of these sets contains no T, and in only one of these sets is the remaining (third) throw also heads. Hence given that we have a set with at least two heads, it is less likely for the last member to be heads as well; the probability is only $1/4$. The same goes for the probability of a set with three tails.

*Example III*

Nicholas Falleta discusses the story of three prisoners sharing the same cell who are condemned to die the next day.[2] Early morning on the fateful day their guard informs them that one of them has been pardoned, but the other two cases are closed. The guard explains to the curious prisoners that he has been forbidden to tell any of them their fate. Given that all three have committed the same crime, come from the same background, are of the same age, etc., prisoner $A$ quickly concludes with the aid of the Principle of Indifference that there is a probability of $1/3$ that he is the one who has been pardoned. Soon afterwards he has a chance to see the guard in private and points out to him that it is already obvious to all that of $B$ and $C$ at least one is going to die, so if the guard told him in strict confidence which one has definitely not been pardoned (without implying that the other one is or is not going to die), he would be violating no regulation. The guard finds the suggestion reasonable and informs $A$ "Prisoner $B$ is sure to die." Falleta concludes:

> Prisoner $A$ reasoned that since he was not certain that $C$ would die, then his chances for survival had improved from $1/3$ to $1/2$, and indeed, they had. (p. 121)

One is bound to feel uncomfortable with Falleta's conclusion. What made $A$'s chances for survival rise? Of course, as we have pointed out earlier, probabilities change with changing information and $A$ has received information concerning one of the prisoners. But is this

---

[2] Nicholas Falleta, *The Paradoxicon* (Garden City, N.Y.: 1983).

information relevant to the probability that $A$ has been pardoned? Suppose, for example, that $A$ knows his cellmates by their numbers only, whereas the guard mentions the actual name of $B$, and $A$ does not know the number that name corresponds to. In this case he was given virtually no substantial information; would his chances still rise from 1/3 to 1/2? Surely if the answer is yes, then $A$ should be able to manage without the guard's help: let him say to himself "I shall call the prisoner who is definitely going to die Tom, and the other Dick. Thus the one who has been pardoned is either Dick or me. Consequently my chances for survival are 50 percent."

The correct interpretation of this puzzle is that in none of the cases mentioned do $A$'s chances for survival increase at all. Once more, the Principle of Indifference was wrongly applied. Before $A$ had his private conversation with the guard, we could think of no reason to make a distinction among the three prisoners, and therefore $A$ was right in concluding that his chances for having received the pardon were 1/3. After the guard's disclosure it is a mistake to continue treating $A$ and $C$ as interchangeable. Now there is sufficient reason to ascribe higher probability to $C$ having been singled out for reprieve rather than $A$. After all it is significant that the guard did not mention $C$ as one of the doomed. There may of course be two different explanations for this: (i) He could not mention $C$, since he is the one to be released, or (ii) neither $B$ nor $C$ have been pardoned, and the guard could only name one of them and he just happened to pick $B$.

Explanation (i) is superior to (ii), for (i) implies, while (ii) does not, that the guard says what he did in fact say. On the other hand, the fact that the guard did not mention $A$ carries no positive implications whatever about his fate, as it was agreed that nothing was going to be said about him. Thus $A$'s chances have not been affected; they remain 1/3. $C$'s chances have risen to 2/3. Furthermore, the very fact that initially we applied the Principle of Indifference to the three prisoners' prior chances for reprieve prevents us from doing so after the guard has spoken. For let

$c = C$ has been pardoned,
$g = $ the guard says $B$ has not been pardoned.

Then by Bayes's Theorem

$$P(c/g) = \frac{P(g/c) \cdot P(c)}{P(g)}.$$

The first factor in the numerator, $P(g/c)$, equals 1, for if $c$ is true, the guard has no choice but to name $B$. The initial probability of $c$ (on the basis of the Principle of Indifference) is $1/3$. The initial probability of $g$ is $1/2$, since if the guard agrees to name one of $B$ or $C$ he is as likely to name the one as the other. Thus $P(c/g) = 2/3$.

"Better is the sight of eyes than the wandering of thoughts," so let us demonstrate the matter visually. In Figure 2 $A$-squares, $B$-squares, and $C$-squares each take up one third of the whole area. One out of the two $A$-squares is also a $G$-square, since if $a$ has been pardoned the probability of the guard naming $c$ is $1/2$. Neither of the $B$-squares is marked $G$, since if $B$ has been pardoned then, of course, the guard will not name

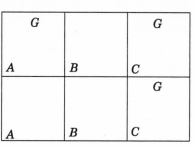

Figure 2

him as one of the unreprieved. Each of the $C$-squares is also a $G$-square, since if it were given that $C$ has been pardoned then the guard cannot but mention $B$ as one of the prisoners who has failed to have been pardoned. The figure thus contains three $G$-squares out of which two are also $C$-squares, and that illustrates the result derived earlier, namely that $P(c/g) = 2/3$.

Thus if the instructions to the guard were to say nothing to $A$ which might affect the assessment of his own chances for survival, the former would act in complete compliance with those instructions if in answering $A$'s inquiry he gave either the name of $C$ or of $B$. The situation would however be altered if $A$ posed his question somewhat differently and asked "name one among the three of us who has received no pardon." In this case, if the guard in his reply named $B$ the Principle of Indifference would continue to apply to $A$ and $C$, and the chances of both would have been equally boosted (to $1/2$) by the guard who might have named either of them instead, and did not. The guard would therefore disobey his instructions if he agreed to reply to $A$'s question. He would also be violating the rules if $A$'s question was "has $B$ been pardoned?" and he replied "no." Now, of course, the form in which the question was put gave him the chance neither for mentioning $A$ nor $C$, still he raised the probability of pardon for each of them simply through eliminating $B$'s chances completely. After the guard has spoken, the only question that remains is whether it is $A$ or $C$ who is to go free, and on the basis of the Principle of Indifference we ascribe $1/2$ to the probability of each.

*Example IV*

In chapter 4 of the book we have referred to earlier, Keynes considers the situation of a standard die that has never been tossed before. Keynes suggests that we could legitimately argue that there is no known reason for expecting it to land with face 6 up rather than 5, 4, etc., and therefore, according to our principle we should assign the same probability to each face. But then we could just as well argue that there is no known reason for expecting a 6 rather than a non-6, and hence consider those exclusive and exhaustive alternatives as equiprobable. Thus we end up with a contradiction; first we assign $1/6$, then we assign $1/2$ to the probability of the same event.

It is not too hard to see how a follower of Laplace would solve this difficulty. The principle, as formulated by Keynes himself, bids us to treat alternatives as equiprobable as long as we know of no reason to distinguish among them. Now it should be hard to think of a more compelling reason than the necessity for avoiding making meaningless probability ascriptions for not regarding 6 and non-6 as equiprobable! Surely, anyone who would regard 6 and non-6 as equiprobable would also have to regard 5 and non-5 as equiprobable, and so on. This would lead him to assign a probability $1/2$ to each one of the six faces and to conclude that the probability that it will land with one of its sides facing upward is the sum of these, i.e. 3, a conclusion devoid of meaning. There is thus clear enough indication what we have to do: we have to assign a probability of $1/6$ to each side.

Suppose, however, that someone were to object in the following manner. Surely, it was wrong to declare each side to be like every other side; face $i$ is different from face $j$ (e.g., it has a different number of dots printed on it). Would a Laplacian reply that such differences were irrelevant for the purposes of determining the chances of each face? That would only reveal the hopelessness of his position; either he has no means for determining what sorts of differences are, and what sorts of differences are not relevant, or if he should claim to have any, then he would have to admit that ultimately his ascription of equal probabilities is grounded in something else than the Principle of Indifference.

I believe that the correct answer would be: If we are to ascribe different probabilities to the different faces then we have nothing to go by as to how much the difference should be. Furthermore, are we to ascribe a higher probability to face $i$ or to face $j$? Any particular answer to such a question would, in the context of total lack of evidence to support it, inevitably be arbitrary. Thus a Laplacian may say that it is in order to avoid unsupported assumptions he refuses to discriminate among the various sides and regards them as equiprobable.

The last point is a most important one. As we shall see in the chapter devoted to the topic, during the present century a great variety of objections have been raised against the Principle of Indifference. It is fair to say that the weightiest reason why so many have thought the principle to be unacceptable is because it seemed to violate the most basic tenet of empiricism, namely that all knowledge about the world is a posteriori, since experience, rather than reason, is the source of whatever we may know about reality. But if we employ the Principle of Indifference, then

> in order to get numerical probabilities, we have to be able to judge that a certain number of cases are equally probable and to be able to make this judgement we need a certain *a priori* principle.[3]

Prior to experience we are ignorant about all matters of fact. We should not be permitted to make positive use of our lack of knowledge and base on it appraisals of the chances of actual events. Thus Reichenbach expresses his objection to the employment of what he calls the Principle of No Reason to the Contrary as it is used to establish that the probability of a standard die to be tossed for the first time to land on any given side is $1/6$:

> Why should the occurrence of physical events follow the directive of human ignorance? Perhaps we have no reason to prefer one face of a die to the other; but then we have no reason either to assume that the faces are equiprobable. To transform the absence of reason into a positive reason represents a feat of oratorial act that is worthy of an attorney for the defense but is not permissible in the court of logic.[4]

Similar sentiments have also been voiced by W. Kneale:

> Instead of knowledge of absence, Laplace and those who agree with him accept the absence of knowledge as a sufficient ground for judgement of probability.[5]

---

[3] D. A. Gillies, *An Objective Theory of Probability* (London, 1973), p. 11.
[4] H. Reichenbach, *Theory of Probability* (Berkeley, 1949), p. 354.
[5] W. Kneale, *Probability and Induction* (Oxford, 1940), p. 173.

However, as I have indicated, a Laplacian would claim that quite on the contrary, he adopts his principle because of his reluctance to make any a priori conjectures. Of course, to suspend judgment and assign no values to the probability of any event would be the perfect way of avoiding postulating any hypotheses whatever. Barring that, the next best thing is surely to keep our unsupported assumptions at a minimum. Thus he would readily concede to Reichenbach that for all we know the faces might not have the same probability. Should we therefore assign a higher or lower probability to one of the sides? Anxious to avoid introducing wantonly any particular distinction for the existence of which there is no evidence, the Laplacian refrains from arbitrarily discriminating among the seemingly interchangeable alternatives.

*Example V*

The following is a rather little known example, though it illustrates effectively a variety of pitfalls one must try to avoid when applying the Principle of Indifference. Fred and Herb are engaged in a disk-throwing competition to see who can throw a certain weight the longest distance. Past experience has shown that the two athletes are precisely of the same skill. On this particular occasion Fred is given two chances by throwing two disks successively while Herb throws once only. What is the probability of Fred winning?

One reasonable-looking approach goes like this: Let,

$F_1 = $ Fred's first disk,
$F_2 = $ Fred's second disk,
$H = $ Herb's disk.

Given that the two players are equally skillful, "$F_1$ is ahead of $H$" should be ascribed the same probability as "$F_1$ is behind $H$," that is each has a probability of $1/2$. Similarly "$F_2$ is ahead of $H$" should be as probable as "$F_2$ is behind $H$." Thus we have

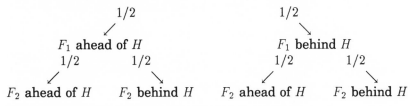

Of these four equipossible combinations only the last one—where both $F_1$ and $F_2$ are behind $H$—is a win for Herb. Hence the probability of Fred winning is $3/4$.

On the other hand, one might argue that since each disk is thrown by equally skillful athletes each disk has an equal chance of traveling the greatest distance. There is therefore a probability of $1/3$ that a given disk is going to be ahead of the other two. But the player whose disk lands ahead of the other two—regardless of the relative positions of those other two—is the winner. Hence the probability of Fred winning is $2/3$.

Since at most only one of these results may be correct, some error was made in at least one of these arguments. It may be claimed that in the first argument the Principle of Indifference was not properly applied. The situation in which $H$ occupies second place has been counted as two equipossible alternatives, namely, once as "$F_1$ ahead of $H - F_2$ behind $H$" and then as "$F_1$ behind $H - F_2$ ahead of $H$." To achieve symmetry it would have been necessary to have four—and not merely two—additional arrangements for the two different ways in which $F_1$ may occupy second place: the one when preceded by $H$ and the other when followed by $H$, and similarly for $F_2$. In this way we would have six equiprobable alternatives, four of which are favorable to Fred. Hence the probability that he is going to win is $2/3$ as shown by the second argument.

Yet, even this is not the whole story. Suppose Fred and Herb have in the past competed against one another 1,000 times (each throwing a single disk), each winning exactly 500 times. Surely this would provide a very solid factual basis for regarding them as equally skilled players. This is, however, compatible with the two being very different *sorts* of players. For example, Herb could be a completely steady pitcher whose throw hardly varies from one time to another, whereas Fred changes from day to day: when he shoots well he shoots very well, but when not he performs rather badly. Thus let us suppose that in all the thousand games they have had so far Herb threw his disk more or less the distance an average athlete would, whereas Fred on 500 occasions did better than the average and won, while on the other 500 occasions did worse than the average and lost. Now if Fred and Herb have been established as two players of equal skill in the manner just described, then the probability that Fred will win the next, special game, where he gets two disks and Herb gets only one, turns out to $3/4$. We are driven to this conclusion because from all the past evidence we may infer that once again Herb will fling the disk an average distance. Fred on the other hand may do (with equal probability) one of four things: he may do extremely well with both disks; extremely badly with both; extremely well with the first and poorly with the second or the other way around. Only in one of these cases would he lose, namely, if he performed poorly with both disks; the three other alternatives represent wins for him.

Consider, however, yet another situation where the two players are judged to be of equal skill but it is Fred whose pitch hardly varies from occasion to occasion whereas Herb's pitch varies as Fred's did, and once more it is on record that out of 1000 games they have played in the past each won 500 times. Reason would bid us in this case to ascribe a probability of $1/2$ to Fred winning in the next special game where he has two disks: he is bound to throw both disks an average distance, while the probability of Herb doing exceptionally well (and win) or exceptionally badly (and lose) is $1/2$.

The conclusion seems to be that players who are correctly judged to be of equal skill are not necessarily interchangeable; such a judgment may be arrived at in a variety of manners. In a problem like ours it is absolutely essential that it be specified in what way the equal skillfulness of the players has been established before we can know which alternatives to treat as equiprobable.

## 4. The Constructive Role of Criticism

The way to wisdom is often the *via negativa*; much of learning is done through unlearning what is wrong. Reviewing and correcting faulty arguments frequently opens the eye, for the flash produced by exploding misconceptions may illuminate the path to understanding.

Graves and Hodge in their classic work on English usage, which cites passages from a great variety of authors to illustrate errors in clear statement and other shortcomings of prose style, make the following comment:

> We have no intention of pillorying the writers whom we include in our list, or of suggesting that the passages chosen are characteristic of their work.[6]

Similarly, the dozens of excerpts from the works of a variety of writers that they claim to contain erroneous arguments are meant to be taken in a constructive spirit, as instructive illustrations. That mistakes proliferate in this domain of reasoning should be no surprise;

---

[6] R. Graves and A. Hodge, *The Reader Over Your Shoulder* (New York: 1971), p. 176.

probability is a notoriously slippery subject. Recently, two leading statisticians had this to say:

> Both of the present commentators make a living by teaching probability and statistics. Over and over again we see students and colleagues (and ourselves) making certain kinds of mistakes. Even the same mistakes may be repeated by the same person many times.[7]

Some years earlier C. S. Peirce, referring to the theory of probability, remarked "This branch of mathematics is the only one, I believe, in which good writers frequently get results entirely erroneous." And the better the writer the more one learns from his mistakes. Surely there is truth in William Blake's assertion "The errors of a wise man make your rule/ Rather than the perfections of a fool."

I should like to emphasize, however, that the commonly acknowledged pitfalls in this domain of reasoning are definitely not due to the complexity of the arguments involved, which is indicated before will, on the contrary, appear relatively elementary. The susceptibility to error is caused by allowing oneself to be guided too much by intuition and common sense. In probabilistic reasoning, more often than elsewhere, things are not what they seem, and untutored innate intelligence may frequently prove an unreliable guide.

---

[7] P. Diaconis and D. Freedman, "The Persistence of Cognitive Illusions," *Behavioral and Brain Sciences* (1981): 334.

# PART ONE

# I

# CONDITIONAL PROBABILITY AND DEPENDENCE

## 1. Statistical Dependence

Two events $A$ and $B$ are called *statistically independent* when knowing that $A$ is true has no effect on the probability of $B$, and vice versa. Thus $A$ is independent of $B$ in case the conditional probability of $A$ given that $B$ equals the unconditional probability of $A$, i.e., if

(i) $P(A/B) = P(A)$.

Many writers on probability have pointed out that a preferable formal definition of independence is to say that $A$ and $B$ are independent if and only if

(ii) $P(A \& B) = P(A) \cdot (B)$

since $P(A/B)$ has no meaning when the probability of $B$ is zero.

We shall now look at examples illustrating some of the typical pitfalls lying in wait for those who are lured into using unconditional probabilities when it is inappropriate to do so.

*Example I*

A tanker is sent from Japan to bring back oil from the troubled waters of the Persian Gulf (in 1986). Any tanker, whether empty or loaded, whether on its way into the gulf or out of the gulf, has a $1/3$ chance of being sunk as it passes through the Straits of Hormuz. What is the probability that the ship will fail to return to Japan?

We may certainly assume that the tanker cannot be sunk on its way back if it has been sunk on its way there, and also that if it sinks on the return journey it could not have sunk on its outward journey. Consequently, if

$O =$ The tanker is sunk on its outward journey
$R =$ The tanker is sunk on its return journey,

19

then $O$ and $R$ are incompatible and thus the abbreviated version of the Disjunctive Axiom seems to apply, i.e.,

$$P(O \vee R) = P(O) + P(R) = 2/3.$$

To many an inexperienced person this result has seemed reasonable until they were presented with a question such as: What if the probability of being sunk on each occasion is $2/3$? Surely, the answer could not be that the total probability of failing to return to Japan is $4/3$!

The error was that we denoted the information that there is a probability of $1/3$ for the tanker to be hit and sink while passing through the straits on its return journey as $P(R) = 1/3$. What in fact is to be seen as given to us as amounting to $1/3$ is, of course, $P(R/-O)$, which means that *given* that the tanker was not sunk on its journey into the gulf and has a chance to embark on a return journey, the probability of then being destroyed is $1/3$.

To obtain the correct answer therefore we should rephrase $R$ slightly: $R^* =$ The tanker fails to get through the Straits of Hormuz on its return journey (either because it never could *begin* its return journey or because it was sunk on its way home), and use the Rule of Elimination:

$$P(R^*) = P(O) \cdot P(R^*/O) + P(-O) \cdot P(R^*/-O)$$
$$= P(O) + P(-O) \cdot P(R^*/-O). \qquad \text{(since } P(R^*/O) = 1\text{)}$$

For if the tanker is sunk on its first journey it certainly fails to sail through on any other journey. Hence,

$$P(R^*) = 1/3 + 2/3 \times 1/3 = 3/9 + 2/9 = 5/9.$$

Thus $P(R^*)$ is less than $2/3$.

This result is quickly obtained through our square-diagram method. In Figure 3 three of the nine squares are marked $O$, indicating that $1/3$ of the outgoing ships are sunk. Two of the squares left unmarked by $O$ are marked $R$, representing the $1/3$ of those which are hit on their return journey. Thus we see that five of the total nine squares are marked either $O$ or $R$, that is, $5/9$ of the ships participating in such a venture fail to return.

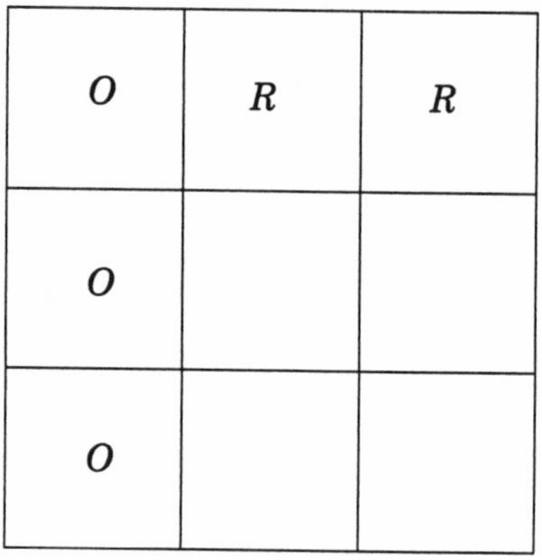

**Figure  3**

*Example II*

Alan and Betty both speak the truth $4/5$ of the time. Thus if

$a = $ Alan is speaking the truth,

and

$b = $ Betty is speaking the truth,

then $P(a) = P(b) = 4/5$. Suppose we are explicitly given that $a$ and $b$ are statistically independent of one another. What is the probability that they are telling the truth when they make the same assertion (the prior probability of which is $1/2$)?

In my experience, many students trying to tackle this question simply multiply $P(a)$ by $P(b)$, since we were assured of the independence of one from the other. But then of course it strikes them as odd that when only one of Alan and Betty affirm a given proposition its credibility is $4/5$, but when both of them do so it loses credibility and its probability is only $16/25$! In a later chapter we shall see that this may actually happen under certain circumstances, but not when $a$ and $b$ are independent.

The mistake was to extrapolate the assumption of independence to the special case in which Alan and Betty make identical statements. Admittedly, when it is given that the prior probability of $p$ as well as that of $q$ was $1/2$, then if Alan asserts $p$ and Betty asserts $q$ then it is correct to conclude that $P(p \,\&\, q) = 16/25$, which is the product of $P(p)$ and $P(q)$. However, when both affirm the same proposition $s$ the probability that one is telling the truth is not independent of the question whether the other is telling the truth. The use of Bayes's Theorem—in which we shall employ instead of '$b$', '$\beta$', denoting "Betty asserts $s$"—will show this:

$$P(s/\beta) = \frac{P(\beta/s) \cdot P(s)}{P(\beta/s) \cdot P(s) + P(\beta/\sim s) \cdot P(\sim s)}.$$

Now if Alan has not asserted $s$, $P(s) = 1/2$, $P(\beta/s) = 4/5$, and $P(\sim \beta/s) = 1/5$ which give $P(s/\beta) = 4/5$ as expected. But if it is given that Alan has asserted $s$, then that has raised the probability of $s$ to $4/5$. In that case, therefore, the probability of $s$ prior to Betty's—but after Alan's—testimony is $4/5$. Substituting into the equation:

$$P(s/\beta) = \frac{P(\beta/s) \cdot P(s)}{P(\beta/s) \cdot P(s) + P(\beta/\sim s) \cdot P(\sim s)} = \frac{16}{17}$$

which is as one would expect considerably higher that the credibility of $s$ supported by a single testimony only.

It may be noted that our square-diagrams method can be put to good use in the present context. In general, when both Alan and Betty make some statement, there are four possibilities and thus the following applies:

$$P(a \& b)+P(a \& {\sim}b)+P({\sim}a \& b)+P({\sim}a \& {\sim}b) = 1$$
$$16/25 + \quad 4/25 \quad + \quad 4/25 \quad + 1/25$$

In Figure 4 we have marked by $S$ those squares which represent situations where they make identical statements. There are seventeen such squares, sixteen of which are $A \& B$ squares, i.e., the probability of their speaking the truth is 16/17.

*Example III*

The following story, though fictitious, closely resembles a somewhat more involved incident that took place in California and was reported in *Time* (April 26, 1968), under the title "Trial by Mathematics":

| S | S | S | S | S |
|---|---|---|---|---|
| A  B | A  B | A  B | A  B | A  B |
| S | S | S | S | S |
| A  B | A  B | A  B | A  B | A  B |
| S | S | S | S | S |
| A  B | A  B | A  B | A  B | A  B |
| S | | | | |
| A  B | A | A | A | |
| | | | | S |
| B | B | B | B | |

**Figure 4**

The driver of a hit-and-run accident was observed by several witnesses, who testified that he was bearded and wore a tweed jacket with elbow patches. They also claimed that he was driving a Volvo and that there were a stack of books on the backseat. Shortly thereafter a person fitting all the details of the description was arrested. At the trial the prosecutor insisted that it was far beyond all reasonable doubt that the culprit had to be the accused, since the chances that another person possessing all his incriminating features existed in the vicinity were negligibly small. He cited several statistical figures obtained from authoritative sources, including the information that the proportion of bearded drivers among all drivers in the area was less than 1/6; of Volvos among all makes of cars less than 1/20; tweed jackets with elbow patches among all jackets 1/100, and cars loaded with books, etc. The prosecutor explained to the jury that by the rules of mathematics the probability of a combination of events is obtained by multiplying together the probabilities of each component event. He then proceeded to multiply all the factors and concluded that the odds were several million to one that some other car and driver were involved in the accident.

The prosecutor's probabilistic reasoning impressed the court and the defense attorney, all of whom at the time could find nothing wrong with it, and a verdict of guilty was returned. Fortunately, in the real case, the California Supreme Court uncovered the error in the computations and overturned the verdict.

The major mistake in the actual case, as well as in our story, was to overlook the statistical interdependence of the various factors. Suppose, for instance, that the frequency of book-carrying Volvos in the neighborhood was merely 1/500; then it would be wrong to argue that the probability of the combination of that event and a tweed-jacketed driver is simply 1/500 × 1/100. The aforementioned features are significantly more common among academicians than among the general population. Thus, given that the car was carrying lots of books, the probability that its driver was wearing what is characteristically academic apparel should have been assigned a substantially higher probability than 1/100.

*Example IV*

$A$ is independent of $B$ and also of $C$. May we therefore assume that $A$ is independent of $B \& C$ and also of $B \lor C$? On the surface there seems little reason to doubt that it is so: my chance of winning the main prize in the local lottery is independent of the economic situation in Poland, of the outcome of the disarmament talks in Geneva, of the weather in Central Asia, etc. The same chances are clearly equally independent of any conjunction of these events as well as of any disjunction formed by them. Furthermore, since we are given that $A$ is independent of both of $B$ and $C$, does that not *mean* that $A$ is independent of $A \& B$ and of $A \lor B$?

It comes therefore somewhat as a surprise to learn that it may be true that $P(A) = P(A/B) = P(A/C)$ while $P(A) \neq P(A/B \& C)$ and $P(A) \neq P(A/B \lor C)$. It is easiest to see this with the aid of the kind of diagram we used before. In Figure 5, clearly, since three of the total six squares are $A$-squares, $P(A) = 3/6 = 1/2$. Also, since there are two $B$-squares of

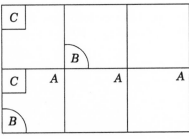

**Figure 5**

which one is an $A$-square and two $C$-squares of which one is an $A$-square, $P(A/B) = P(A/C) = 1/2$. And yet both $P(A/B \lor C) \neq P(A)$

and $P(A/B \& C) \neq P(A)$. As there are three squares which are either $B$ or $C$ one of which is also an $A$-square, $P(A/B \vee C) = 1/3$; and there is only one square which is a $B \& C$-square, but which is also an $A$-square, hence $P(A/B \& C) = 1$.

Finally, one more small point. Several writers have suggested[1] that an additional way for defining statistical independence exists: If $A$ and $B$ are independent, then a person who contemplates betting on $A$ should be indifferent to whether $B$ happens to be true.

The definition is inaccurate. For suppose $A$ and $B$ have absolutely nothing to do with one another, and thus $P(A) = P(A/B)(\neq 1)$. It is invariably the case that there exists some $C$ such that $P(A) = P(A/B \& C)$ (e.g., when '$C$' stands for "If $B$ then $A$", $A \& B$ implies $C$ and thus $P(A/B \& C) = 1$. Thus, a rational wagerer who believes that $C$ is true or is highly probable should be interested in finding out whether $B$ is true. A person who contemplates betting on $A$ should not be indifferent to whether $B$ happens to be true, for though by both criteria (i) and (ii) $A$ is independent of $B$, $B$ has a *relevance* to $A$.

Nor would it be correct to say the converse, that if $A$ is dependent on $X$ then a rational person who contemplates betting on $A$ should *not* be indifferent to whether $X$ happens to be true. Suppose $A$ is independent of $B$ and $B$ has no relevance to $A$, that is, acquiring the knowledge that $B$ is true or false would not affect the probability of $A$. Then it is always possible to find a $C$ such that, even though $P(A) = P(A/B)$, $P(A) \neq P(A/B \vee C)$(and $B \vee C = X$). Now since by the Law of Addition $B \rightarrow B \vee C$, by acquiring the knowledge that $B$ is true one also secures the knowledge that $B \vee C$ is true. Hence, regardless what $B$ stands for, one who contemplates betting on $A$ should not be indifferent to whether $B$ happens to be true; in other words, $B$ is relevant to $A$ no matter what $B$ is. Stated thus, however, the notion of relevance is rendered vacuous. The answer therefore must be that though the inequality $P(A) \neq P(A/B \vee C)(= P(A/X))$ ensures that $A$ is dependent on $X$, it does not make $X$ relevant to $A$.

---

[1] E.g., M. Davis, *Mathematically Speaking* (New York, 1980), p. 82.

## 2. Base Rates

The journal *The Behavioral and Brain Sciences* devoted more than a hundred pages in 1981 and 1983 to a debate among philosophers, statisticians, and psychologists over some examples in which there was no agreement even among experts on which conditions must be taken into account and which may be neglected when evaluating the probability of certain events. One of the most discussed examples concerned a story that originated in the works of A. Tversky and D. Kahaneman, which also involves a hit-and-run accident occurring at night and involving a cab. It was given that two cab companies, Green and Blue, operate in the city and 85% of the cabs are Green, 15% are Blue. A witness of an accident involving a cab testifies having observed that the color of the car was blue. The witness has been subjected to extensive testing, under conditions comparable to those prevailing at the site of the accident, and proved himself fairly, though not completely, reliable: he was able to make correct identifications 80% of the time, and erred in 20% of the cases.

Tversky and Kahaneman, who have made it their speciality to investigate how laymen form probability judgments, report that they have presented this story to several hundreds of people and asked what in their opinion was the probability that the cab involved in the accident was blue rather than green.[2] The reply of the great majority was: 80%. The result may be taken to indicate that from the point of view of common sense the only factor to be taken into account is the attestor's degree of reliability, while the base rate, that is, the relative frequency of blue cabs (which after all determines the probability of that kind of cab involved in the collision, prior to the testimony we were given), may be ignored.

The two investigators cite these results to illustrate how frequently untutored probabilistic arguments go wrong and that even the most elementary forms of reasoning under uncertainty are infested by cognitive illusions. I believe it is possible to argue convincingly, though informally, that the view expressed by the majority of people was indeed mistaken. Let us suppose that, when our witness was subject to the suitable conditions with several hundreds of cars, half of which were green and the other half blue, he was found to

---

[2] "Causal Thinking in Judgement Under Uncertainty," in *Basic Problems in Methodology and Linguistics*, Pt. III, ed. R. E. Butts and J. Hintikka (Dordrecht, 1977), pp. 174–175.

make correct identifications as often as not. Such a witness would be entirely useless, since his judgment appears to have no causal connection with the actual color he is confronted with; to pay any attention to his testimony would be no better than if we allowed the outcome of the tossing of a coin to play a role in determining the cab's color. Now if there happened to be not a single witness, and all we knew was the ratio between the different colored cabs, then virtually everyone would readily agree that the probability of a blue cab is determined by their relative frequency, and thus it is 15%. Thus when we have a completely useless witness—which is no different than having no witnesses at all—practically no one would find it reasonable to say that since our witness has a fifty–fifty chance of making a correct observation, then never mind that there are far fewer blue cabs than green cabs, the probability that the accident was caused by a blue car is 50%!

Next we consider the question of how to regard the testimony of a deponent who has not proven perfectly incompetent, who has been able to make correct color identifications in 51% of all cases and erred only 49% of the time. Surely, it would be absurd to say that, because of the minute advantage of the last witness over the one before, the credibility of the claim that the culpable individual was driving a blue cab abruptly jumped from 15% to 51%. What may, however, seem reasonable is that it should rise *slightly* above 15%. Thus with a witness who has proven reliable 51% of the time we end up assigning his testimony a probability far below 51%, and when we have a witness with a record of 85% success we will of course give greater credence to his testimony, but certainly not 85%. It should therefore be fairly evident that to determine the probability that the accident-causing car was blue two factors have to be taken into account: (a) the weight of the evidence given by the witness, which in this case (where we apparently do not suspect the witness intentionally giving a false report) is determined by subjecting him to an extensive test, and (b) by the prior probability, which is given by the relative frequency of blue cabs.

To accommodate these two factors to the precise degree required we shall denote,

$B$ = The cab involved in the crash was blue,
$W$ = The witness testifies that $B$.

Substituting into Bayes's Theorem:

$$P(B/W) = \frac{P(B) \cdot P(W/B)}{P(W)}.$$

Substituting in the denominator from the Rule of Elimination:

$$P(B/W) = \frac{P(B) \cdot P(W/B)}{P(B) \cdot P(W/B) + P(\sim B) \cdot P(W/\sim B)}$$
$$= \frac{15/100 \times 880/100}{15/100 \times 80/100) + 85/100 \times 20/100)}$$
$$= \frac{12}{29}.$$

Some doubts may still linger in our minds. We have been told that the witness has a reliability of 80%, and we were given to understand that this meant both that when under the specified circumstances he is presented with color $C$ he identifies it as color $C$ 80% of the time, and when he claims to have observed color $C$ then that is in fact what he has observed. This implies that $P(B/W) = 0.80$; how then is it possible to conclude with the aid of Bayes's Theorem, or indeed with the aid of any theorem, that $P(B/W)$ equals only 12/29? The answer is, that $P(B/W) = 0.80$ was said to be the case in general and not when it is clearly stated that we are dealing with a case where either blue cabs or green cabs preponderate.

And yet it may not be so easy to overcome the tendency to disregard the base rate. One of the arguments of L. J. Cohen, who wrote the target article of the debate we mentioned, goes as follows:

> A probability that holds uniformly for each of a class of events because it is based on causal properties, such as the physiology of vision, cannot be altered by facts, such as chance distribution, that have no efficacy in the individual events.[3]

But of course by ascribing only 4/9 probability to the witness who really has seen a blue cab we are not lowering in our estimate his powers of vision. Even though in general we estimate his rate of success to be 4/5, it is conceded that 1/5 of the time he fails to identify the color of a cab. It stands to reason that we should conjecture that his failures to make the correct identification are more likely to have occurred in a situation such as ours, where the proportion of blue cars is small, and therefore there is considerable presumption that his testimony is mistaken.

---

[3] L. J. Cohen, "Can Human Irrationality Be Experimentally Demonstrated?," *Behavioral and Brain Sciences* (1981).

It is interesting to note that one of the discussants, I. Levi, launches a vehement attack on Kahaneman and Tversky, an attack that misses its target by a remarkably wide margin. Among other things he charges that,

> the experimental subjects studied by Kahaneman and Tversky et al. seemed to have a better grasp of the matter—even from a Bayesian point of view—than do the experimental psychologists.[4]

Levi insists (and in later works he continued to insist) that the investigators were wrong in focusing merely on the percentage of blue cabs as such, and that it is imperative that an additional factor be taken into account, namely, the percentage of cabs *involved in accidents* that are blue.

One may be wondering why Levi did not also make several further demands, such as (supposing that the collision occurred during the rush hour and when it was raining) that we must not ignore the percentage of blue cars involved in accidents when it is raining, and specifically in those occurring between 5:00 P.M. and 6 P.M. Wet roads, low visibility due to rain, and the busy traffic during rush hour are all important factors in an accident and in their presence the difference between good and bad drivers, between one type of car and another, becomes more accentuated. The percentage of blue cabs involved in collisions under such circumstances is likely to be appreciably different than when such circumstances do not obtain. Thus information concerning them is highly relevant. Indeed, what Levi should have advised is that we make sure we take into account the ratio of blue cars involved in this specific accident now under review, and the value of which is either 1 or 0. But of course the truth is that we should make use of every bit of relevant information on which we can lay our hands. In the example we were given we were supposed to assume that the frequency of blue cars alone is known. Probability theory does not demand that we also take into account information we do not possess.

To top all this, Levi goes on to suggest, "it is precisely in situations of this sort that principles of insufficient reasons are invoked," and thus a good Bayesian should proceed on the assumption that a blue cab is no more and no less likely to be involved in an accident than a green cab.

There is of course no reason to think that Levi would treat any differently a situation in which, for example, there is but a single

---

4 Ibid., p. 343.

blue cab while there are 10,000 green cabs, and thus the fact that there are 10,000 times more green than blue cabs provides insufficient reason to ascribe any different probabilities to the two types of cabs!

A brief review of Levi's attack on Kahaneman and Tversky may be useful in that it shows that if one insists on holding the wrong view it is best not to try offering articulated reasons for it. Mistakes tend to look more mistaken when explicitly argued for.

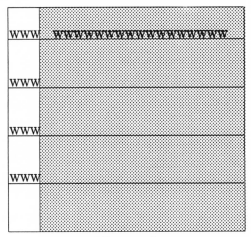

**Figure 6**

We may also examine the situation with the aid of square-diagrams. Figure 6 is to be looked upon as consisting of one hundred squares, fifteen of which represent blue cars, and eighty-five (the shaded area) non-blue cars. We mark twelve of the $B$-squares by $W$, since we were told that 4/5 of the blue cars are identified correctly by the witness. We also mark seventeen of the $\sim B$-squares by $W$, since in 1/5 of the cases the witness misjudges the color, and thus he takes 17/85 of the green cars to be blue. We thus see that in twenty-nine out of one hundred cases $W$ holds and only twelve of the $W$-squares are also $B$-squares. In other words, $P(B/W)$ is only 12/29.

## 3. Correlations and Indicative Conditionals

The difference between the two conditional probabilities, $P(C/A)$ and $P(C/\sim A)$—to be denoted by $Sc(C/A)$—stands for the important notion, "the strength of correlation between the antecedent $A$

and the consequent $C$."[5] The value of that difference indicates the amount which $A$ (when it is true) would contribute to the probability of $C$. In other words, the value of $\mathrm{Sc}(C/A)$ is the degree to which $A$ ensures, as well as it is required for, the truth of $C$. When $\mathrm{P}(C/A) = \mathrm{P}(C/\sim A)$, then $A$'s truth or falsity is of no relevance to the probability of $C$ (nor, of course, to that of $\sim C$). In that case, therefore, $\mathrm{Sc}(C/A) = \mathrm{Sc}(C/\sim A) = 0$.

The inequality $\mathrm{P}(C/A) > \mathrm{P}(C/\sim A)$ implies that the truth of $A$ raises the probability of $C$ from what it would be otherwise, and thus $\mathrm{Sc}(C/A) > 0$. On the other hand, $\mathrm{P}(C/A < \mathrm{P}(C/\sim A)$ indicates that $A$ lowers $C$'s probability from what it would be in case $\sim A$ were true. That means that $A$ negatively correlates with $C$, i.e., $\mathrm{Sc}(C/A) < 0$.

Now suppose we are given the indicative conditional:

> "If Fred is a smoker, his insurance premium will increase next year."

(1) This conditional is certainly not to be equated with the material conditional $K \supset N$ (where $K$ = Fred is a smoker; $N$ = Fred's insurance, etc.), since the mere falsity of $K$ ensures the truth of $K \supset N$. But of course $K$'s falsity, as such, does not render $K \Rightarrow N$ true.

(2) Nor should we want to say that $K \Rightarrow N$ is true just because $\mathrm{P}(N/K) = 1$, since if, for example, next year everybody's premium rises, then the truth of $N$ ensures both that $\mathrm{P}(N/K)$ and $\mathrm{P}(N/\sim K)$ equal one. On the other hand, for the indicative conditional $K \Rightarrow N$ to be true, it is not sufficient that $N$ be true, since '$\Rightarrow$' indicates a specific connection between smoking and higher insurance cost. But if the rise in cost affects everyone equally, that is, if $N$ is true regardless of whether $K$ or $\sim K$ is the case, then $K$ has no bearing on $N$, and we should not want to concede the truth of $K \Rightarrow N$.

(3) Clearly, however, asserting $K \Rightarrow N$ amounts to asserting both: (i) $\mathrm{P}(N/K) = 1$, for it definitely affirms that given that $K$,

---

[5] R. N. Giere, in *Understanding Scientific Reasoning* (New York, 1984), p. 184., defines "$\mathrm{Sc}(C/A)$" as a magnitude proportional to the difference between the percentage of $a$'s that are $c$'s (where $A =$ a certain particular exemplifies $a$), and the percentage of $\sim a$'s that are $c$'s. Those who do not subscribe to the frequency interpretation and translate "$\mathrm{P}(C/A)$" to mean "the degree of $C$'s certainty given $A$," might go along with this, thanks to Bernoulli's Theorem, linking probability to frequency (cf. Chapter 9).

$N$ follows, and (ii) $P(N/\sim K) = 0$, i.e. the insurance premium for nonsmokers is not going to rise next year.

Given (i) and (ii), $Sc(N/K) = P(N/K) - P(N/\sim K) = 1$, i.e., the strength of correlation between $N$ and $K$ is of maximum degree. This amounts to an unqualified affirmation of the indicative conditional $K \Rightarrow N$. An indicative conditional such as $K \Rightarrow N$ may be seen as the claim that $K$ is both a sufficient and a necessary condition for $N$. On the other hand, suppose it is not entirely certain that the insurance premiums for all smokers will rise next year, but that the probability that it will is 0.9. Furthermore, there is also a small probability of 0.1 that even nonsmokers will have to pay more next year. Here, $P(N/K) - P(N/\sim K) = 0.9 - 0.1 = 0.8$, and thus $Sc(N/K) = P(K \Rightarrow N) = 0.8$. This value reflects the fact that smoking is neither a fully sufficient condition nor an absolutely necessary condition for $N$.

To sum up:

(1) When the value of the difference $P(N/K) - P(N/\sim K) \geq 0$, it equals the value of $P(K \Rightarrow N)$, and
   (i)   as long as that value equals one, $K \Rightarrow N$ is true;
   (ii)  when that value is between 1 and 0, $K \Rightarrow N$ is of finite probability, less than one;
   (iii) when it equals zero, $K$ is entirely irrelevant to $N$; thus $K \Rightarrow N$ is false.
(2) If the value of $P(N/K) - P(N/\sim K) < 0$, then $K$ is negatively correlated with $N$, and hence $K \Rightarrow N$ is definitely false.

Stalnaker, Adams, and several other philosophers have been much concerned about the correct analysis of an indicative conditional such as "If Oswald did not shoot Kennedy then someone else did" (denoted: $\sim O \Rightarrow E$). According to what we have said earlier, $\sim O \Rightarrow E = Sc(\sim O \Rightarrow E) = P(E/\sim O) - P(E/O)$. It is common to ascribe a fairly high value to the probability of $\sim O \Rightarrow E$, (since there is hardly any doubt that Kennedy *was* actually shot), while we are virtually certain that no more than a single person took part in the assassination, and thus $P(E/O) = 0$. In that case $P(\sim O \Rightarrow E) = P(E/\sim O) - P(E/O) = P(E/\sim O)(\approx 1)$.

In general, then, if $P(C/\sim A) = 0$, the probability of the indicative conditional $A \Rightarrow C$ is equal to the conditional probability $P(C/A)$.

It should be clear that in cases in which $C$ is known to be true $P(C/A)$ need not equal one, for "$P(C/A)$" denotes the probability of $C$ when only $A$, and not $C$, is given. To put it differently, a certain individual may definitely be known to exemplify the property $c$, nevertheless the percentage of $c$'s among particulars characterized by $a$'s may be low.

This brings us to the highly acclaimed paper of David Lewis in which he argued:

> there is no way to interpret a conditional connective so that with sufficient generality, the probabilities of conditionals will equal the appropriate conditional probabilities.[6]

Part of his famous *reductio* proof runs along the following lines:

·(6)   $P(A \Rightarrow C = P(C/A)$, if $P(A)$ is $+ve$. (Using Lewis's numbering. For him '$\Rightarrow$' stands for the indicative conditional.)

On the next page Lewis states,

(9)   $P(A \Rightarrow C/C) = P(C/AC) = 1,$
(10)   $P(A \Rightarrow C/{\sim}C) = P(C/A{\sim}C) = 0.$

Next he cites the well known elementary theorem:

(11)   $P(D) = P(D/C) \cdot P(C) + P(D/{\sim}C) \cdot P({\sim}C)$, for any $D$. (Which theorem we called RE).

In particular, let $D$ stand for $A \Rightarrow C$ and substitute (6), (9), and (10) into (11),

(12)   $P(C/A) = P(C/A\&C) \cdot P(C) + P(C/A{\sim}C) \cdot P({\sim}C)$
   $= 1 \cdot P(C) + O \cdot P({\sim}C) = P(C).$

Lewis points out however that in practice there are indefinitely many cases where $P(C/A)$ does not equal $P(C)$. Thus (12) is unacceptable and assumption (6) must be incorrect.

Lewis's argument is erroneous. First of all, if indeed, as he thought, substituting into (11), $A \Rightarrow C$ for $D$, yielded (12), then surely substituting $A \vee C \Rightarrow C$ for $D$ should give us:

(13)   $P(C/A \vee C) = P\{(C/(A \vee C)\&C\} \cdot P(C)$
   $+P\{C/(A \vee C)\&{\sim}C\} \cdot P({\sim}C)$
   $= P(C)$

---

[6] David Lewis, "Probabilities of Conditionals and Conditional Probabilities," in *Ifs*, ed. W. L. Harper et al. (Dodrecht, 1981), p. 130.

But by Bayes's theorem,

$$P(C/A \vee C) = \frac{P(A \vee C/C) \cdot P(C)}{P(A \vee C)}.$$ Combine this with (13):

$P(A \vee C/C) = P(A \vee C)$. Applying the Axiom of Disjunction to the left hand side:

$P(A/C) + P(C/C) - P(A\&C/C) = P(A \vee C)$ i.e.,
$P(A/C) + 1 + P(A/C) = P(A \vee C)$ i.e.,
$1 = P(A \vee C)$,

which is contrary to the first axiom of probability according to which $0 \geq P(X) \geq 1$, while according to our last expression $P(A) = P(C) < 1/2$ is impossible! Thus Lewis's (12) is wrong not merely because of mere empirical considerations, but because it leads to an incoherent theory of probability.

To exhibit the root of Lewis's fallacy, let us go one step back and affirm that by the Rule of Elimination,

(14)   $P(C/A) = P(C/A\&B) \cdot P(B/A) + P(C/A\&\sim B) \cdot P(\sim B/A)$,

and not

(15)   $P(C/A) = P(C/A\&B) \cdot P(B) + P(C/A\&\sim B) \cdot P(\sim B)$

is the correct equation.

To reassure ourselves on this point we observe in Figure 7, that of the three A-squares two are also C-squares and thus $P(C/A) = 2/3$. We can also see that $P(B/A) = 1/3$; $P(C/A\&B) = 1$; $P(\sim B/A) = 2/3$; $P(C/A\& \sim B = 1/2)$. Substituting these values into (14):

$2/3 = 1/3 \times 1 + 2/3 \times 1/2$,

which is correct. On the other hand given that $P(B) = 1/4$ and $P(\sim B) = 3/4$, (15) yields:

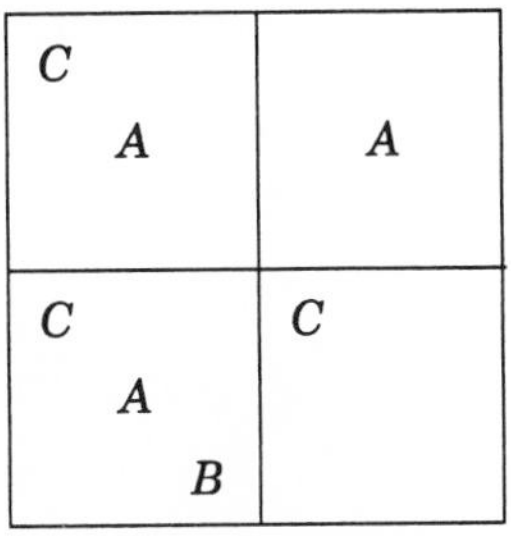

**Figure 7**

$2/3 = 1/4 \times 1 + 3/4 \times 1/2$,

which is incorrect. Now if we substitute into (14) $C$ for $B$ we get:

(16)   $P(C/A) = P(C/A\&C) \cdot P(C/A) + P(C/A\&\sim C) \cdot P(\sim C/A)$,

which of course reduces to the completely innocuous: $P(C/A) = P(C/A)$.

Lewis's incoherent (12) may be obtained only in the illegitimate way of substituting $C$ for $B$ into (15). It is illegitimate since equation (15) is invalid.

There is good reason for not wanting to equate the probability of the indicative conditional with conditional probability i.e., for not wanting to say $P(A \Rightarrow C) = P(C/A)$. The reason is that $P(C/A)$ may equal 1 even when $A$ has no relevance to $C$ as when the prior probability, $P(C)$ equals 1. We do not wish to equate $P(A \Rightarrow C)$ with one unless the $C$ owes its truth to $A$. However, in the more restricted case where it is given that $A$ is definitely a necessary condition for $C$ i.e., $P(C/\sim A) = 0$, then we may well equate the probability that it is also a sufficient condition to the conditional probability. Thus if '$P(A \Rightarrow C)$' stands for 'given that $A$ is necessary for $C$, the probability that it is also sufficient'. We may therefore write: $P(A \Rightarrow C) = P(C/A)$.

# II

# THE USEFULNESS OF
# THE RULE OF ELIMINATION

The Rule of Elimination

(RE)   $P(A) = P(B) \cdot P(A/B) + P(\sim B) \cdot P(A/\sim B)$

which is obtained by combining the Law of Excluded Middle, the Conjunctive Axiom, and the Disjunctive Axiom is an indispensable tool in probabilistic reasoning. On those occasions when we are not given the value of $P(A)$ and are unable to carry out our calculations without it, we can obtain it from RE, provided we know the values of the four expressions on the right-hand side.

Recall that in the previous chapter we were trying to evaluate $P(B/W)$, that is, the probability of the cab involved in the accident being blue, given that the witness testifies so. We employed Bayes's Theorem, which gave us:

$$P(B/W) = \frac{P(B) \cdot P(W/B)}{P(W)}.$$

However, this simple version of Bayes's Theorem was no help to us, for we were not given the value of $P(W)$. Our difficulty here, as in so many similar cases, was solved through the use of the Rule of Elimination, according to which

$$P(W) = P(B) \cdot P(W/B) + P(\sim B) \cdot P(W/\sim B).$$

Since the values of all the four expressions on the right-hand side were known to us we were able to find the value of $P(W)$.

RE may also provide help in some cases in which we not only lack information about the value of $P(A)$ but about $P(A/B)$ and $P(A/\sim B)$ as well. For we may write,

$$P(B) = P(A) \cdot P(B/A) + P(\sim A) \cdot P(B/\sim A)$$

i.e.,

$$P(B) = (A) \cdot P(B/A) + [1 - P(A)] \cdot P(B/\sim A).$$

In case we know the values of $P(B)$, $P(B/A)$, and $P(B/\sim A)$, we have an equation with a single unknown, $P(A)$, which is easily solved.

## 1. Alternative Ways of Elimination

Normally RE makes use of the Law of Excluded Middle. This, however, is not always necessary, and in some cases alternative ways of eliminating the troublesome expression are preferable. The following example may serve as an illustration.

A small deck contains the four top cards, $J$, $Q$, $K$, and $A$ of a single suit. A player is asked to pick at random one card, conceal it from us, and hold it in his right hand and pick another to hold in his left hand. His instructions are: In case either of his hands holds a face card (a $K$ or a $Q$), tap the table with that hand; should he happen to hold a face card in both hands, tap the table with the hand that holds the $K$. Our player does as told, looks at the cards he has drawn, and taps the table with his right hand. Question: What is the probability that $Lq$ (that the left hand holds a queen)?

I believe this example to be singularly instructive. Apart from illustrating a special way of making use of RE, it shows how such a simple situation involving no more than four possibilities with equal prior probabilities is capable of harboring a variety of pitfalls for the unwary. We shall review four different approaches to the question, each yielding a different value for the probability.

A rather casual reasoner might propose to solve the problem in the following manner. Let $Rt$ = the player's right hand taps the table; then $P(Lq/Rt)$ simply equals $1/4$, since there were four cards in the deck, and each one of them (i.e., either one of the two left in the deck, as well as the card held by R, and the one held by L) has an equal chance to be the $Q$.

This would amount to a gross misuse of the Principle of Indifference. The four cards cannot be treated on an equal footing. The player has tapped the table with his right hand, thus the card held in that hand must be either the $K$ or the $Q$. None of the remaining three cards is restricted to those two possibilities only.

A more sophisticated way of going astray would be the following. The card in the right hand needs to be singled out for special attention. We have evidence that it is a face card, the only question is whether it is the $K$ or the $Q$. It seems reasonable to say that

$P(Rk) = P(Rq) = 1/2$. What is left over should surely be equally divided among the other three on the basis of the Principle of Indifference, and thus each card, except the one held in the player's right hand, has $1/2 \times 1/3 = 1/6$ of a chance to be the $Q$.

The more subtle error in this case was to treat the alternatives (that the right hand holds the $K$ and that it holds the $Q$) as equiprobable. Admittedly, there is no reason why the prior probabilities $P(Rk)$ and $P(Rq)$ should not be assigned the same value. But here we are dealing with $P(Rk/Rt)$ and $P(Rq/Rt)$, and once $Rt$ is given we have sufficient reason to favor $Rk$ slightly over $Rq$. After all, if $Rk$ is the case then the player is bound to tap the table with his right hand, regardless of what he may hold in his left hand, whereas if $Rq$ is true then it is not certain that he will do so, since if the $K$ is in his left hand his right hand will not touch the table.

A third approach would involve the use of Bayes's Theorem and RE to eliminate the expression $P(Rt)$ from the denominator, in the standard fashion:

$$P(Lq/Rt) = \frac{P(Rt/Lq) \cdot P(Lq)}{P(Rt/Lq) \cdot P(Lq) + P(Rt/\sim Lq) \cdot P(\sim Lq)}.$$

There is little difficulty in evaluating $P(Rt/Lq)$ and $P(Lq)$. If it is given that the left hand holds the $Q$, then any of the three remaining cards may be the $K$. There appears to be no reason to distinguish between those three possibilities and therefore they are to be treated as equiprobable: $P(Rt/Lq) = 1/3$. But $P(Lq)$ is obviously $1/4$, and hence $P(\sim Lq) = 3/4$.

But when it comes to evaluating $P(Rt/\sim Lq)$, one might be tempted to argue thus. Given that the $Q$ is not held by the player's left hand, his right hand could have tapped the table either because $it$ had the $Q$ or because it had the $K$. Thus $Rt$ implies the disjunction of $Rk \vee Rq$. Since the two disjuncts are incompatible with one another, the probability of $Rt$ is simply the sum of the probabilities of the disjuncts, i.e., it is $1/4 + 1/4 = 1/2$.

Once again we have committed the error of treating dissimilar probabilities as if they were indistinguishable. While the prior probabilities of $Rk$ and $Rq$ are, of course, equal, the probabilities of these propositions when $\sim Lq$ is given are unequal: $P(Rq/\sim Lq)$ is surely greater than $P(Rk/\sim Lq)$, since $\sim Lq$ is compatible with the $K$ being held by the left hand, but it leaves for the $Q$ only two alternative places to be if not in the player's right hand.

The fourth (and the correct) approach involves the elimination of $R_t$ from the denominator of the Bayesian fraction above, not via the standard RE, but rather through our knowledge of the prior circumstances of the example before us:

$$P(Rt) = P(Rk) + P(Rq) \cdot P(\sim Lk/Rq).$$

The above equation is implied by the condition laid down for the game that the player is to strike his right hand against the table when either of two incompatible events takes place: he draws the $K$ with his right hand, or he draws the $Q$ with his right hand while not holding the $K$ in his left hand. Now, $P(Rk) = 1/4$, $P(Rq) = 1/4$ and $P(\sim Lk/Rq) = 2/3$. Thus,

$$P(Rt) = 1/4 + 1/4 \times 2/3 = 5/12.$$

Substituting this into Bayes's equation we get,

$$P(Lq/Rt) = \frac{1/3 \times 1/4}{5/12} = 1/5.$$

A diagram is particularly helpful here, as it allows us to confirm very quickly the various claims made in the course of the four suggested solutions. There are twelve rectangles of which three are marked $Rk$, $Rq$, $Lk$, and $Lq$ respectively (each representing one quarter of the possibilities). The combination $Rk \& Lq$ as well as that of $Rq \& Lk$ has the probability $1/4 \times 1/3 = 1/12$. The occasions on which the player is to tap the table with his right hand and those on which he is required to tap it with his left hand are also marked $Rt$ and $Lt$, respectively.

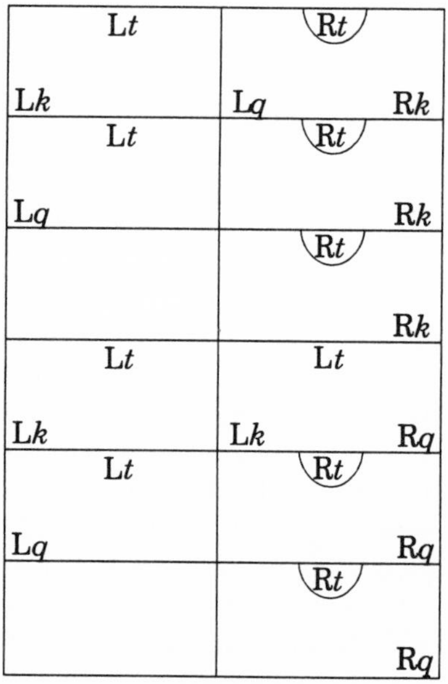

Figure 8 shows us first of all that while indeed $P(Lq) = 1/4$, $P(Lq/Rt)$ is, as we said, less: there are five $Rt$-rectangles and only one of these is marked $Lq$ and therefore the value of $P(Lq/Rt)$ is only $1/5$.

**Figure 8**

Figure 8 also shows clearly that it was a mistake to assume the equality of $P(Rk/Rt)$ and $P(Rq/Rt)$. Of the five rectangles marked $Rt$ three are also marked $Rk$, but only two are marked $Rq$. Thus the probability of the first is $3/5$, which is somewhat greater than the second, which is only $2/5$.

We may also verify at once that $P(Rq/\sim Lq)$ is indeed greater than $P(Rk/Lq)$ by reading off the diagram the precise value of each. Nine rectangles are not marked $Lq$ and thus they represent $\sim Lq$, and of these three are $Rq$ while only two are $Rk$. Thus $P(Rq/\sim Lq) = 3/5$, while $P(Rk/\sim Lq) = 2/5$.

Finally, we may satisfy ourselves that we calculated the value of $P(Rt)$ correctly: the sample space contains twelve rectangles and five of these are marked $Rt$, thus $P(Rt) = 5/12$.

In this chapter we shall look at two noteworthy uses of RE by philosophers. Our first example involves the study of the foundations of knowledge and the second the nature of a certain type of combined evidence.

## 2. 'Nothing Is Probable Unless Something Is Certain'?

One of the most celebrated debates in the history of the American Philosophical Association took place in 1952 between the eminent philosophers C. I. Lewis and Hans Reichenbach. The subject of their discussion was the question: Could one ever justifiably hold an empirical statement $e$ under circumstances in which the assertion that $e$ is probable to such and such a degree is itself not certain but merely probable to a given degree relative to *its* ground, and so on, endlessly? Lewis argued that if a statement can be established only as probable then it must have a ground. But if the ground itself is only probable then *it* must have a ground, which in turn must have a ground. It follows, therefore, that in order to assign a value to the probability of $e$ its probability relative to its ground must be multiplied by the probability of that ground's probability relative to its own ground, which in turn must be multiplied, etc. We would thus end up assigning virtually zero to the value of $e$'s probability. Lewis thus made his famous pronouncement, "nothing is probable unless something is certain." Given that we do regard a considerable number of empirical statements as fairly probable, we have to conclude that in many cases the succession of insecure grounds stops somewhere; it has to be reasonable to regard some fundamental statements as true beyond question.

Reichenbach claimed that Lewis's argument was based on a rather elementary mistake. He pointed out that there is no danger in assuming that nothing is certain, since Lewis's fear that such an assumption inevitably leads to a process of ever decreasing probabilities was ill-founded. James van Cleve is one philosopher who has presented Reichenbach's reasoning in a brief and clear manner.[1] Before entering into any technical details, however, let us note that in the context of commonsense reasoning we often encounter situations which seem to vindicate Lewis's position. Consider the fairly well-known story of the young man who was called up to serve in the Czar's army at the onset of the Russo-Japanese war. Lacking in fighting spirit, the youth was considerably perturbed by the prospect of being killed in battle. A wise friend, wishing to allay his fears, told him: First of all, it is by no means certain that you will pass the physical; even if you do, it is not certain that the war will still be on by the time you will have finished your basic training; but supposing it is, you may not be sent to the front; and assuming that you are assigned front-line duty, there is a good chance that you will never see battle; but even if you do, etc.

Clearly, the judicious friend uttering these soothing words meant to imply that the variety of uncertainties *reinforce* one another so that ultimately the probability of perishing in battle becomes negligible. And what is significant in this story is that it has the characteristic structure envisaged by Lewis. For what are the grounds for fearing injury in battle, $(A)$? Surely the fact that one may have to serve in a spot where there is fighting going on, $(B)$. And we may take it that $P(A/B)$ is not negligible, and hence the fear of $A$ may seem well founded. But then we ask what are the grounds for $B$, to which the answer is, the fact of not being given a desk job but sent to the front, $(C)$. But, of course, even $C$ itself has a chance to materialize only if the war does not end before he finishes his basic training, $(D)$, and so on. Thus it seems that $P(C) < P(D)$, since even it if were certain that he finishes his basic training soon enough, there is a good chance that he is not sent to the front. Similarly, $P(B) < P(C)$ and so on, that is, every successive eventuality is less probable than its ground, hence if there is a large enough number of intermediate grounds between $A$ and the last ground in the series, $P(A)$ may cumulatively dwindle down to practically zero.

Where then is the elementary mistake claimed by Reichenbach? To see his point let us once more assume that some proposition $B$ constitutes the probabilistic grounds for $A$, so by Theorem (RE):

---

[1] James van Cleve, "Probability and Certainty: A Reexamination of the Lewis–Reichenbach Debate," *Philosophical Studies* (1977): 323–334.

$$P(A) = P(B) \cdot P(A/B) + P(\sim B) \cdot P(A/\sim B).$$

If we take into account the first term on the right-hand side then we certainly should conclude that $P(A)$ must be less than $P(B)$, since $P(A)$ equals $P(B)$ multiplied by $P(A/B)$, which is a number less than 1. But we must not overlook the second term, which if it is large enough together with the first term adds up to something bigger than $P(A)$.

Figure 9 illustrates Reichenbach's claim. $P(A/B) = 3/4$, since the four top squares are $B$-squares. We also see that $P(A/\sim B) = 1/2$. At the same time, while only one third of the whole board contains $B$-squares, and thus $P(B) = 1/3$, $P(A) = 7/12$, which is not smaller but considerably greater than $P(B)$.

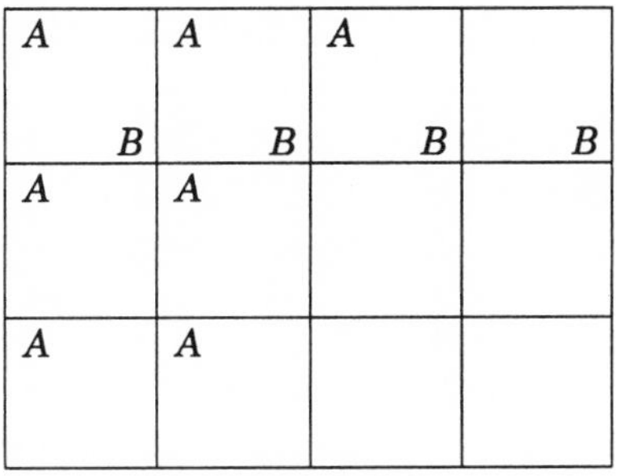

**Figure 9**

It has been agreed by most that the debate was won by Reichenbach. Van Cleve, in the essay just cited, attempts to mitigate Lewis's defeat by contending that Lewis was indeed wrong if he feared that the probability of $e$ is bound eventually to dwindle down to nothing, but he was right if what he feared was that because of the infinite regress we are prevented from determining the value of $e$'s probability.

Lewis was one of the leading philosophers of his time, yet keeping in mind Peirce's pronouncement of our special proneness to lose our way in the context of probabilistic reasoning, it is not entirely unbelievable that he should have overlooked the implications of a most elementary theorem such as RE. Be that as it may, it seems to me possible to argue that he may not have committed such a simple error. In presenting his argument I shall not pretend to know what Lewis actually had in mind and shall merely attempt to draw attention to the fact that on certain assumptions about the foundations of knowledge his insistence on the need for an ultimate and certain basis for our probable beliefs may be reasonable. I shall start with a few noncontroversial practical examples which illustrate some circumstances under which RE definitely fails to prevent the probability of a belief statement from continually decreasing.

### 3. Concrete Examples Where Probability
### Keeps Eroding

Let me begin by considering a children's game, very popular in some places, in which the object is to transmit a verbal message from one end of a row formed by the members of a team to its other end. In one of the variations of the game, the referee whispers a message into the ear of the first member of one of the competing teams, who has to pass it on to the second child, who in turn has to tell it to the third, and so on. Each participant must try to speak loud enough for the next to be able to hear the message correctly, but not so loud that the referee—who is standing nearby—hears it and stops the game. The last member of the team is required to announce the message he heard. The team wins if the final announcement was identical with the referee's original message.

Experience has shown that even though the probability is considerably high that a given child hears correctly what has been whispered in his ear, as proven by the fact that in eight out of ten cases he will be able to reproduce precisely what he has just heard, the last member of a large team will hardly ever utter a sentence that bears much resemblance to the original sentence. The very reason why many children find this game fun to play is the grotesquely distorted versions of the referee's message that are often announced at the end of a game. It is not too difficult to see why a successful transmission with a sizable team is unlikely to occur. Let,

> $E$ = The original message of the referee was $m$,
> $A$ = 1st child on the team whispers $m$ into the ear of the 2nd,
> $B$ = 2nd child on the team whispers $m$ into the ear of the 3rd,
> $C$ = 3rd child on the team whispers $m$ into the ear of the 4th,

and so on. Employing the equation Reichenbach has drawn our attention to,

$$P(E) = P(E/A) \cdot P(A) + P(E/{\sim}A) \cdot P({\sim}A),$$

let us assume that $P(E/A) = 0.8$. The crucial point to note here is that $P(E/{\sim}A)$ is exceedingly small, indeed negligibly so. On the assumption, for instance, that the referee is required to formulate a sentence consisting of ten words, the number of possibilities is immensely large. ${\sim}A$ implies that the first child heard some sentence other than $m$, namely $m^*$. Thus we have to consider the question: If the first player believes that he was given $m^*$, given that he is mistaken, can we guess what the actual sentence whispered into his ears might have been? Now even though our choices are somewhat restricted, since the actual sentence is highly unlikely to have been one that sounds very different from $m^*$, still we are faced with a vast number of possibilities and the correct answer that it was $m$ is merely one among many. In other words, the probability that it was $m$ of all the possible sentences that might have been whispered into his ears, given that he believes it to have been $m^*$, may be denoted by $\epsilon$, where $\epsilon$ is very small. Thus we have:

$$P(E) = 0.8 \times P(A) + \epsilon \times P(\sim A) \approx 0.8 \times P(A) \tag{i}$$

Where the second term, $\epsilon \times P(\sim A)$ is small enough to be neglected. We also have:

$$(A) = 0.8 \times P(B) + P(A/\sim B) \cdot (\sim B),$$

which by the same argument as before reduces to

$$P(A) \approx 0.8 \times P(B) \tag{ii}$$

where of course:

$$P(B) \approx 0.8 \times P(C)$$

and so on. Substituting the last result into (ii), we get: $P(A) \approx 0.64$. And substituting this into (i) we get: $P(E) \approx 0.512 \times P(C)$. Thus it is evident that the probability of the team's last member correctly reproducing the original sentence rapidly decreases with the number of participants.

The probability mechanism we have just examined may also be said to be at work in the more common situations of gossip being spread around. Given that there is always some chance that a person passing on some report he has heard over the back fence exaggerates or embellishes it slightly, the chances increase as the rumor is spread that eventually the tale told bears little resemblance to anything that actually took place.

Now we can see why the story of the youth who was called up to the Russian army has to be analyzed according to similar lines. Here too we are presented with a situation where the second term in the successive equations representing RE may be ignored. We need not be concerned with the term in the relevant equation in which one of the two factors is the probability that the young man is rejected as unfit to serve in the army: that term is virtually zero, since there is no chance for a civilian thousands of miles away from the fighting zone to become a war casualty. Similarly the corresponding term in the next equation, which has as one of its factors the probability that the war will have ended by the time he is trained for battle, is also practically zero, and so on.

## 4. The Status of Knowledge Claims in General

Let us try to see whether a plausible theory of knowledge might be constructed that would lead to Lewis's conclusion that in order to avoid total skepticism uncertainty must cease at a certain level. Suppose $E$ denotes the hypothesis that an event $e$ is going to happen, e.g., a certain particle will be found at a certain location $s$ at time $t$. Suppose also that we offer a probabilistic justification for our belief that $E$, and claim that our ground for accepting $E$ is the statement $A$ (where $A$ might be the currently accepted laws of mechanics conjoined with a description of the relevant initial conditions). We may assume that the probability of $E$ given $A$ is very high. When we come to the question of why we subscribe to $A$, we might once more offer a probabilistic justification, and maintain that, given $B$, $A$ is highly probable. Clearly, $B$ would stand for the great number of experimental results plus the principles of scientific method. Likewise, we might suggest that $B$ itself is grounded in $C$, which confers high probability on $B$. $C$ would have to be some metaphysical principle which one might cite in justifying a belief in scientific methodology. Then a higher-order metaphysical principle $D$ would be invoked for the justification of $C$, and so on. Once more we would have,

$$P(E) = P(E/A) \cdot P(A) + P(E/\sim A) \cdot P(\sim A).$$

The crucial question is whether we may claim here, as in the previous cases, that the value of $P(E/\sim A)$ is negligibly small?

The following argument, which supports an affirmative answer to this question, may seem reasonable. Spot $s$ is merely one of indefinitely many places where our particle could be found at time $t$. If all we are given is that we have made a mistake in inferring from the laws of mechanics and the initial conditions where the particle will be at $s$, then we have no reason to believe why it may not be situated at any one of the indefinitely many alternatives to $s$. Thus we should assign equal probability to each one of the many possible resting places for the particle, i.e., an indefinitely small probability to each, including $s$. Thus $P(E/\sim A) = 0$. Thus if $P(E/A) = n$ and our last equation representing RE reduces to

$P(E) = nP(A),$

then employing RE once more we obtain,

$P(A) = P(A/B) \cdot P(B) + P(A/\sim B) \cdot P(\sim B).$

Now, of course, it is only the commonly practiced scientific method that looks reasonable to us, but there exist any number of other logically possible methods, e.g., those according to which we predict the location of a particle at any given time with the aid of this or that crystal ball, or horoscopy, etc. It stands to reason that if we were to predict the location of a particle through any such weird method, then the probability that—instead of one of the indefinitely many alternative positions—the outcome will be $s$ is negligibly small. Thus if $\sim B$ stands for the disjunction of all the "irrational" methods of scientific inquiry then $P(A/\sim B)$ might well be claimed to approach zero. Thus assuming that $P(A/B)$ equals $m$ (where $m$ is somewhat less than 1),

$P(A) = mP(B).$

Substituting for $P(A)$ from our earlier equation, we get

$P(E) = nmP(B).$

Clearly it should be possible to fabricate some metaphysical principles which—absurd as they may appear to us—offer a justification for any of the above-mentioned esoteric ways for divining future events. The question is: If $\sim C$ stands for the disjunction of all the justifications for different predictive methods, is it plausible to maintain that $P(A/\sim C) = 0$? There seem good reasons to deny this, since dozens of different justifications for traditional scientific method have been offered by philosophers ever since Hume raised the problem of induction, and if $\sim C$ includes all these with the exception of one particular variant $C$, then we cannot maintain that $P(A/\sim C)$ equals zero.

To avoid this difficulty we might introduce $C^*$, which stands for the disjunction of all those metaphysical doctrines which offer a justification for $B$. Thus $\sim C^*$ stands for the disjunction of all doctrines that justify some alternative to the commonly practiced scientific method. It follows that $P(B/\sim C^*) = 0$, and if $P(B/C^*) = k$ (where $k$ is slightly less than 1) then we end up with,

$$P(E) = kmnP(C^*).$$

It is not hard to see how one could continue in this vein, and find the value of $P(E)$ decreasing with every succeeding step. Thus if the above approach to the foundations of empirical knowledge claims has any plausibility then Lewis's pronouncement, "Nothing is probable unless something is certain," need not be assumed to have involved his overlooking the Rule of Elimination; on the contrary, it might be claimed to have been based on it.

## 5. The Issue of Combined Evidence

The following is a more straightforward example of the use of RE, since unlike the previous section, where we dealt with disjunctions of certain *kinds* of propositions, here our symbols will denote clearly specified propositions. It involves an argument of Ian Hacking, a leading expert on the history of probability. Hacking discusses the problem of how to combine pieces of evidence whose effects are clearly not additive. In the course of his study he treats at considerable length the following problem:[2]

We are traveling by overnight train from Washington, D.C., to Chicago, and in the morning we find in the parlor car a scrap of newspaper with the date of issue torn off which predicts "cold weather in Chicago tomorrow." If the paper is yesterday's then cold weather for today is a virtual certainty (because we assume the paper to be an infallible forecaster). If not, then it provides us with no useful information. We also see that the scrap is so clean and fresh that it is reasonable to assess the probability of its being from the latest issue of the paper as 90%. It is also known that during the particular time of the year in which this story took place meteorologists have determined the probability of a cold day in Chicago to be 20%.

Thus we are in possession or two different pieces of evidence, the scrap of paper which provides 90% support for the belief that today is going to be cold, and the general meteorological information which serves as a basis for assigning a 20% probability to the same event. How are we to combine them?

Hacking begins his discussion by stipulating that the chance of a cold day within a given period $t$ is constant, and that the newspaper was issued some time during the same period. Subsequently he considers the following four propositions:

---

[2] Ian Hacking, "Combined Evidence" in *Logical Theory and Semantic Analysis*, ed. S. Stenlund (Dordrecht, 1974), pp. 113–123.

(F)   Exactly one piece of paper including a weather report has been found in the parlor car, and this scrap must be from period $t$.

(C)   We are now in $t$, and it will be cold tomorrow in Chicago.

(N)   The newspaper mentioned in (F) predicts cold on the day following the publication.

(T)   It is today's newspaper.

Next, Hacking presents ten equations, after which he introduces an expression (∗) which he claims to be essential for deriving the solution:

(∗)   $P(N/\sim T \,\&\, C \,\&\, F) = P(N/\sim T \,\&\, \sim C \,\&\, F) = P(C)$.

To justify (∗) he explains that as long as we are assured that the newspaper has been issued on some day within the period $t$, then since we are given its infallibility we may regard the frequency with which it predicts cold to be precisely the frequency with which cold does occur in period $t$. In other words,

> the probability, that an infallible weather forecast taken at random from $t$ predicts cold, is the same as the probability, that a day in $t$ taken at random should be cold. That seems unexceptionable. (p. 119)

After deriving four more equations Hacking finally concludes that $P(C/N \,\&\, F) = 1 - P(\sim C) \cdot P(\sim T/F)$, which (given that $P(C) = 0.2$) equals $1 - 0.8 \times 0.1 = 0.92$.

A relatively minor objection to Hacking's presentation is that it seems so unlikely that it should require so many steps to arrive at the correct result. A more serious objection concerns his reliance on (∗). Situations are quite conceivable where (∗) is definitely false and yet the answer is the same as under the conditions stipulated by Hacking. Imagine, for example, that the newspaper in question is not entirely infallible, and on certain days when there are not enough signs to go by the policy is to forecast warm weather. Thus sometimes the paper predicts warm weather and it turns out to be cold, but it never happens that a cold day is incorrectly predicted.

If this were the situation in which we found ourselves, then instead of (∗),

(∗∗)   $P(N/\sim T \,\&\, C \,\&\, F) < P(C)$

would be true, since there are more actual cold days than predicted ones. Yet since the paper can fully be trusted when it predicts cold weather and everything else remains as in the original story, the probability of cold weather should be the same as that arrived at by Hacking. Is there no way to prove this formally?

To be more realistic, however, it has to be admitted that while some weather forecasters are more competent than others, none can be fully relied on, whether they predict a hot or a cold day. Thus in a practical situation it would not be true that the frequency with which any human agent made a given weather prediction would precisely equal the frequency with which in fact that sort of weather occurred in period $t$. In an actual situation (∗) would not be available.

But the hardest thing to understand about Hacking's approach is this: Admittedly, the general statistical information concerning the usual weather at this time of the year constitutes a very different kind of evidence, relating to our question, than the particular weather forecast printed in the newspaper. But why should that be of any concern to us? After all, RE is a theorem of elementary probability and is valid regardless of what the various symbols appearing in it stand for. But by RE we have

$$P(C/N \& F) = P(C/T \& N \& F) \cdot P(T/N \& F) + P(C/\sim T \& N \& F) \cdot P(\sim T/N \& F). \qquad (\alpha)$$

The only question we need to be concerned with is: Can we evaluate every expression on the right-hand side of $(\alpha)$? Evidently we can. If we go along with Hacking then we accept what he said, namely, that $P(C/T \& N \& F) = 1$. He has also pointed out that since the weather is independent of the question whether a newspaper is timely, $P(C/\sim T \& N \& F) = P(C)$. Thus,

$$P(C/N \& F) = P(T/N \& F) + P(C) \cdot P(\sim T/N \& F).$$

It seems legitimate to assume that $P(T/N \& F) = P(T/F)$, since the fact that the newspaper predicts cold on the day following publication does not affect the probability of it being today's paper, as we know of no reason why it should make such a prediction today rather than on some other day within period $t$. Hence we end up with

$$P(C/N \& F) = 0.9 + 0.2 \times 0.1 = 0.92,$$

which is also the result Hacking obtained.

Among the advantages of our method are the following points. First of all, its encouraging brevity, showing that on occasion probabilistic reasoning may actually be simpler than it appears at first; it does not involve the introduction of fourteen equations. Secondly, as long as we may assume that $P(C/T \& N \& F) = 1$, we arrive at Hacking's result without having to invoke the problematic expression (∗). Finally, and perhaps most importantly, our method is not confined to the special situation—one which in fact we shall never encounter—where we are ministered to by perfectly inerrant predictors. It matters not if $P(C/T \& N \& F) = n$, where $n$ has any value between zero and one, since we obtain the value of $P(C/N \& F)$ at once by substituting $n$ for $P(C/T \& N \& F)$ in equation ($\alpha$).

The most important issue this whole discussion raises involves the question of whether Hacking's example is unique in introducing a *special* problem of how different kinds of evidence interact. The answer seems to be that his example represents a fairly common situation, which we have dealt with before. For example, in the famous incident described in the previous chapter where a blue or green cab has been involved in a crash, we were confronted with radically different types of evidence: the relatively small number of blue cabs supports the hypothesis that the accident was caused by a green cab, while evidence of quite a different nature, namely the testimony of an eyewitness, supports its denial. We combined the two pieces of evidence, neither by adding them or subtracting one from the other, but through the use of Bayes's Theorem: The only small difficulty in the present context is that we could not straightforwardly employ the equation,

$$P(C/N \& F) = \frac{P(N \& F/C) \cdot P(C)}{P(N \& F)},$$

since we have no way of estimating the probability of $F$. One way of circumventing this problem is, as we have just seen, by using equation ($\alpha$).

I shall conclude with a somewhat simpler example which has, in the relevant sense, a structure identical to Hacking's story. One day in 1916 Mata Hari receives a letter expressing admiration for her dancing. She is used to receiving fan mail, but this particular letter is couched in strange, ungrammatical terms, and therefore she suspects it is in a coded language. When interpreted through the code she knows, the letter seems to be indicating that a zeppelin raid on Paris is imminent. What is the probability that such a raid is indeed being planned? Let

$(L) =$   A letter in strange, ungrammatical language is received, etc.

$(D) =$   The letter is meant to convey in code that a raid on Paris is imminent.

$(Z) =$   A zeppelin raid is imminent.

We shall assume that $P(Z/L \& D) = 1$, since if the letter does predict an air raid then we may be certain that it came from the authorities who know with virtual certainty what the Germans are going to do. In general, $P(Z) = \epsilon$, where $\epsilon$ is a small fraction. Also, on the basis of her past experience, in which 90% of this kind of weird letter she has received turned out to be espionage message, Mata Hari estimates $P(D/L)$ to equal 0.9. To evaluate $P(Z/L)$ we need to assess the interaction of two different types of evidence: on the one hand, there exists strong evidence that we need fear no air attack since such attacks in the past have been rather rare; on the other, the letter just arrived points toward a high probability of impending aerial bombardment.

We shall assume that Hari has no idea about the value of $P(L/Z)$, since it is only recently that she has proven herself trustworthy enough to be notified about forthcoming zeppelin raids, and she has no means of knowing whether in the future she will be informed about every impending attack nor whether such information is going to be conveyed by mail. Thus to evaluate $P(Z/L)$ she is not able simply to use Bayes's Theorem,

$$P(Z/L) = \frac{P(L/Z) \cdot P(Z)}{P(L)}.$$

It is however possible to use RE in the same manner as before:

$$P(Z/L) = P(Z/L \& D) \cdot P(D/L) + P(Z/L \& \sim D) \cdot P(\sim D/L)$$
$$= 1 \times 0.9 + \epsilon \times 0.1.$$

The only assumption additional to those already set forth is the rather innocuous one that $P(Z/L \& \sim D) = P(Z)$, i.e., that the probability of an imminent air raid is not affected by Mata Hari's receiving a strangely worded letter from one of the admirers of her stage performance.

# III

# COMPARING CREDIBILITIES

Many philosophers equate the credibility of a scientific hypothesis with its probability. They still find it hard to ascribe a numerical value to the credibility of a hypothesis and feel much more confident about the relative degrees of credibilities. Thus they will often assert univocally that the credibility of $H$, in the light of the evidence, is greater (or less) than it was before, and thus the evidence confirms (or disconfirms) $H$. They may also claim that the evidence has had a different confirmatory effect on $H$ than on $K$, i.e., it changed the probabilities of the two hypotheses by different degrees. In this chapter we shall deal with some aspects of comparative probabilities.

## 1. The Positive Instance Criterion of Confirmation

It has seemed natural to most to accept the principle that a universal generalization is confirmed by its positive instances. A hypothesis of the form "Every individual having property $F$ also has property $G$" is confirmed or has its credibility raised by observing the truth of $Fi \& Gi$, i.e., by observing that an individual $i$ exemplifies both $F$ and $G$. Thus the generalization "All mammals have livers" is confirmed to some degree by observing a mammal having a liver.

This elementary and intuitively fairly compelling criterion came under successful attack not so long ago by Ellery Eells. In his book *Rational Decision and Causality*[1] he constructs the following counterexample. Let it be given that we have before us two urns, each containing one hundred marbles. I know that urn 1 contains fifty

---

[1] Ellery Eells, *Rational Decision and Causality* (Cambridge, 1982).

glass black marbles and fifty glass white marbles, while urn 2 contains five glass black and ninety-five plastic white marbles. I pick at random a marble from one of the urns, which is just as likely to be urn 1 as urn 2, and I observe: $e = Ga \& Ba$, i.e., the marble I selected is glass and black. What effect does $e$ have on

$h$ = All the glass marbles in the urn before me are black?

On the one hand, $e$ constitutes a positive instance of $h$. On the other hand, however, the probability of $h$ in the light of $e$ is smaller than its prior probability:

$$P(h) = P(\text{urn 2 is before me}) = 1/2,$$

while in view of the fact that there are altogether fifty-five glass and black marbles, and only five of them in urn 2 as required by $h$,

$$P(h/e) = 1/11 < 1/2.$$

Thus $e$ disconfirms $h$. Eells concludes therefore that the positive instance criterion does not universally hold.

As Eells himself points out this is an artificial example, but that does not render it ineffective. Scientific examples modeled on his story may easily be imagined. A zoologist, for instance, could be studying habitat 1 and habitat 2 for which urn 1 and urn 2 may serve as parallels, while glass and plastic would stand for mammals and reptiles and the two colors for carnivorous and herbivorous.

Eells also suggests two provisos under which the positive instance criterion does hold. He maintains that a hypothesis "All $F$'s are $G$'s" $(= h)$ is confirmed by $Fa \& Ga(= e)$ provided: (i) $P(Fa/h) = P(Fa)$, and (ii) $P(Ga/Fa) < 1$.

He demonstrates this as follows. By Bayes's Theorem,

$$P(h/Fa \& Ga) = \frac{P(h) \cdot P(Fa \& Ga/h)}{P(Fa \& Ga)} \tag{B}$$

By definition, $e$ confirms $h$ if and only if,

$$P(h/e) > P(h) \quad \text{i.e.,} \quad P(h/Fa \& Ga) > P(h) \tag{C}$$

i.e., iff

$$\frac{P(Fa \& Ga/h) \cdot P(h)}{P(Fa \& Ga)} > P(h) \qquad \text{(substituting the right hand side of (B) into the left hand side of the inequality)}$$

$$\frac{P(Fa \& Ga/h)}{P(Fa \& Ga)} > 1 \qquad \text{(dividing both sides by } P(h)\text{)}$$

$$\frac{P(Fa/h) \cdot P(Ga/Fa \& h)}{P(Fa \& Ga)} > 1$$

(expanding the numerator by applying the Conjuctive Axiom)

$$\frac{P(Fa/h)}{P(Fa \& Ga)} > 1$$

(since $Fa \& h \to Ga$, and thus $P(Ga/Fa \& h) = 1$)

Eells concludes his proof by saying:

> Now, let us make the assumption that $Fa$ and $h$ are probabilistically independent. Then $e$ confirms $h$ if, and only if,

$$\frac{P(Fa)}{P(Fa) \cdot P(Ga/Fa)} > 1 \dots \text{(D)}$$

{$P(Fa/h) = P(F/a)$ and applying the multiplication rule to the denominator}

> if and only if,

> $P(Ga/Fa) > 1$.[2]

Eells points out that given his revised criterion the example with the two urns no longer creates any difficulties: the probability that the selected marble is glass is not independent of the hypothesis that all the glass marbles in the urn before us are black. Thus condition (i) is violated and the positive instance confirmation criterion does not apply here.

I believe, however, that the argument Eells has offered in support of the new criterion is not entirely correct. While his proof does indeed show that given (i) and (ii) the observation of a positive instance confirms $h$, it does not show that *only* if. That is, while he has shown that his two conditions are sufficient to ensure that the evidence supports the hypothesis, he has not shown that they are jointly necessary. To see exactly what has and what has not been shown, it is best to work our way backwards, by beginning with $P(Ga/Fa) > 1$, and then assume (i) $P(Fa/h) = P(Fa)$, which will lead us to Eells's first step, $P(h/e) > P(h)$. It should be clear that it is advantageous and not disadvantageous if (i) is false, and $P(Fa/h) > P(h)$ is true, for obviously given (D) (that is, given that the fraction with the numerator $P(Fa)$ is greater than 1), then surely a fraction with the same denominator but with numerator $P(Fa/h)$ must be greater than 1!

What has to be conceded, though, is that the same proof cannot be used to show that the positive instance criterion holds even

---

[2] Ibid., p. 61.

when $P(Fa/a) < P(Fa)$. But even in that case no proof has been provided that it is *not* the case that $P(h/e) > P(h)$. In fact, sometimes it is the case and sometimes it is not. The following shows that the positive instance criterion may hold even when $P(Fa/h) < P(Fa)$.

Suppose we have before us two urns. Let it be given that half of the contents of urn 1 are black glass marbles, and the other half are plastic marbles. Urn 2 contains an equal number of marbles and they are all glass and white. We select at random one marble $a$ for inspection and it turns out to be black and glass. This confirms $h$: All the glass marbles in the urn before us are black. Indeed it conclusively verifies $h$, since a black glass marble could

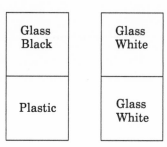

**Figure 10**

not have come from anywhere else but urn 1. Now $P(Fa/h)$, the probability that $a$ (the marble to be selected) is glass given that $h$, i.e., given that we have urn 1 in front of us, is $1/2$. On the other hand $P(Fa)$, the probability that $a$ is glass when $h$ is not given and thus the marble has the same chance of coming from either urn equals—as can be seen from Figure 10—$3/4$. Thus here we encounter a situation where a positive instance of $h$ confirms it even though $P(Fa/h) < P(Fa)$.

Seeing that Eells's condition (i) is not required, we need to inquire what is the real explanation of why, in the example he has produced, the positive instance criterion is violated. To do so we have to take notice of the fact that in his example $h$ logically implies $h'$, where $h'$ is disconfirmed by the evidence: $h$ logically implies that we have urn 1 before us which was said to contain plastic marbles as well, i.e., $h$ implies

$h'$ = Not all the marbles in the urn before us are glass.

The prior probabilities of $h$ and of $h'$ are both $1/2$. On the other hand, $P(h'/e)$ is less than that, it is $1/3$. Thus the evidence disconfirms $h'$. I would claim therefore that the positive instance criterion applies regardless of how $P(Fa/h)$ and $P(Fa)$ are related to one another, except where the positive instance constitutes disconfirmatory or nonconfirmatory evidence for a hypothesis implied by $h$.

## 2. The Special Consequence Condition

What I have just said seems to assume the validity of the Special Consequence Condition (SCC). That widely discussed condition has been formulated as follows:

(SCC)  If $e$ confirms $h$, and $h$ logically implies $h'$, then $e$ also confirms $h'$.

By applying Modus Tollens to the SCC we obtain that if $e$ does not confirm (or disconfirms) $h'$ then $e$ does not confirm $h$.

The SCC sounds plausible, yet it is agreed by virtually everyone that it is false. Eells provides a nice example illustrating this. Consider a subscriber to a newspaper whose deliverer is so unreliable that only for 0.8 of all days is the paper delivered, and only on 0.25 of these days is it delivered before eight A.M.

$h = $ The paper will arrive before eight A.M. today.

$h' = $ The paper will arrive today.

$e = $ Due to a paper shortage only half of the usual number of copies have been printed and thus the deliverer has considerably fewer papers to deliver today and also fewer to deliver on his route to our subscriber.

Given $e$, we may assume that the paper will arrive today, if at all, before eight A.M. It may be reasonable to say that $P(h'/e) = P(h/e) = 1/2$, since only half of the subscribers will get the paper today. Thus $e$ lowers the probability of $h$, while it raises the probability of $h'$.[3]

Other writers have cited even stronger reasons why the SCC must be rejected. The distinguished philosopher Mary Hesse in her *The Structure of Scientific Inference* claims, like others before her, that the acceptance of that condition would lead to the absurd result of allowing any proposition to confirm any proposition whatever. Suppose, for example, that $h$ entails $f$, and $k$ is the conjunction of $h$ and $g$ (where $f$ and $g$ have absolutely nothing to do with one another); then $k$ also entails $f$. Thus $f$ confirms $k$ which logically implies $g$ therefore the SCC would instruct us to regard $f$ as providing evidential support to the randomly chosen $g$. This shows that the SCC is untenable "for it contradicts the tacit condition that confirmation must be a selective relation among propositions."[4]

---

[3] Ibid., pp. 56–57.

[4] Mary Hesse, *The Structures of Scientific Inference* (Berkeley, 1974), p. 143.

For a concrete illustration of Hesse's objection, let

$f =$ All observed ravens until now were black.
$g =$ Borrowed garments never fit well.
$h =$ All ravens are black.
$k = h \& g$.

Establishing $f$ confirms not only $h$ but $k$ as well (in an innocuous, obvious sense since the probability of a conjunction rises if the probability of one of its conjuncts rises). And we have to agree with Hesse that it would be intolerable if our past observations of the color of ravens were to be acknowledged as supporting the proverb concerning borrowed garments.

All this, however, does not invalidate my suggested solution to the problem of positive instance confirmation. Nobody has provided any reason why the SCC should be rejected *in toto*. In fact there exist plainly statable circumstances under which the SCC is valid, and others under which it is not.

Let us first be reminded that,

(I)   When $h \rightarrow h'$, then $P(h) \leq P(h')$ and (regardless of what $x$ stands for) $P(h/x) \leq P(h'/x)$.

It follows at once that when there is evidence to raise the probability of $h$ so much so that $P(h/e) > P(h')$, then the probability of $h'$ must also rise so that in compliance with (I), $P(h/e) \leq P(h'/e)$ will hold, and $e$ which confirms $h$ also confirms $h'$, i.e., the SCC applies. Otherwise it does not apply. Thus we may state the Restricted Special Consequence Condition:

(RSCC)   Given that $h \rightarrow h'$, $e$ confirms $h$, and $e$ raises $h'$s probability to a value higher than $P(h')$, then and only then, $e$ also confirms $h'$.

Hesse's objection, for example, can now be seen to disappear. She had $k = h \& g$ and $h \rightarrow f$ and therefore $P(k/f) > P(k)$, which means that $f$ confirms $k$; but $k \rightarrow g$, so that if the SCC applies we end up with the absurdity that an arbitrary $f$ (= All ravens observed in the past were black) confirms $g$ (= Borrowed garments never fit well). Clearly, however, $P(k/f) = (h \& g/f) = P(g/f) \cdot P(h/g/f) = P(g) \cdot P(h/g \& f)$, since $P(g/f) = P(g)$, $f$ being irrelevant to $g$. Also, since $P(h/g \& f) \leq 1$ it follows that $P(k/f) < P(g)$, and consequently by the RSCC $f$ does not confirm $g$, and the feared absurdity does not materialize.

Before leaving the subject of the qualified version of the Special Consequence Condition, I should like to mention that P. Horwich has raised an interesting issue in the course of his inquiry as to whether evidence $E$ (which is the discovery that a randomly selected person is a great philosopher from Ohio), confirms or rather disconfirms $T$ (which postulates that *all* great philosophers come from Ohio). On the one hand, we are inclined to say that it confirms it, since $E$ instantiates $T$. On the other hand, there seems to be good reason for maintaining that $E$ disconfirms $T$: the fact that we happened to come across a great philosopher indicates that there exist more than a few of them, and if so it would be a very unlikely coincidence if they all came from Ohio. Thus $E$ supports the conjecture that the world contains a considerable number of great philosophers, implying that they are likely to be scattered all over the globe, which in turn supports the denial of $T$.[5]

The answer to the inquiry whether $E$ confirms or does not confirm $T$ is actually neither simply affirmative nor negative but as before it depends on the relevant probabilities. Let,

$e = $ A randomly selected great philosopher turns out to be from Ohio.

$H = $ $\text{P}(e) < n$.

We shall assume with Horwich that $T \rightarrow H$, i.e., that if no great philosophers are nurtured anywhere outside Ohio, then the probability of meeting such a personage through a random encounter is less than a given small fraction $n$. Now $\text{P}(H/e)$ is less than $\text{P}(H)$, that is, observing $e$ to be true lowers the probability of $H$, i.e., $e$ disconfirms $H$.

All this shows that the answer to Horwich's question depends on the initial probability of $H$ and on the amount by which $e$ lowers it. In case $\text{P}(H)$ was not higher than $\text{P}(T)$ to start with, it matters not to what degree $\text{P}(H)$ is lowered by the discovery of $e$; $\text{P}(T)$ (because $T$ logically implies $H$) is inevitably lowered as well. If however the prior probability of $H$ is higher than that of $T$ then there are two possibilities: (i) the discovery of $e$ lowers $H$'s probability below $\text{P}(T)$, or (ii) the discovery of $e$ lowers it less than that. If case (i) holds, then observing the great philosopher from Ohio disconfirms not merely $H$ but $T$ as well. On the other hand, if merely (ii) is the case, then while $e$ disconfirms $H$ it confirms $T$.

---

[5] "Explanations of Irrelevance," in *Testing Scientific Theories*, ed. J. Earman (Minnesota, 1983), p. 64.

### 3. Comparing Posterior to Prior Credibility

The degree to which the evidence confirms a given hypothesis is the amount of change the credibility of the latter has undergone through the evidence. The degree of confirmation is obtained by comparing the posterior credibility of the hypothesis to its prior credibility. There have been several suggestions how to define precisely the degree to which evidence supports a hypothesis. The following two are the most widely accepted ones:

(I) The ratio of the posterior probability to the prior probability of a hypothesis is the measure of the change of credibility the evidence brought about in the hypothesis. Thus the degree of confirmation is $P(H/E)/P(H)$. When this fraction is greater than 1 the evidence confirms the hypothesis; when less than 1 it disconfirms it; and when it equals 1 the evidence is said to be irrelevant.

(II) According to this suggestion it is the difference rather than the ratio between the two quantities that stands for the degree of confirmation, i.e., it is the expression $P(H/E)-P(H)$. Thus when this quantity is greater than zero $E$ confirms $H$; when less it disconfirms it; and when it equals zero it is irrelevant.

Some philosophers are of the opinion that it is important that we regard (II) as representing the degree of confirmation. Donald Gillies claims that it cannot be right to define the measure of support as $P(h/e)/P(h)$ since

$$\frac{P(h/e)}{P(h)} = \frac{P(e/h)}{P(e)},$$

and thus when (as is generally the case) the hypothesis logically implies the evidence, $P(e/h) = 1$, and therefore $P(h/e)/P(h) = 1/P(e)$. This would mean that the degree of support $h$ receives depends solely on $e$. To Gillies, however, it seems obvious that the support must also depend on $h$, and Criterion (I), which fails to reflect this, is wrong.[6]

Gillies then proceeds to demonstrate some further absurd consequences to which the adoption of Criterion (I) as the measure of the degree of confirmation leads. Suppose $e$ stands for the statement that the large number of ravens so far observed were all black, and

---

[6] Donald Gillies, "In Defense of the Popper–Miller Argument," *Philosophy of Science* (1986): 110–113.

$g$ for any arbitrary hypothesis, say, a detailed version of the big bang theory. Then, according to the advocates of Criterion (II), both the simple theory $h$ and the conjunctive theory $h \& g$ are supported by $e$, and the degree of support in both cases is $1/P(e)$, which he says is unacceptable. Gillies maintains that, on any reasonable position, the more a hypothesis $h$ goes beyond the evidence $e$ the less it is supported by $e$. This crucial requirement that is violated by the criterion he rejects is, however, satisfied by his own criterion, for from Bayes's Theorem he obtains that

$$P(h/e) - P(h) = \left( \frac{1}{P(e)} - 1 \right) \cdot P(h),$$

which is the degree of confirmation on Gillies's view. He argues that

> [o]n the reasonable assumption that the more sweeping and general a hypothesis $h$ the less its prior probability, we have the result that the more $h$ goes beyond $e$, the smaller will be [the] support $e$ provides for $h$. (p. 112)

At this stage I shall point out only that Gillies is naturally right in maintaining that the more $h$ goes beyond $e$ the smaller the support $e$ provides for $h$. But this only means that ultimately we end up with a very small value for $P(h/e)$, which is the final credibility of $h$ in the light of the evidence $e$. But if $h$ is an extravagant hypothesis, $P(h)$ (the prior probability with which $h$ starts) is proportionately just as small. Consequently, it is only to be expected that we shall end up with the same value for the ratio $P(h/e)/P(h)$ when both the numerator and denominator are large, as when they are both diminished by the same factor.

## 4. Which of the Two Criteria of Confirmation Is Preferable?

It is of no vital importance to choose one criterion rather than the other, since when it comes to the question whether a piece of evidence confirms, disconfirms, or is irrelevant to a hypothesis, each gives the same answer. We also get the same result on either criterion when we wish to determine whether $e$ confirms $h$ as much, more, or less than it does $k$. Nevertheless, it is possible to argue that Criterion (I) may have a certain edge over its rival. The following example shows how it may.

In a gambling casino players are confronted by two urns each of which contains a single red marble. Through a random mechanism another marble is introduced in each urn and the chances are equal that the second marble is either white or red. Let,

$h$ = Both marbles in urn 1 are red,
$k$ = Both marbles in urn 2 are red.

We thus have $P(h) = P(k) = 1/2$, and $P(h \& k) = 1/4$, since $h$ and $k$ are independent of one another. I am allowed to pick at random a marble from urn 1, and I observe it to be red. Through this evidence the probability of $h$ increases and now equals 2/3. As 2/3 divided by 1/2 equals 4/3, we should say that the posterior probability of $h$ is 4/3 higher than was its prior probability. Clearly, the probability of $P(h \& k)$ has also increased because of my observation, and is now $1/2 \times 2/3 = 1/3$. Dividing 1/3 by 1/4 results also in 4/3 and thus the final probability of the conjunction $h \& k$ is also 4/3 higher than its initial probability, even though $h$ is completely irrelevant to $k$.

The rules of the game are that a player receives a prize of \$$N$ if prior to any evidence he bets correctly on $h$. His expected utilities are therefore \$$N \times 1/2 = $\$$N/2$. Given that the casino wishes to treat all wagerers even-handedly, it must offer 2\$$N$ to anyone who bets on the conjunction $h \& k$, so that his expected utilities are also $($\$$2N \times 1/4 =)$\$$N/2$. In order to remain even-handed, following the drawing of a red marble from the urn the house will offer 3/4 (the inverse of 4/3) times \$$N$, if I bet on $h$ and win, for then my expected utilities are $(3/4 \times $\$$N) \times 2/3 = $\$$N/2$, as before.

For those who wish to bet on $h \& k$ after observing the red marble drawn from the urn, the bank will reduce the prize by exactly the same factor, since $(3/4 \times $\$$2N) \times 1/3 = $\$$N/2$, and thus betting on either outcome is worth the same. We may state generally that if $u$ is the measure to which $e$ raises the probability of $h$ from what it was before, and $N$ the reward for betting correctly on $h$, then to treat bets even-handedly $1/u$ should be the reward for winning with $h$ when $e$ is given, and similarly whatever the prize for betting successfully on $h \& k$ subsequent to observing the evidence of the red ball. Thus Criterion (I) has the significant feature that the numerical value of the degree of confirmation it measures can serve to determine the change the evidence brought about in the expected utilities associated with a given outcome. Criterion (II) does not seem to have this feature.

Additional grounds for preferring Criterion (I) over (II) have been provided by a philosopher, R. Rosenkrantz, who interestingly enough happens to come to the opposite conclusion on the very same grounds. His discusses, a situation where $h$ entails $e$, and $k$ is an arbitrary hypothesis that has nothing to do with $e$. Now since P($e/h$)=1 it follows that $P(e/h \& k)$ equals 1 as well, and thus $P(h/e) : P(h) = P(h \& k/k) = 1/P(e)$. It follows therefore that if we adopt Criterion (I) as our measure of the degree of confirmation, then the support $e$ provides for $h \& k$ is precisely the same it provides for $h$ alone.

> That seems objectionable when $k$ is extraneous, and even more objectionable when $k$ is probabilistically incompatible with $h$ in the sense that $P(k/h)$ is low. Personally, I have always considered this reason enough to reject the ratio measure in favor of the difference measure:
>
> $$dc(e, h) = P(h/e) - P(h)$$
>
> writing $dc(e, h)$ for the *degree of confirmation* $e$ accords $h$.[7]

Rosenkrantz finds this result particularly appropriate since in addition to implying that $e$ confirms $h \& k$ less than it does $h$, it also shows that $dc(e, h \& k)$ varies with $P(h/k)$, that is, the degree of compatibility of $k$ with $h$ "control[s] the rate of depreciation."

Now, of course, the value of $P(k/h)$ plays a crucial role in determining the value of the probability of the conjunction of $h$ and $k$ both before and after $e$ is given. But surely, to the extent the statistical dependence of $h$ on $k$ affects the value of $P(h \& k)$, precisely to the same extent it also affects the value of $P(h \& k/e)$ and should therefore have *no* effect on their ratio. It is thus a disadvantage, rather than an advantage, that by Criterion (II) the degree of confirmation does vary with $P(k/h)$.

To reassure ourselves that this is indeed so, we observe that by the Conjunctive Axiom,

$$P(h \& k) = P(h) \cdot P(k/h) \quad \text{and} \quad P(h \& k/e) = P(h/e) \cdot P(k/h \& e).$$

For a moment the impression may be had that the dependency of $h$ on $k$ does affect the ratio of the posterior and prior probabilities since there are different factors involved in the denominator and the numerator, i.e., in one case $P(k/h)$ and in the other $P(k/h \& e)$. But by RE,

$$P(k/h) = P(e/h) \cdot P(k/h \& e) + P(\sim e/h) \cdot P(k/h \& \sim e).$$

And since we were given that $P(e/h) = 1$, it follows that $P(\sim e/h) = 0$, and thus $P(k/h) = P(k/h \& e)$. Hence the two factors are identical

---

[7] R. Rosenkrantz, "Why Glymour Is a Bayesian," in *Testing Scientific Hypotheses*, ed. J. Earman (Minneapolis, 1983), p. 92.

and the value of the relevant ratio is as claimed, independent of the way the probabilities of $h$ and $k$ are related to one another.

There is a third argument in favor of Criterion (R) ('R' stands for ratio), which is perhaps the strongest one. It often happens in practical research that a scientist investigates a theory $T$ which is a conjunction of $h$, the main hypothesis, and its auxiliary hypothesis, $a$. The scientist knows that by performing a certain kind of experiment there is a good chance for him to obtain result $e$, which would be irrelevant to $a$, but would raise the probability of $h$ and therefore also of $T$ which is equivalent to $h \& a$. He is also aware that by performing another kind of experiment there is an equally good chance of obtaining result $f$, which though irrelevant to $h$ would raise the credibility of $a$ and hence of $T$. Both experiments may be expensive and so he can afford to carry out but one of them. Everything else being equal the rational thing for him to do is to perform that experiment which if successful will yield a higher degree of confirmation for what he is after, viz. $T$.

Let us suppose that $P(h) = 1/8$ and $P(h/e) = 1/4$. Then the degree to which $e$ confirms $h$ by Criterion R, $P(h/e)/P(h) = 2$, while the degree to which $e$ confirms $h$ by Criterion D ('D' stands for difference), $P(h/e) - P(h) = 1/8$. Suppose further that $P(a) = 1/3$ and $P(a/f) = 1/2$. Then the degree to which $f$ confirms $a$ by Criterion R, $P(a/f)/P(a) = 3/2$, and the degree to which $f$ confirms $a$ Criterion D, $P(a/f) - P(a) = 1/6$. We see that according to Criterion R it is true both that $e$ confirms $h$ (since the relevant ratio is 2) and that $f$ confirms $a$ (where the ratio is $3/2$)—both numbers being higher than 1. Similarly, by Criterion D, $e$ confirms $h$ (where the relevant difference is $1/8$) and $f$ confirms $a$ (where the difference is $1/6$)— both numbers being positive. Thus far the two criteria agree with one another.

They clearly disagree, however, on the question of whether $e$ confirms $h$ to a higher or a lower degree than $f$ confirms $a$: according to Criterion R $e$ confirms $h$ more than $f$ confirms $a$ since $2 > 3/2$. According to Criterion D, however, it is the other way round, since $1/6 > 1/8$.

Thus Criterion R seems to indicate that it pays more to perform the experiment which may yield $e$ rather than the one that would yield $f$, whereas Criterion D indicates the opposite.

We shall assume that $h$ is independent of $f$ and $a$ is independent of $e$. Clearly, then,

$$P(T/e) = P(h \& a/e) = 1/4 \times 1/3 = 1/12$$

while

$$P(T/f) = P(h \& a/f) = 1/8 \times 1/2 = 1/16$$

So it is unquestionable that it is more useful to do the experiment that may yield $e$ (as implied by the comparison made—from the standpoint of Criterion R—between the effect of $e$ on $h$ and the effect of $f$ on $a$ through Criterion R) for it will result in a higher confirmation of $T$. This provides support for Criterion R.

### 5. Comparing the Confirmation of Different Hypotheses

When we are considering different hypotheses not all of which imply the observations, then there is a simple principle by which we may compare the relative effect of the evidence on the hypotheses:

(E)   $P(e/h) > P(e/h')$ iff $e$ confirms $h$ more than it confirms $h'$.

Principle (E) follows from both criteria we have just discussed. To see this in the case of the criterion which regards the ratio between the posterior and prior probabilities of the hypotheses as the proper measure of the degree of confirmation, all we do is substitute $h$ and then $h'$ into Theorem (B), thus obtaining two equations which give us $P(h'/e)/P(h') > P(e/h)/P(e)$ iff $P(e/h')/P(e) > P(e/h)/P(e)$, i.e., iff $P(e/h') > P(e/h)$, which amounts to (E). According to the other criterion, which regards the difference rather than the ratio as the relevant measure, we obtain: $P(h'/e) - P(h') > P(h/e) - P(h)$ iff $P(e/h')/P(e) > P(e/h)/P(e)$, which also amounts to (E).

Principle (E) may also look objectionable for reasons fairly similar to the reason why Gillies objected to the first criterion for the measure of evidential support. M. Martin, in a paper on confirmation, claimed that (E) leads to absurd results. He considered the example in which,

> $h =$ 99% of all ravens are black,
> $h' = k \& l =$ All ravens are black *and* some roses are black,
> $e =$ Of the five ravens hitherto observed all were black.

Martin claims:

> Surely there is nothing initially less credible about $h'$ than $h$. Nevertheless since $P(e/h') > P(e/h)$, then $e$ confirms $h'$ more than $h$. This is absurd.[8]

---

[8] M. Martin, "Does the Evidence Confirm Theism More Than Naturalism?" *International Journal for Philosophy of Religion* (1984): 261.

It is plausible to conjecture that Martin was arguing along the following lines. There is very little difference between $h$ and the first conjunct of $h'$, $k$, while its second conjunct is entirely irrelevant to $e$, and hence $l$'s credibility should not at all be affected by the discovery that $e$. Consequently, he may have gained the impression that establishing the truth of $e$ raises the credibility of $h$ more (upon which it has full bearing) than it raises that of $h'$ (with one half of which it has nothing to do). But in fact since $P(e/h) = .99 \times .99 \times .99 \times .99 \times .99 \approx .96$ while $P(e/h) = 1 > P(e/h)$, according to (E) $e$ confirms $h'$ more than $h$.

I may add that even without the aid of arithmetic it can be shown by common sense that Martin is not right. After all, clearly if all ravens are black, there is a slightly greater chance for the five observed ravens to be black than if only 99% of them are. Hence the probability of $k$ rises somewhat more than that of $h$ through the materialization of $e$. True enough, $e$ has nothing to do with $l$, and hence *its* probability is unaffected by $e$. But $e$ raises the probability of $k$ by exactly the same factor when it is, as when it is not, conjoined by $l$, that is, by a factor greater than by which it raises the probability of $h$.

A special case in which Principle (E) may be found to be useful is where $h'$ is simply the denial of $h$. The following is a true story illustrating conditions under which the principle may be applied. The world bridge championship was held in Buenos Aires in May 1965. The British team's members were accused of cheating, by signaling to each other the number of hearts the players had. The matter was serious enough to warrant a hearing resembling a genuine legal proceeding . The prosecutor had a full list of the specific hands played by the British team and showed that their playing these hands was consistent with the hypothesis that the two British competitors had illicit knowledge of the heart suit. The defense attorney pointed out that their playing was also consistent with their customary way of playing. The prosecutor insisted that what mattered was that their play was consistent with the charge that they cheated and therefore it supported that charge.

Sheldon Ross, in concluding his discussion of this incident, explains that the play of the cards could have been regarded as supporting the hypothesis of cheating only if it were the case that $P(E/H) > P(E/\sim H)$, i.e., if $E$ (the way the hands that were played) was more probable on $H$ (the hypothesis of guilt) than on its denial.[9] But the prosecutor never made this claim, so his assertion that the evidence confirms the charge against the players is invalid.

Here then is a simple illustration of the special use of Principle (E). Somewhat peripherally, however, I might point out that from the manner in which Ross presents the story it is not entirely clear that the inequality does not hold. Admittedly, the way the hands were played was *consistent* with both the hypothesis that $H$ and the hypothesis that $\sim H$. In general, however, a complete lack of knowledge of which cards one's partner holds is a handicap, and even a life master may adopt a line of play he would have realized to be a mistake had he been aware of the number of hearts in his partner's possession. Thus, while the particular way the hands were actually played may have been consistent with a master's strategy, the relevant question is, whether there may not also have been some additional strategies consistent with a state of complete ignorance and not with the possession of relevant information. If such an alternative strategy does exist, then the prosecutor may have been right after all: $E$ was consistent with $H$. It follows therefore that $P(E/H) > P(E/\sim H)$, since on $\sim H$ there were other reasonable strategies that could have been adopted and which were inconsistent with $H$.

## 6. Justified Belief

A considerable number of philosophers agree that when a hypothesis has been confirmed strongly enough so that its credibility has reached a certain number $n$, where $n$ is somewhere between $1/2$ and $1$, then that hypothesis becomes rationally acceptable, or one is justified in believing it. There are two factors that make for the vagueness of the notion of justified belief: (i) there is no general agreement what the precise value of $n$ is supposed to be, and (ii) even if that value were fixed we have no criterion whereby to assign numerical values to the probabilities of scientific hypothesis. Nevertheless, one may profitably compare different hypotheses with respect to their warrantedness. Let us look at some examples illustrating this.

(I) Suppose it is given that $\sim E(H/K)(=$ It is not the case that one is justified in believing that $H$, given that $K$), is it then also possible that $\sim E(\sim H/K)$? The answer is: it depends on whether $n$ is greater than $1/2$. Consequently it is possible that both $P(H/K)$ and

[9] Sheldon Ross, *A First Course in Probability* (New York, 1984), p. 69.

$P(\sim H/K)$ should be less than $n$. Thus $\sim E(H/K)$ and $\sim E(\sim H/K)$ are compossible.

(II) Is it possible for both $E(H/K)$ and $E(H/\sim K)$ to be true? The answer is, Yes. For example, when $P(H) > n$, and $H$ is probabilistically independent of $K$, then the probability of $H$ is at least $n$ regardless of whether $K$ is true or false.

(III) Suppose $E(H/K)$ and $E(K/L)$, does it follow that $E(H/L)$? This question amounts to asking whether the relation of justification between evidence and hypothesis is transitive. One way to go about answering this is by assigning numerical values to the various expressions involved. We may, for instance, assume that $n = 3/4$, and postulate $P(H/K) = 1$, $P(K/L = 3/4$ and $P(H/L) = 0$. There are various ways to show that these values are compossible. The easiest way is perhaps with the aid of Figure 11, where we see that four of the $K$-squares are also $H$-squares, i.e., $P(H/K) = 4/5$, and three out of the four $L$-squares are also $K$-squares, hence $P(K/L) = 3/4$, and two of the $L$-squares are $H$-squares, and therefore $P(H/L) = 1/2$. This then shows that justified belief is not transitive, since here we have an example where $E(H/K)$ and $E(K/L)$ hold but it is not the case that $E(H/L)$.

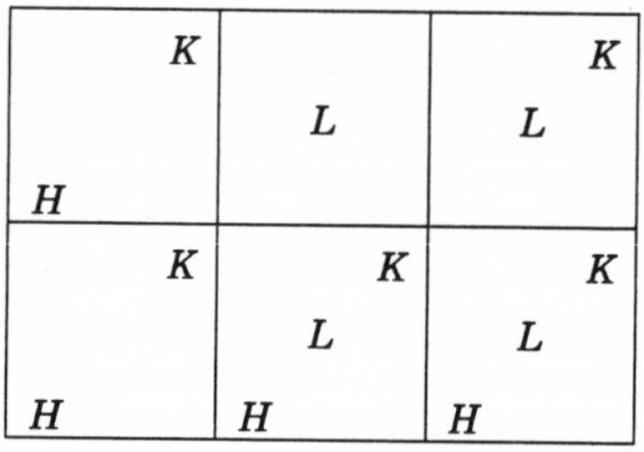

**Figure 11**

(IV) Given that $E(H \vee K/L)$ and $E(\sim H/L)$, does it follow that $E(K/L)$? One is inclined to say that it does, in line with what is known as the Hypothetical Syllogism, i.e., the rule that from $H \vee K$ and $\sim H$ one may infer $K$. However, as we saw in the previous example, where the Law of Transitivity failed to apply, Hypothetical Syllogism does not apply to what are only highly credible—but not certainly true or false—sentences either. In Figure 12 we see that three out of the four $L$-squares are $H \vee K$-squares. Thus $P(H \vee K/L) = 3/4$ and therefore $E(H \vee K/L)$; also, three out of the four $L$-squares are $\sim H$-squares and hence $E(\sim H/L)$, and yet only two out of the four $L$-squares are $K$-squares, and therefore $\sim E(K/L)$.

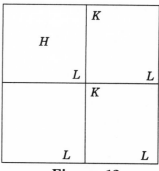

**Figure 12**

## 7. A Rational Justification of Total Skepticism

Keith Lehrer has offered an interesting justification of complete skepticism which requires him to maintain that he knows absolutely nothing. He insists that his ignorance is so all-inclusive as to embrace even itself, that is, he admits to his failure to actually *know* that he knows nothing. He concedes, of course, like everybody else that there are a great number of propositions which seem obviously true to him; however, he feels unjustified in ruling out the possibility that there may exist some highly intelligent, powerful, and malevolent beings who are deceiving him into imagining things that are not so. Lehrer's argument is similar to the famous argument of Descartes, except that he does not resort to any supernatural agencies.

In order to assess the exact nature of Lehrer's argument and the presuppositions upon which it is built it will be best to follow a very clear and detailed exposition of it by Risto Hilpinen.[10] Hilpinen calls the hypothesis that there exist extraterrestrial tricksters, the "sceptical hypothesis" and denotes it by $s$. He believes it to be reasonable to assert:

(L1)  $s \rightarrow \sim Eh,$

where $h$ stands for anything. I believe we would not want to deny that if it were actually given that our perceptions and thought processes are distorted by powerful manipulators then no evidence and no reason for believing anything to be true could be regarded as reliable.

Hilpinen also supposes on behalf of Lehrer:

(S2)  $\sim E \sim s.$

Though (S2) does not go so far as to claim that a belief in mischievous extraterrestrial beings is warranted, it is a controversial claim; many would grant that we are *not* positively justified in denying the existence of such beings.

Finally he enunciates the theorem:

(S3)  *If $p \rightarrow q$, then $\sim E \sim p \rightarrow \sim E \sim q$.*

Subsequently Hilpinen proceeds to reconstruct formally Lehrer's proof:

---

[10] Risto Hilpinen, "Scepticism and Justification," *Synthese* (1983): 165–174.

   (1)  $s \rightarrow \sim Eh$                                               (L1)

   (2)  $\sim E \sim s$                                                 (S2)

   (3)  If $s \rightarrow \sim Eh$, then    (S3), substituting $s$ for $p$ & $\sim Eh$ for $q$

       $\sim E \sim s \rightarrow \sim E \sim \sim Eh$

   (4)  $\sim E \sim s \rightarrow \sim E \sim \sim Eh$          (1), (3), Modus Ponens

   (5)  $\sim EEh$                           (2), (4), Modus Ponens

   (6)  $\sim EEh \rightarrow \sim Eh$        (L2): $Eh \rightarrow EEh$ by counterposition

                                   ((L2) is a somewhat controversial rule)

   (7)  $\sim Eh$                                 (5), (6), Modus Ponens

This then is an interesting and instructive illustration of how the notion of 'probable to high enough degree to warrant belief' may be employed in deriving basic philosophical theses.

In my *Range of Epistemic Logic*, I produced what seemed to me an objection to Lehrer's argument as presented by Hilpinen. I began by enunciating a fairly trivial theorem:

(L2*)  $\sim Eh \rightarrow E \sim Eh$.

Anyone who subscribes to (L2) will not fail to subscribe to its twin theorem (L2*), which says that if, objectively speaking, there is no justification for me to hold $h$, then there is a rational basis for believing that I have no justification for holding $h$.

Now Lehrer has introduced the hypothesis $s$, concerning the existence of very powerful creatures who are capable of manipulating our minds and see to it that we form no correct beliefs about anything. He did not regard $s$ too implausible and claimed that as long as we have no positive proof of its falsity he is entitled to assert

(S2)  $\sim E \sim s$.

It stands to reason, therefore, that Lehrer would not object if, emulating him, we entertained the thought that perhaps even more powerful creatures existed as well, who happen to be benevolent and disapprove of the mischievous machinations of Lehrer's tricksters and make sure that their evil designs are frustrated. We seem to be entitled to assume that there are no positive arguments showing our hypothesis to be less likely true than Lehrer's, and therefore we may assert

(T2)  $\sim E \sim t$,

where $t$ stands for our statement concerning the benevolent superbeings. It also seems that we may assert, parallel to (L1),

(L1*)  $t \rightarrow Eh$,

since $t$ means that all the interferences of the malevolent beings are neutralized. Thus we have:

| | |
|---|---|
| (1') $t \rightarrow \mathrm{E}h$ | (L1*) |
| (2') $\sim\mathrm{E}\sim t$ | (T2) |
| (3') If $t \rightarrow \mathrm{E}h$ then$\sim\mathrm{E}\sim t \rightarrow \sim\mathrm{E}\sim\mathrm{E}h$ | (S3) $t/p, \mathrm{E}h/q$ |
| (4') $\sim\mathrm{E}\sim t \rightarrow \sim\mathrm{E}\sim\mathrm{E}h$ | (1'), (3'), Modus Ponens |
| (5') $\sim\mathrm{E}\sim\mathrm{E}h$ | (2), (4), Modus Ponens |
| (6') $\sim\mathrm{E}\sim h \rightarrow \mathrm{E}h$ | (L2*), contraposition |
| (7') $\mathrm{E}h$. | (5'), (6'), Modus Ponens |

*Proof:* (1')–(7') is of course the mirror image of Hilpinen's (1)–(7) and leads to the contradictory result that should be taken as an indication that (L1) was incorrect. After all, given the truth of $t$, the truth of $s$ does not imply that $\sim\mathrm{E}h$.

David Shatz, in reviewing my argument, has raised what seems to me a very strong objection.[11] He has pointed out that Lehrer could well reply by attacking my very first premise, (1') $t \rightarrow \mathrm{E}h$, by reminding us that truth does not guarantee justified belief, that is, the bare fact that $t$ may be true is not sufficient to warrant my belief that $t$. In fact, it is not even necessary that $t$ be true; what is relevant to justified belief is the existence of adequate supporting evidence.

I do not see how I could fault Shatz's point. However, although he has convincingly shown that my argument directed against Lehrer—as interpreted by Hilpinen—is invalid, he has at the same time inadvertently shown that my argument was also superfluous, since Hilpinen's own reasoning was unsound to begin with. It is unsound, since Hilpinen's first premise, (1) $s \rightarrow \sim\mathrm{E}h$, is not true. To give a concrete illustration, let

$s^*$ = Mars is devoid of all oxygen,
$h^*$ = The canals of Mars that are visible through terrestrial telescopes have been constructed by human-like creatures.

In the nineteenth century there was no evidence that $s^*$ was true and hence there were quite a number of scientists who were prepared to believe that $h^*$ was true, since the canals looked too straight to be the result of blind coincidence. Be that as it may, we shall suppose that the way the surface of Mars appeared to astronomers made $h^*$ probable enough and thus rationally justified a belief in it. Nowadays, of course, we know (or have sufficient

---

[11] David Shatz, *Philosophia* (October 1987).

evidence to be justified in believing) that $s^*$ is true, and that it was true in the last century as well. Does it follow that in the last century those who believed in the existence of life on Mars were irrational? Perhaps they were, for one reason or another, but certainly not because $s^* \rightarrow \sim Eh^*$, as they were not in the possession of any significant evidence that Mars lacks life-sustaining elements.

Thus if we wish to defend Lehrer's argument we will have to do it in some way other than that attempted by Hilpinen. The following procedure might seem feasible and is at the same time instructive for our purposes, since it illustrates once more how elementary probability theory may play a role in an issue which prima facie seems considerably removed from its domain.

Once more we postulate that $Eh \rightarrow (P(h) > n)$, and claim on behalf of Lehrer that we are unjustified in believing that $\sim s$ (provided of course that $t$ is false). In other words, we are to consider the conjecture that the assumption that $P(\sim s/\sim t) = n - \epsilon$, where $\epsilon$ is some number small enough to render a belief in any $h$ unjustified. We assume that Lehrer would grant that $t$ has the same status as $s$ and therefore $P(\sim t) = n - \epsilon$. Then by RE:

$$P(\sim s) = P(t) \cdot P(\sim s/t) + P(\sim t) \cdot P(\sim s/\sim t) \qquad \text{(I)}$$
$$P(h) = P(s) \cdot P(h/s) + P(\sim s) \cdot P(h/\sim s) \qquad \text{(II)}$$

By definition $P(h/s) = 0$. Substituting into (II):

$$P(h) = P(\sim s) \cdot P(h/\sim s). \qquad \text{(III)}$$

Also by definition, $P(\sim s/t) = 1$. Substituting into (I):

$$P(\sim s) = P(t) + P(\sim t) \cdot P(\sim s/\sim t). \qquad \text{(IV)}$$

If $h$ stands for what we normally take to be clearly evident propositions then I believe it is safe to assume that, according to Lehrer, as long as we did not have to worry about those extraterrestrial manipulators we could be certain that $h$ was true. Hence $P(h/\sim s) = 1$. Substituting into (III):

$$P(h) = P(\sim s). \qquad \text{(V)}$$

Substituting from (V) into (IV):

$$P(h) = P(t) + P(\sim t) \cdot P(\sim s/\sim t). \qquad \text{(VI)}$$

Substituting the numerical values established earlier into the right-hand side of (VI):

$$P(h) = 1 - (n - \epsilon) + (n - \epsilon)^2. \qquad \text{(VII)}$$

Now of course,

$$(1 - (n - \epsilon))^2 > 0 \qquad \text{(since all perfect squares are greater than zero)}$$

i.e., $\quad 1 - 2(n - \epsilon) + (n - \epsilon)^2 > 0$

i.e., $\quad 1 - (n - \epsilon) + (n - \epsilon)^2 > n - \epsilon$

This result together with (VII) shows that it may be rational to believe in $h$ in spite of the possibility of $s$. To be more precise, if $\epsilon$ is of a minimum magnitude, just sufficient to render a belief in the nonexistence of Lehrer's demons unjustifiable, then on the assumption that even-handedness requires that the same treatment be accorded to our own demon, then since we have just shown that $P(h) > n - \epsilon$ it follows that $Eh$. Of course, Lehrer is at liberty to assign a greater than minimum value to $\epsilon$. It is noteworthy, in that case, that even if for the sake of fairness we correspondingly increase the value of $P(t)$ it will not result in the refutation of Lehrer's skeptical thesis, since now the fact that $P(h)$ is greater than $n - \epsilon$ no longer implies that it is rational to believe in $h$.

# IV

# PROBABILITY AND INDUCTION

## 1. Bayes's Theorem and Induction

In his *Human Knowledge: Its Scope and Limits*, Bertrand Russell discussed what is generally regarded as one of the most dramatic episodes in the history of nineteenth century science, the discovery of Neptune. He sought to determine whether the great increase of general confidence in Newton's law of gravity resulting from this discovery was really justified. The following is a paraphrase of Russell's exposition. Let

$G$ = Newton's law of gravity,
$E$ = A new planet (Neptune) is going to be found in the spot specified by Adams and Leverrier.

Then by Bayes's Theorem

$$P(G/E) = \frac{P(E/G) \times P(G)}{P(E)}.$$

Now the value of $P(E/G)$ may be taken to be 1, since Adams and Leverrier used $G$ in their premises from which they mathematically determined the spot in the sky where a new planet should be found. On the other hand, $P(E)$ is exceedingly small in view of the fact that since early antiquity only one new planet (Uranus) had been discovered, and in addition $E$ says not merely that another planet is going to be sighted somewhere in the sky but gives the precise position where it is going to be sighted. It follows therefore that $P(G/E) > P(G)$, i.e., that the discovery of Neptune (that is, $E$'s turning out to be true) has immensely increased the probability of $G$. Does it also follow that $G$ is now to be regarded as highly credible? No, Russell explains:

> This argument . . . apparently shows that, if the law of gravitation had even a very small probability at the time when it was first enunciated, it soon became virtually certain. But it does nothing to help us gauge

73

this initial probability, and therefore would fail even if valid, to give
us firm basis for the theoretical inference from observation to theory.[1]

The difficulty pointed out by Russell is one we did not take into
account in our discussion in the previous chapter of the confirmation process based on Bayes's Theorem. The difficulty, of course,
presents scientists with a basic problem in every situation they
may face: they may obtain evidence that is highly improbable unless their hypothesis is true, but clearly, as Russell has argued,
that evidence is incapable of increasing the probability of that hypothesis if initially it was zero. This then is the perennial problem
of induction.

To be more precise, this is only half of the problem of induction.
For even if we were granted that $P(G) > 0$, it would still not follow
that the accumulation of evidence $E$ such that $P(E/G) = 1$ would
indicate the preferability of $G$ over any of its rivals. As we have
seen in the previous chapter, at every stage of experimentation the
degree of confirmation the data confers upon each of the infinitely
many competing hypotheses, fully capable of accounting for them,
is precisely the same.

There have been many proposals concerning the best way of tack-
ling the problem of justifying our belief that evidence increases
the credibility of any given empirical hypothesis, and supports it
to a different degree than it supports rival hypotheses. On the one
extreme we find what perhaps we may call the most "optimistic" approach, as initiated by H. Jeffreys, and on the other extreme the one
associated with K. R. Popper. Jeffreys admits that there are always
infinitely many hypotheses capable of accounting for any finite set
of observations; but from that it does not follow that the probability
of each is 1 divided by infinity, i.e., 0. According to Jeffreys's famous
postulate, the various possible hypotheses are not all equiprobable;
the simpler a hypothesis the higher its probability, and the sum of
the probabilities of the infinitely many hypotheses that fit the data
converges to one.

Jeffreys's postulate would overcome both parts of the problem
of induction. In Russell's equation just mentioned, $P(G)$ stands for
the simplest hypothesis accounting for past observations and it is
considerably higher than zero. Secondly, $\sim G = g_1 \vee g_2 \vee \ldots$, where

---

[1] Bertrand Russell, *Human Knowledge: Its Scope and Limits* (London,
1948), p. 429.

$g_1, g_2,$, etc. represent the various alternative hypotheses contrary to $G$ (and are arranged in order of decreasing simplicity). As the set of our observations increases and continues to accord with $G$ as well as with $g_1, g_2$, etc. although they all rise in credibility to the same degree, since $G$ started off with a higher initial probability it is the first to reach the highest a posteriori probability in the light of the favorable evidence.

Radically opposed to this is the Popperian view. According to Popper the solution to the problem of induction is that there is no solution. He insists that, in view of the fact that there exist infinitely many possible hypotheses to account for any given phenomenon, all universal lawlike statements have zero prior probability (i.e., the probability correctly assigned to them prior to the existence of any relevant evidence), and therefore also zero posterior probability, regardless of the amount of accumulated supporting evidence at a later stage. Popper's position has been so often subjected to criticism that there is not much point in going into details, and I shall only mention what seem to be the two most obvious objections. First of all, it is to be noted that Popper himself relies on inductive reasoning, not only in everyday life, which of course is inescapable, but also in subscribing to the new scientific method with which he proposes to replace the old. According to the revolutionary method advanced by Popper, all scientific knowledge is to be viewed as mere conjecture which one can never confirm as true or even as probable. All that is possible is to falsify hypotheses and eliminate them from consideration. But of course falsification itself cannot be achieved without reliance on inductive reasoning!

For example, Aristotle held that the heavier a terrestrial body the greater its downward acceleration. Nobody believes this anymore to be true, for since the time of Galileo there have been thousands of experiments involving different objects in different locations showing that the acceleration of freely falling bodies near the surface of the earth is independent of weight. But we should ask the followers of Popper: Surely all these adverse results have been obtained in the past, so what basis is there for believing that the hypothesis that from tomorrow onwards heavier bodies will fall faster than lighter bodies is false? Their answer would of course have to be that, "In the future heavier bodies fall faster than lighter bodies" is a hypothesis that has repeatedly been falsified in the past." This however is unacceptable now merely because—to paraphrase a well-known quip by Russell—all the evidence we have concerns past futures, and now for the first time we are postulating something about future futures, but because the Popperian defense relies on the principle that the kind of past conjecture that has been refuted is bound to be refuted again. In other words, they have to invoke the principle that the future will be like the past, or the unobserved like the observed; in brief, they are forced to rely on the inductive principle.

The second obvious objection is that there seems to be absolutely no logical basis for insisting that the prior probability of every hypothesis is 0. It is to be admitted that there are infinitely many hypotheses capable of accounting for any finite set of observations, but from this it does not follow that the probability of each one of these is 1 divided by infinity. The prior probabilities of the infinitely many alternative hypotheses may (as Jeffreys held) vary, and their sum may converge to 1. There is of course no proof that this is so; thus, from a logical point of view Jeffreys's conjecture is on equal footing with Popper's thesis, while from the point of view of common sense it is vastly superior.

## 2. Proving the Impossibility of Inductive Probability

In a more recent move Popper has gone beyond merely voicing disapproval of inductive practices and has offered what is to be taken as a deductive argument showing that "induction is a myth." In a 1983 paper, which caused a minor sensation in the philosophical community, Popper and Miller advanced what they claimed to be a proof, a conclusive proof, that inductive probability is logically impossible![2]

Their argument begins by defining the notion of a 'support measure', $S(h/e)$, as the difference between the posterior probability of a hypothesis in the light of the evidence obtained and its prior probability (which is identical with what we denoted by $dc(e, h)$ according to Criterion (II) in the previous chapter):

$$S(h/e) = P(h/e) - Ph. \qquad \text{(II)}$$

Given this definition, their argument may be represented thus:

(1) $S(h \vee e/e) = P(h \vee e/e) - P(h \vee e)$      Substituting $h \vee e$ for $h$ into (II)

(2) $S(h \vee \sim e/e) = P(h \vee \sim e/e) - P(h \vee \sim e)$      Substituting $h \vee \sim e$ for $h$ into (II)

(3) $S(h \vee e/e) + S(h \vee \sim e/e) = P(h \vee e/e)$

---

[2] K. R. Popper, "Note,'" *Nature* (1983): 687.

$$+P(h \vee \sim e/e) - [P(h \vee e) + P(h \vee \sim e)] \qquad \text{Adding (1) \& (2)}$$

(4)
$$= P(h/e) - P(h) \qquad \text{i.e.,}$$

(5) $S(h \vee e/e) + S(h \vee \sim e/e) = S(h/e)$ \qquad From (II) & (4)

The last result shows clearly, according to Popper, that the degree of support $h$ receives from $e$—as measured by $S(h/e)$—consists of two parts: $S(h \vee e/e)$ (the first term of (5)'s left-hand side) which is purely deductive support (since $e \rightarrow h \vee e$); and $S(h \vee \sim e/e)$, which is the only term that might represent the much-hoped for inductive support. But the latter is surely a negative number! In case we do not see this right away, the usual square-diagram method will once again clarify matters for us. In Figure 13, the two middle squares are $h$-squares and all the three bottom squares are $\sim e$-squares, four out of the six squares are either $h$ or $\sim e$, hence $P(h \vee \sim e)$ $= 4/6$. But there are only three $e$-squares, none of which is a $\sim e$-square, and only one $h$-square, hence $P(h \vee \sim e/e) = 1/3$. But $1/3 - 4/6$ is a negative number, which according to the Popper-Miller argument demolishes the whole idea of inductive evidence providing positive probabilistic support for any hypothesis.

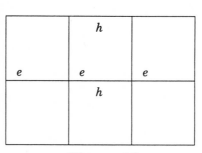

**Figure  13**

This remarkable argument has been defended by quite a number of philosophers, even though so implausible. However, since in the past similarly outlandish arguments to discredit induction have as a rule created considerable philosophical commotion, Popper and Miller astutely assumed (by using induction, of course) that their latest effort would not fail to please some and tantalize others.

Let me mention briefly one of the more obvious objections to these maneuverings. Popperians call $S(h \vee e/e)$ the "deductive support" $e$ gives $h$, and leave it to the reader to figure out precisely why it is called this. What aspect of $S(h \vee e/e)$ might be said with some justification to be "deductive"? It is true, of course, that in order to evaluate $P(h \vee e/e)$ we require no empirical information; by the Law of Addition, $e \rightarrow h \vee e$, and thus indeed it follows deductively that $P(h \vee e/e) = 1$. But is it possible to arrive also at the value of $S(h \vee e/e)$ without using factual data or logically unwarranted assumptions? We have been given:

$$
\begin{aligned}
S(h \lor e/e) &= P(h \lor e/e) - P(h \lor e) \\
&= 1 - P(h \lor e) && \text{Since } e \to h \lor e \\
&= 1 - [P(h) + P(e) - P(h \ \& \ e)] \\
&= 1 - [P(h) + P(e) - P(h)] && \text{Since } P(e/h) = 1 \\
&= 1 - P(e).
\end{aligned}
$$

Now it is true that $e \to (P(e) = 1)$ and therefore it might occur to someone to maintain that $1 - P(e) = 0$ is after all a result that may be reached purely by deduction. But as we shall see later in this book (and there is really no room for thinking otherwise), $P(e)$ in Bayes's equation does not refer to the probability of any given evidence when we already know it to exist; $P(e)$ stands for the *prior* probability of $e$, the value of which depends on the empirical circumstances surrounding the issue. More specifically, by the Rule of Elimination, $P(e) = P(h) \cdot P(e/h) + P(\sim h) \cdot P(e/\sim h)$, and hence,

$$
\begin{aligned}
1 - P(e) &= 1 - [P(h) \cdot P(e/h) + P(\sim h) \cdot P(e/\sim h)] \\
&= 1 - [P(h) + P(\sim h) \cdot P(e/\sim h)].
\end{aligned}
$$

Thus $S(h \lor e/e)$ is a function of three quantities:

(i)   $P(h)$, which by the very definition of inductive reasoning cannot follow deductively from $e$;

(ii)  $P(\sim h)$, which is exactly in the same boat as $P(h)$; and

(iii) $P(e/\sim h)$, where $\sim h = k \lor l \lor m \lor \ldots$, and $k, l, m$, etc. are hypotheses incompatible with $h$ and could legitimately account for $e$. But of course what constitutes a legitimate hypothesis is determined by the principles of scientific methodology, not by deductive reasoning.

Now even if the value of $S(h \lor e/e)$ were merely not logically dependent on every one of (i), (ii), and (iii), that would be sufficient to refute the claim that $P(e)$ determined its value by pure logic. But as we see the value of $S(h \lor e/e)$ is not logically dependent on any one of those three factors! A distinguished logician such as Popper could hardly be suspected of failing to have seen that though we can deduce by deductive logic and one of the axioms of probability theory that $P(h \lor e/e) = 1$, that has no bearing on the status of $S(h \lor e/e)$. It is thus not easy to see what the splitting of $S(e, h)$ into its two component disjuncts is supposed to have achieved.

However, perhaps the most puzzling aspect of this whole exercise is that it is impossible to think of a plausible objective the two writers might have been hoping to achieve. Surely their intention was not to derive the truism that induction is not deductively valid. Nor is it likely that they were planning to show that induction is not inductively valid. But what else is there? So when they said that they had set out to show that inductive support is not probabilistic support, what could they possibly have meant? That from the axioms of probability alone no empirical hypotheses can be derived is already widely known. Now as we have seen at the beginning of this chapter, on the Bayesian approach inductive reasoning in general rests on the assumption that there exists a set of hypotheses that have a finite chance of being true, and each member of this set has a different prior probability. Popper and Miller have not attempted to produce arguments showing why these assumptions are invariably, or at least sometimes, false. Thus even if their essay has validly proven something, it is not so clear what that something might be.

### 3. Using the Elementary Theorems of Probability in Justifying Induction

In the spectrum of opinions concerning the status of inductive reasoning, at the opposite end to that of the Popperians, who have attempted to deny that it exists at all, we find the view that induction is not merely a universally practiced and legitimate form of reasoning, but that it can be rigorously shown to be valid. Of special interest to us is a remarkable recent attempt in which the elementary theorems of probability theory are employed in an effort to establish the logical validity of induction. Ken Gemes proposes to show through a *reductio* argument that what he calls Hume's Inductive Scepticism (H.I.S.) is false.[3] Gemes begins with the following definition:

(H.I.S.)  $P(h/e \& t) = P(h/t)$, for all $e$ and $h$ such that the argument from $e$ to $h$ is inductive for all tautological $t$.

We may note that (H.I.S.) as understood by Gemes is a somewhat more moderate position than Popper's. The latter insisted that the prior probability of all hypotheses is zero, while the former holds that the probability of $h$ fails to rise through favorable evidence, which may be due to $h$'s zero prior probability, but need not be, since it may be due to the second reason we have given (why even with a finite initial probability, $h$'s credibility cannot rise with the accumulation of evidence). We should also note that since (H.I.S.) asserts that no amount of empirical evidence raises the probability

---

[3] Ken Gemes, *Australasian Journal of Philosophy* (1983): 434–438.

of an inductive generalization, Gemes is quite right in believing that a successful proof of the falsity of (H.I.S.) amounts to a deductive justification of induction.

The proof is presented essentially as follows:

(1)  There exist propositions $A$, $B$, and $C$ such that the arguments from $A$ to $B$, from $A$ to $A \& B \& C$, from $A \& B$ to $C$, and from $A \& B$ to $A \& B \& C$ are all inductive (e.g., $A$ is "There is a sunrise on the first day of this week," $B$ is "There is a sunrise on each of the second through sixth days of this week," and $C$ is "There is a sunrise on the seventh day of this week.")

(2)  $P(A \& B \& C/A \& t) = P(A \& B \& C/t)$ (By (H.I.S.) the evidence that $A$ is true has no confirmatory power)

(3)  $P(A \& B \& C/A \& B \& t) = P(A \& B \& C/t)$ (By (H.I.S.), as before)

(4)  $P(A \& B \& C/A \& t) = P(A \& B \& C/A \& B \& t)$ ((2), (3) by the transitivity of equivalence)

(5)  $P(A \& B \& C/A) = P(A \& B \& C/A \& B)$ ((4), irrelevance of $t$)

(6)  $P(A/A \times P((B \& C/A \& B) = P(A \& B/A \& B) \times P(C/A \& B \& A \& B)$ (Applying the Conjunctive Axiom to both sides of (5))

(7)  $P(B \& C/A \& A) = P(C/A \& B \& A \& B)$ (The first factor in the expressions on both sides of (6) equals 1)

(8)  $P(B \& C/A) = P(C/A \& B)$ (Simplifying (7))

(9)  $P(C/A \& B) = 0$ (Assumption)

(10)  $P(B/A) \cdot P(C/A \& B) = P(C/A \& B)$ (Applying the Conjunctive Axiom to the left-hand side of (8))

(11)  $P(B/A) = 1$ (Dividing both sides of (10) by $P(C/A \& B)$)

(12)  $P(C/A \& B) = 0 \rightarrow P(B/A) = 1$ ((9)–(11) by Conditional Proof)

(13)  $\sim[P(C/A \& B) = 0] \vee P(B/A) = 1$ ((12), definition of Material Implication)

First we should note that step (9) was necessary, since unless $P(C/A \& B)$ is assumed not to equal zero it is illegitimate to divide both sides of equation (10) by it.

After arriving at conclusion (13) Gemes explains that we have two options: (a) conclude that $P(C/A \& B)$ is indeed equal to zero, which amounts to extreme counterinduction; or (b) infer the thesis of inductive infallibilism, i.e., that in view of evidence $A$, $B$ becomes absolutely certain, which is what $P(B/A) = 1$ means.

Gemes argues that both (a) and (b) are absurd. He claims (b) to be absurd since it implies that inductive arguments can be fully conclusive. In any case, given the choice a Humean should prefer abandoning (H.I.S.) to embracing the radically antiskeptical (b).

Conclusion (a) may be even less tolerable: it entails that the argument from "There is a sunrise on the first day of this week" to "There is a sunrise on each of the second through sixth days of this week" has the lowest probability. But surely the argument from "It is not the case that there is a sunrise on the seventh day of this week" to "There is a sunrise on the seventh day of this week" has a lower probability!

It might occur to someone to object that $P(C/A \& B)$ could equal zero not because of counterinduction being at work here, and thus what is normally regarded as supporting evidence for $C$ actually lowers its probability to zero. To this Gemes would reply that he has on purpose chosen not to deal with universal hypotheses accounting for the data, of which there are always infinitely many. Here if $C$ is false $\sim C$ must be true, thus if we insisted on assigning zero to the prior probability of $C$ we must accept with complete certainty that there is *no* sunrise on the seventh day of this week, which would be completely unwarranted.

Seeing that Gemes's reasoning leads to the unacceptable conclusions (a) and (b), we are forced to infer that it started out with wrong premises. He identifies (H.I.S.) as the wrong premise.

This ingeniously devised, elegant argument comes as near to an ideal justification of induction as one might wish for. Though it is somewhat lengthy, ultimately it is very simple as it uses only the most elementary principles. It does not attempt to do too much; it sets out only to prove (so to speak) one half of the problem of induction. As indicated before this problem may be viewed as consisting of two parts, namely, how to show that: (i) the prior probability of any hypothesis is other than zero; and (ii) the posterior probability of a hypothesis can increase with evidence. Gemes proposed only to solve (ii).

It is truly regrettable that reality has decreed otherwise and does not seem to permit us to achieve even this much. Step (2) is unfortunately incorrect. By the Conjunctive Axiom $P(A \& B \& C) = P(A) \cdot P(B \& C/A)$, which of course is less than $P(B \& C/A)$, since we do not assume $P(A)$ to equal 1. On the other hand, $P(A \& B \& C/A) =$

$P(A/A) \cdot P(B \& C/A \& A)$, which *is* equal to $P(B \& C/A)$ (since $P(A/A)$ $= 1$). Thus, contrary to Step (2), $P(A \& B \& C) < P(A \& B \& C/A)$. Similarly, Step (3) is also incorrect.

## 4. Establishing Prior Probabilities by Analogical Arguments

Wesley C. Salmon, possibly the most lucid contemporary writer on the role of probability in scientific method, is one of the leading philosophers to have addressed the problem of on what basis we might assign nonzero prior probabilities to hypotheses. On several occasions he has asserted that analogical arguments relying on previously established results may profitably be employed to assign finite values to the probability of newly proposed hypotheses. One of the examples Salmon uses to illustrate how the analogical argument works is Coulomb's theory of electrostatics. He claims that there are good grounds for saying that from the very beginning that theory had higher than zero probability, since a strong analogy exists between it and Newton's gravitational theory, the credibility of which by the time Coulomb advanced his hypothesis was firmly established.[4] Another example he cites concerns the many known similarities between humans and other mammals, which entitle us to assign a finite probability to various postulates concerning human physiology. Furthermore, anthropologists are disposed to entertain seriously hypotheses about extinct societies on the basis of analogous, well-established hypotheses concerning our own society. Salmon points out that through such analogical arguments it is not possible to determine the numerical values prior probabilities are to be assigned, but this is of little importance; all we need in order to help the Bayesian method of confirmation get off the ground is that those probabilities should be different from zero.

Salmon's is a simple and rather attractive idea. Unfortunately, there is no chance for it to bring us any nearer to the solution of our problem. To begin with, we may note that his examples have been carefully selected and it would surely be hard to produce many more like them. Moreover, it is very easy to cite any number of examples of hypotheses for which—at the time they were first put forward— one could not have had a clue where to turn in search of a suitable

---

[4] W. C. Salmon, *Scientific Explanation and the Causal Structure of the World* (Princeton University Press, 1984), p. 234.

analogy. In fact matters seem even worse. If it were indeed the case that the initial probability of every putative hypothesis was to be determined by some analogous, established hypothesis, then not only would scientists often fail to find an adequate basis for their conjectures, but well-confirmed laws similar to the lawlike statement under consideration would often positively rule out the latter as having no chance of being true. Consider, for example, the situation in which Einstein proposed his famous hypothesis that light travels at the same velocity relative to all systems, regardless of their different speeds. Not only was there nothing analogous in the whole of science as it stood at the beginning of the present century, but in all parallel examples where something travels fast or slow invariably the contrary is true: it is never the case that velocity as measured in different systems is the same. Although Einstein's hypothesis proved immensely fruitful—it is after all the cornerstone of the special theory of relativity—nevertheless it would seem that according to Salmon it was not legitimate to advance it in the first place as a viable candidate to play any scientific role.

But these are relatively minor objections. Salmon's attitude (which incidentally is shared by several other philosophers) is based on what must surely be regarded an illusion, namely, that scientific method may somehow be able to pull itself up by its own bootstraps, that is, that all conjectures may be grounded in solid facts and that at no stage does science require the introduction of a priori postulates. In practice, however, it turns out that Salmon's own approach is based on contrary tacit assumptions. Among other things, Salmon clearly takes for granted the most basic tenet of inductive reasoning (which he has just set out to justify), namely, that similar conditions are likely to be governed by similar laws. Without such a presupposition he would not, for example, be able to assume that, just because both Coulomb and Newton deal with attractive forces of one kind or another, an inverse square law is likely to obtain in the latter if it obtains in the former. As Hume pointed out, the central principle of induction, the assumption that like things are alike, cannot be shown to be true or even probable.

If possible, then, an even greater difficulty is presented by the fact that even if it were granted that for every hypothesis an analogue could be found among those we already hold, and that for some reason this analogue may be assumed to provide sufficient justification for assigning nonzero probabilities to novel hypotheses, Salmon's enterprise still could not be set in motion. Let us concede that Coulomb's law acquires its initial probability from Newton's;

what then about Newton's law itself? Even if one could find some established hypothesis which lent finite prior probability to Newton's law of gravity, and so on, it would certainly not have been possible to establish the first hypotheses advanced in history, since there was then nothing to compare them to. Thus the hypotheses coming after them had nothing to be grounded in either. It follows, therefore, that at this very moment science is yet to begin, since we do not have a single suitably established hypothesis to analogize with. We can speak only of having numerous adopted theories, without any of them having a finite chance of being true, if indeed nonzero probabilities can only be assigned through comparison with some statement that is already known to be probable to an appreciable degree.

### 5. Laplace's Rule of Succession

Before leaving the topic of justifying inductive reasoning with the aid of probability theory I should like to refer briefly to the classic example provided by Laplace's rule of succession. The details of his proof lie beyond our scope as they involve slightly more than the most elementary theorems we have confined our attention to. I shall thus cite what is called Laplace's *special* rule of succession, which is restricted to ascribing a value for the probability, not that a given hypothesis which has never been violated and has been satisfied many times in the past is true, but merely a value to the probability that the next observation will conform to $h$. The special rule says:

$$P(A/B) = \frac{n+1}{n+2}$$

where

    $A =$ Our next observation will satisfy hypothesis $h$,
    $B =$ Hypothesis $h$ is known to have been satisfied $n$ times in the past and never to have been violated.

Emanuel Parzen in his textbook *Modern Probability Theory and Its Applications* illustrates the reasonableness of the special rule of succession with a story about a tourist who finds himself in a foreign city and who does not understand the language spoken there. He is very concerned as to how safe the local food might be. After a considerable amount of worry he goes to a restaurant he deems superior to the others and eats there ten successive meals. Consequently he would seem rather well-justified in ascribing at least

11/12 probability that he is not going to get sick from eating the next meal there.

Yet Parzen raises the objection (an objection several others have also raised) that in many contexts the rule of succession leads to absurd results. Consider a boy who is ten years old. According to Laplace, having lived ten years justifies our ascribing the probability of 11/12 to his living one more year. But then his eighty-year-old grandfather has probability of 81/82 of living one more year. However, as everyone knows there is a considerably greater chance for a young boy to continue living another year than for his wizened progenitor!

I do not believe that this particular objection is very damaging to Laplace's formula. We must remember that his approach goes hand in hand with his Principle of Indifference and applies therefore in contexts where there exist no reasons whatever either to prefer $h$ to $\sim h$ or vice versa *except*, of course, the $n$ instances in the past in which $h$ has been instantiated. Thus when we have what looks like a perfectly symmetrical coin that has never been tossed before, then since $n$ is zero, Laplace's formula ascribes $0 + 1/0 + 2 = 1/2$ to its showing heads or to its showing tails when we are about to toss it the first time. Incidentally, the formula does not apply when we are about to roll for the first time a perfect die and wish to evaluate the probability of its showing six or not showing six. As we have explained in the Introduction, the hypothesis that it will be six and the hypothesis that it will not are not symmetrically related since there *is* sufficient reason to ascribe higher probability to non-six than to six. And finally in the case of what looks like a perfect coin after it has been tossed a number of times and shown heads each time, then because of this positive evidence in favor of heads, and in the absence of any additional evidence, the probability of the next toss resulting in heads increases as $n$ increases. In the case mentioned by Parzen, of course, a vast accumulation of data indicates that the proportion of ten-year-olds surviving another year is considerably greater than the proportion of eighty-year-olds living another year. Thus there exists very strong inductive evidence, which takes into account relevant instances not limited to the two cases under investigation, that the ten-year-old child has a much greater chance to survive. In a case like this, Laplace would not apply his formula.

Laplace's famous application of his rule was to calculate the probability that the sun will rise tomorrow. He asks us to assume that the biblical account of world history is correct and accordingly the solar system is 5,000 years or 1,826,213 days old. Since the sun has risen on each day in the past it is rational to bet 1,826,213 against 1 that it will rise again tomorrow.

This particular example has often been cited as a paradigm of wrong-headed probabilistic argument, but I do not think all the criticism directed against it has been equally fair. In a well-respected textbook William Feller, for instance, univocally rejects Laplace's argument and says:

> it pretends to judge the sun's rising tomorrow from its *assumed* risings in the past. But the assumed rising of the sun on February 5, 3123 B.C. is by no means more certain than that the sun will rise tomorrow. We believe in both for the same reason.[5]

This objection does not seem too damaging. Laplace could reply that his belief in the occurrence of a sunrise on February 5, 3123 B.C. is not purely an inductive conclusion based on the recently verified instances of such occurrences; had it failed to have risen on any day in the past 5,000 years or so, that would have been a momentous enough catastrophe for its echoes to reach as far as our own days. In any case Laplace merely bids us to assume that the sun has invariably risen every day for the last 5,000 years. If Feller is reluctant to do so, would he be willing to allow that there has been no day without a sunrise for the last 1,000 years? In that case, we are still in the favorable position of being able to bet more than 365,000 to 1 that the sun is going to rise tomorrow.

There seem, however, to be other, perhaps more serious difficulties. Laplace, who is best known for his monumental work *Celestial Mechanics*, certainly held that the rising of the sun is a phenomenon required by Newtonian dynamics and gravitational theory. Clearly the more confirmation there is for these latter the more confidently we are entitled to anticipate tomorrow's sunrise. How many instances had there been at Laplace's time that confirmed Newtonian mechanics? Given the immense variety of terrestrial and celestial phenomena that are accounted for by, and hence confirm, Newton's theories, no sensible answer can be expected to such a question. This need not be looked upon as such a damaging flaw. We may not even approximately know the value of $n$, but as long as we know that it is a large number we are assured that $n + 1/n + 2$ is close to 1, and that is really what is significant for our purposes. But the major point to remember is that given a finite set of data there

---

[5] William Feller, *An Introduction to Probability Theory and Its Applications* (New York, 1962), p. 114.

always exist an infinite number of hypotheses each capable of accounting for the data, and each of which makes different predictions concerning our next observation. Since it is impossible that each of these contrary hypotheses should be equally probable, we must interpret Laplace's rule not as saying that any given hypothesis has a probability of $n+1/n+2$, but that the disjunction $h_1 \lor h_2 \lor \cdots \lor h_n$, where each disjunct equally satisfies all the data so far obtained, has a probability $n+1/n+2$. Laplace, however, provides no further guidance as to how to assign probabilities to any of these individual hypotheses.

## 6. The "New" Problem of Induction

Philosophers have become so habituated by the spectacular successes of elementary probability notions in such a vast variety of conditions, that on occasion they have rashly assumed the useful applicability of basic probabilistic methods to problems which in fact were altogether unsusceptible to such treatment. The following is a fairly detailed description of such an incident which I found fascinating and most revealing of some aspects of the contemporary philosophical climate.

So far we have focused mainly on the following problem. How are we to justify the principle that the unobserved will be like the observed? As indicated before, there exists a more radical difficulty, namely, the principle may not merely be unjustified but vacuous, since no matter how much data we have collected the principle will never lead to a unique hypothesis, but to an indefinite number of equally well-supported generalizations. A finite set of observations can always lend itself to be described as exhibiting any number of regularities, each one leading to a different generalization and to sets of predictions and each incompatible with those every other description leads to.

This kind of objection was raised in the 1920's by Harold Jeffreys and has been made famous by Nelson Goodman. He presents it by starting with the following definition:

> A certain thing $X$ is said to be *grue* at a certain time $t$ iff
> $X$ is green at $t$ and $t$ is before the year 2000
> or
> $X$ is blue at $t$, and $t$ is after the year 2000.

Now if we were speaking a language which did not have a word for green but only for grue, we would say that each of the many thousands of emeralds we have observed in the past were grue. Employing the Principle of the Uniformity of Nature would then lead us to conclude that all emeralds are grue and thus predict that after the year 2000 observed emeralds would appear to us as having a color which in the language we speak is called blue. Thus according to Goodman and his many followers we have here a more radical problem than the traditional problem of induction, a problem they call "the new riddle of induction." On their view even if we could rest assured that the future is going to be like the past this would get us nowhere because we never know how the past itself was. That is, past observations will always lend themselves to different descriptions, descriptions that are equally compatible with everything so far observed but yield incompatible predictions about what is going to be observed.

People who have not yet been exposed to the extensive literature extolling the revolutionary significance of this problem are usually tempted to offer a very simple solution, which, however, the earnest followers of Goodman dismiss as too simple-minded. The common-sense reply invariably is, that once we accept the Principle of the Uniformity of Nature, then we assume that the color of emeralds which has so far always been the same will remain the same in the future as well. The Goodmanian regards this not so much as a solution as a basic failure to grasp what the problem is. He will explain that he wishes to follow the Principle of the Uniformity of Nature as scrupulously as anyone else: given that the color of every emerald observed in the past has been grue, the principle may be said to bid us to assume that the color of every emerald to be observed in the future will also be grue. The simple-minded person might persist and venture to suggest that the issue of whether surfaces are or are not of identical color should not be settled by determining whether one and the same word or two different words are being used to denote their color, but rather by the way they actually appear to us. Grue surfaces are simply perceptually different before the year 2000 than after the year 2000. However, those who have succeeded in convincing themselves of the gravity of the grue problem have been heard to brush off this kind of suggestion as a further defect of comprehension. They point out that the crucial point to realize is that to those who speak the grue-language emeralds have precisely the same appearance at all times; they are just as grue before as after the year 2000. And in general, as Brian Skyrms explains:

(1) Whether we find change or not in a certain situation may depend on the linguistic machinery we use to describe that situation.

(2) Which regularities we find in a sequence of occurrences may depend on the linguistic machinery used to describe that sequence.

Our artless friend may still not feel quite reassured. Is it really all a matter of convention and determined by the way we speak? Is there no such thing as two surfaces being "naturally" of identical color, independent of any linguistic machinery? According to the French Academy there are about 2,800 separate languages in the world today. How are we to explain that in not one of these do any words like grue exist? Also, numerous experiments have been performed with animals capable of distinguishing between various colors and the results clearly indicate that surfaces which we called, for instance, green yesterday as well as today, were similarly recognized by the animals (e.g., after having learnt that food is always to be found in green containers), even though presumably they neither used the same nor a different word to denote those surfaces. Is it thus not appropriate to maintain that to the primitive, untutored perception emeralds appear directly green and not grue?

It is quite possible that our friend, after acquainting himself with the copious literature on this issue and seeing that these questions are not only left unanswered but have hardly even been raised, would conclude that the solution to his problems—whatever it may be—is too simple to have required any attention.

We will not discuss any further aspects of Goodman's problem. But let us concentrate only on a single suggestion of how with the use of the simple theorems of probability it may at last be solved, without resorting to any "simple-minded" maneuvres.

G. Rosenkrantz, a well-known writer on the philosophy of probability, treats Goodman's problem with great gravity. In discussing this problem he does not feel the need to defend at all the complete symmetry between the predicates 'green' and 'grue'. He probably takes Skyrms's explanation for granted, and dismisses the thought that colors may be simple or compound *per se* as stemming from a bias inculcated in us through the language we are used to. Rosenkrantz believes that through a judicious use of the theory of probability he can at last suggest a way out of the problem. He starts by denoting,

(H) All emeralds examined before time $t$ are green,

($K$) All emeralds examined after time $t$ are blue,

and he points out that Goodman's alternative hypothesis may be represented by $H \& K$. He then introduces the concept of 'degree of confirmation' which is the increase in the probability of a hypothesis due to evidence $E$, i.e., the difference between the probability the hypothesis has after the evidence and what it had before. Thus,

$$dc(E, H) = P(H/E) - P(H)$$

which as will be remembered is just Criterion (II) we discussed in Chapter Three. Next he enunciates a theorem which we meet now for the second time, so let us verify that it is indeed valid. By Rosenkrantz's definition:

$$dc(E, H \& K) = P(H \& K/E) - P(H \& K)$$
$$= P(H/E) \cdot P(K/E \& H) - P(H) \cdot P(K/H).$$
$$\text{(by the Conjunctive Axiom)}$$

Given that $H \to E$, $P(K/E \& H) = P(K/H)$ and thus,

$$dc(E, H \& K) = P(H/E) \cdot P(K/H) - P(H) \cdot P(K/H)$$
$$= P(K/H) \cdot dc(E, H). \qquad \text{Q.E.D.}$$

With his apparatus in place he now denotes,

$E =$   All the emeralds examined so far were green.

Then assuming that the year 2000 is still in the future, we have before us a case where $H - E$. We therefore may assume the validity of Rosenkrantz's theorem just proven. But according to that theorem,

$$dc(E, H \& K) = P(K/H) \cdot dc(E, H),$$

since that theorem equates $dc(E, H \& K)$ with the product of $dc(E, H)$ and the fraction $P(K/H)$, and the *latter is obviously much smaller than 1*. To quote exactly what he says:

> our little theorem also shows that the degree of confirmation $E$ accords the conjunction, $H \& K$, is the fraction $P(K/H)$ of the degree of confirmation it accords $H$ alone. And given our knowledge of the colour constancy of emeralds, the probability $P(K/H)$ that emeralds unexamined before $t$ are green, is minute.[6]

---

[6] G. R. Rosenkrantz, "Does Induction Rest on a Mistake?" *Journal of Philosophy*, (1982): 85.

The most astounding statement in this passage is that $P(K/H)$ must be minute! The explanation given why it must be minute is that it follows from "our knowledge of the colour constancy of emeralds." But according to its advocates, the very essence of the new riddle is that grue is as full-fledged a color as what we happen to call green or blue. Consequently, our knowledge of the color constancy of emeralds implies no less that if emeralds have been grue in the past they will continue to be grue in the future, i.e., $P(K/H) = 1$.

The conclusion is inescapable that Rosenkrantz at this stage has suddenly and inadvertently permitted his thinking to be overwhelmed by common sense and so takes it for granted that something that has been green both before and after the year 2000 remains constant in color, while if it is grue both before and after that date then (whatever you may decide to call it) in reality it has undergone a change. But, of course, if Rosenkrantz is willing to assume the Principle of the Uniformity of Nature (and his assumption of the constancy of colors is but a special case of that principle), as well as that the status of green is different from the status of grue, not only relative to the language we speak, but from an objective point of view, then the riddle of the new induction does not arise in the first place, and there is absolutely no point in the entire ingenious argument using elementary probability theorems which Rosenkrantz devised for its solution!

I believe that the moral of this story is an encouraging one. Many have been wondering about the nature of our discipline: what restraints are there in philosophy to prevent it from becoming the scene of complete intellectual chaos, where anybody can say anything? Now, while it has to be conceded that Cicero may not have been far off the target when he said "There is nothing so absurd but some philosopher has said it," nevertheless, although they may be uttered, philosophical absurdities are unlikely to be held for too long; even their advocates cannot help but see sooner or later what they are. Common sense and sound intuition provide a fairly reliable defense mechanism through which we will come to reject untenable ideas. Here we have seen a philosopher earnestly trying to go along with a very strange idea, though sanctioned by a considerable portion of the philosophical community as a highly sophisticated idea, concerning what is a single color and what is not.

Goodman's point may be said to be a variation on Jeffreys's point made thirty years earlier. Jeffreys showed that as soon as we can suggest a hypothesis (represented by a certain equation) that accounts for any finite set of experimental results, we have an easy way of producing infinitely many other hypotheses (represented by some equation generated out of the original equation through a simple method), each accounting equally well for the same data, while incompatible with all the other hypotheses. There are, however, important differences between the two writers. Whether one agrees or not with Jeffreys's solution, according to which all the rival hypotheses may be ranked according to their increased complexity and hence decreased prior probability, there can be no dispute that he has highlighted what amounts to one of the most fundamental problems in the philosophy of science. On the other hand, it is by no means clear why Goodman's problem, though having had a remarkably higher dramatic impact, presents a serious source of worry.

Jeffreys did not make any attempt to make his problem more acute by claiming that nothing substantial distinguishes one hypothesis from another; he acknowledged that they differ in complexity and based his solution on this very fact. Goodman attempts to go further, insisting that in reality 'grue' is precisely as good a predicate as 'green' and that there is no other difference between the two than that the former is more entrenched in our language than the latter. It is true that the term 'green' is vastly more entrenched than the relatively freshly minted term 'grue', but that is merely an offshoot of something much more substantial: the property of being green is substantially different from the property of being grue, indeed so conspicuously so that, as we have seen, even with the most arduous effort it is hard to remain oblivious to this difference.

# PART TWO

# V

# EXTRAORDINARY PHENOMENA
# AND CONFIRMATION

A great deal of science is devoted not so much to showing that the unexpected was in fact to be expected but rather to explaining why what seems not merely improbable but also out of the ordinary, and hence astonishing, is really a common occurrence. It is the central aim of science to do away with mysteries and shield us against surprises. Thus a strange event or series of events which we find bewildering prompts us to look for a reasonable hypothesis, which when adopted will remove the grounds for puzzlement and transform the inexplicable into the inevitable. We have to begin by clarifying the distinction between an improbable but common event, and what may not be less improbable, and yet is an uncommon, astonishing event.

## 1. The Credibility of Extraordinary Stories

All extraordinary events are highly improbable but few improbable events count as extraordinary. To illustrate the difference between the two kinds of events, let us take a close look at an example involving nonscientific hypotheses. In 1785 the Marquis de Condorcet considered the question of what credibility to assign to a testimony, when $t$ is the probability that the witness tells the truth and $p$ is the prior probability of an event $E$ he claims to have taken place. According to Condorcet the posterior probability of $E$ is given by,

$$\frac{pt}{pt + (1 - p)(1 - t)}.$$

Condorcet's formula, as has been pointed out by I. Niiniluoto,[1] is an application of Bayes's Theorem. We can see this by denoting,

---

[1] I. Niiniluoto, "L. J. Cohen versus Bayesianism," *Behavioral and Brain Sciences* (1981): 349.

$W = $ A witness asserts that $E$ has taken place,

and substitute into Bayes's Theorem:

$$P(E/W) = \frac{P(E) \cdot P(W/E)}{P(E) \cdot P(W/E) + P(\sim E) \cdot P(W/\sim E)}.$$

Niiniluoto says this result is controversial and claims that the issue "is in fact closely related to an old controversy on the credibility of extraordinary stories." He cites Todhunter, who found Condorcet's formula objectionable. For suppose we have before us a person of considerable reliability, such that $t = 0.99$, who announces that ticket #267 has won in a fair lottery with 10,000 tickets; then by the above formula we are led to ascribe no more than $1/102$ probability to the credibility of his claim. It is hard to accept that the testimony of a reputable witness should be so "enormously depreciated," and thus that reason should require us to refuse to believe it.

Some people may not think there is much to be puzzled about: the more unlikely a story the less rational it is to believe it. Thus even though our informant may have the highest reputation for truthfulness, once he indulges in telling us a story too fantastic to be credible it is only just on our part to cease trusting him. It is, however, not a very plausible explanation, since though the prior probability of any particular lottery number being chosen was admittedly small, this was to be expected from the very beginning; it was bound to be the case, and thus should not puzzle us in any way that the result is going to be some highly improbable number.

However, what is perhaps hardest to reconcile with common sense is that ever day thousands of people—the majority of whom are sufficiently rational—buy lottery tickets where the chances of winning the main prize are over a hundred times smaller than 1 in 10,000. Yet a typical customer will not hesitate, soon after the drawing, to make inquiries concerning the number of the winning ticket. But if the calculations of Condorcet and Niiniluoto were correct then even if the ticket holder should consult an authority ten or twenty times more reliable than the witness these authors refer to, he would have to dismiss the information—regardless of what number the witness mentions—as most likely incorrect. Can it really be the case that I, a ticket holder, when in the presence of dozens of my highly reliable friends, all of whom know the lottery results, should find it pointless to ask any of them about it, knowing that most likely none of them would be telling the truth?[2]

The solution lies in realizing that we have committed an error in computing the value of $P(E/W)$. Consider the last factor in the second term of the denominator, $P(W/\sim E)$. We went along with the suggestion that the value of that factor was $(1-t)$ or $1-0.99 = 0.01$, and this was a mistake. The event that indeed has a probability of $0.01$ is that the witness is reporting falsely. But given that he is not providing us with the right information, does it follow that he was bound to pick #267? That number is not the only one to have failed to win the prize!

In actuality, the value of $P(W/\sim E)$ varies from context to context. If our friend's report is incorrect, then under circumstances which offer no reason for treating one set of numbers unlike any other, we should treat each of the 9,999 wrong numbers as having had an equal chance to present themselves to his mind. Thus even if we assume with complete certainty that our friend is lying, the probability that he will settle upon ticket #267 was only 1/999. But of course '$P(W/\sim E)$' stands for "the probability that our informant is giving us the wrong number *and* in so doing he is going to pick the number 267." Clearly the value of that expression is the probability that he is not telling the truth, multiplied by the probability that of the many possibilities he will choose to represent #267 as the winning number. Thus $P(W/\sim E) = 1/100 \times 1/9999$. It follows that the second term of the denominator, $P(\sim E) \cdot P(W/\sim E)$, amounts to $9,999/10,000 \times 1/100 \times 9,999 = 1/1,000,000$. Hence $P(E/W)$ turns out to equal a fraction with numerator $1/10,000 \times 99/100 = 99/1,000,000$ and denominator $99/1,000,000 + 1/1,000,000$, which equals $99/100$. Thus there has been no depreciation whatever in the credibility of our witness, even though the prior probability of $E$ was so minute, and we shall equate the credibility of his assertion to the degree of his trustworthiness.

It is important to point out that here we had a typical case where an event, though highly improbable, is not extraordinary and thus requires no special explanation. If I pull out a banknote from my pocket and observe its serial number to be B20586291M I would be facing the same kind of situation. The prior probability of observing this particular serial number was less than 1 in $10^{10}$, yet it would occasion no surprise and consequently I should not be inclined to

---

[2] Cf. Chapter 17 "Credibility of Extraordinary Stories" in John Venn's *The Logic of Chance* (London & New York, 1888).

postulate that someone who said this was its serial number must be deliberately playing a trick on me or to seek any explanation why such an incredibly rare event happened to me. The reason is that although this particular serial number was exceedingly unlikely, that *some* number of similar rarity would be observed was not unlikely. In the lottery case too, although my friend mentioning the particular number 267 was highly improbable, that he would mention some equally improbable number—if he is going to mention any number at all—was practically a certainty. I am therefore not facing anything extraordinary and need not seek to explain what happened by ascribing high probability to our friend lying or to something else.

Returning to the banknote story, suppose that after glancing at its number I call upon a student to name the first serial number that comes to his mind and he replies "B20586291M." It would strike me as something remarkable, even mysterious. But why? Surely the probability of his naming the number on the bill was precisely the same as that of my finding it on the bill in the first place!

The answer is that in the second case what we have observed was not merely a highly improbable instance of a common type of event that was bound to happen anyway. Here we have been witnessing something where the very *kind* of event which has been instantiated was of a very rare sort. That the number I observe and the number the student calls out are identical represents the kind of occurrence that is itself extraordinary and thus unanticipated. We are therefore faced with an exemplification of an uncommon class of events that perplexes us and demands an explanation.

A parallel situation would arise in the lottery case if the number 267 my friend claims is the winning ticket happens to be the ticket I have purchased. In that case I would be witnessing not an improbable, common occurrence, but one both improbable and exceptional: my friend mentioned a number that has the unexampled feature of corresponding to my ticket number. It is therefore an extraordinary and striking event which demands an explanation. A plausible explanation might be to say that my informant is deliberately trying to deceive me into believing that I have come into a great amount of money. Here the computation of the probabilities has to proceed differently. The assumption that I am intended to be a victim of a hoax implies that of all the wrong numbers, #267 is the only one I would be given. The value of $P(W/\sim E)$ is therefore not less than 0.01 while the value of the denominator is high and consequently that of the whole fraction is low. In this special case, Niiniluoto's statement about a drastic reduction in the credibility of the witness is correct. And of course the absurd consequence that it is pointless to ask anyone about the winning ticket (since whatever the reply we shall have to reject it) does not apply: it is highly improbable that in answering our inquiry the number of our ticket will be mentioned.

It may be worth pointing out that rationality does not require that I refuse to believe the claim that my ticket won the main prize if I read it in an impersonal medium such as the *Wall Street Journal*. Being informed by that public organ that I am the lucky winner is not an extraordinary event. It is no more than one of a great number of possible instances of a common occurrence that was bound to take place; a newspaper is expected to inform some ticket holder or another that he has won the lottery.

## 2. Is the "Extraordinary" What Is More Probable on an Alternative Hypothesis?

Paul Horwich is one of the few philosophers who has attempted a rigorous treatment of the vital issue of extraordinary, puzzling, or what he calls "surprise" events. He advances the principle that an event, regardless of how improbable it is on hypothesis $C$ (the favored background assumption), does not qualify as a genuine surprise when there is no candidate for the role of $K$—which is at least a "remotely plausible alternative to $C$"—relative to which that event is more probable. According to his principle, an event is to be thought as genuinely surprising if it is highly improbable in the context of normal circumstances, and in addition "there is some initially implausible (but not wildly improbable) alternative view $K$, about the circumstances relative to which [it] would be highly probable."[3]

Horwich is not the only philosopher to have held this view. I. J. Good, in reviewing Horwich's book, claims it to be the view he had held for some years:

> we tend to be surprised... when the result of an observation has much greater probability on some other, not entirely untenable, hypothesis.[4]

---

[3] Paul Horwich, *Probability and Evidence* (Cambridge, 1982), p. 102.
[4] I. J. Good, "A Bayesian Approach in the Philosophy of Inference," *British Journal for the Philosophy of Science* (1984): 161–173.

The Good–Horwich explication of the notion of a surprise is very effective in accounting for a considerable number of situations. Consider the story of a pet woodpecker and the electric typewriter that has been placed in its cage. We should not find it extraordinary if the bird (for lack of anything better to do) kept pecking at the various keys, but we should be dumbstruck if as a result of its continued tapping it correctly reproduced the entire poem "The Owl and the Pussycat." I take it for granted that everyone would be very reluctant to entertain the hypothesis that the woodpecker actually intended to print Lear's poem. Birds are of relatively low intelligence among animals and even among humans there are few who know the whole poem by heart and could produce a perfect copy.

Another hypothesis which most of us would not willingly embrace is that the printed poem is the result of an incredibly improbable accident. The explanation we would most readily accept is that even though the cage may have been under constant surveillance, some person, possibly a prankster, had smuggled a copy of the poem into the cage, or if not, through remote control had manipulated the machine to produce the text he was sure would stupefy us.

One might be wondering: Why should we find this whole incident so tantalizing? Surely, if the probability that random pecking at the keys of a typewriter will produce a sequence of symbols amounting to "The Owl and the Pussycat" is one in many trillions, so too is the probability of the emergence of any completely jumbled sequence of as many symbols. How is it to be explained that while the former event would produce an immense shock, the latter would stir no emotions at all? Good and Horwich have a ready answer: when we are confronted with a fully meaningful text we have an alternative $K$ to the hypothesis that what we see is the outcome of random process such that both (a) $K$ is not too unlikely, and (b) given $K$, the appearance of the poem had high probability. $K$ is the hypothesis that the typing was arranged by a practical joker, and even though we may have watched the cage and the typewriter carefully "$K$ is not too unlikely" in the sense that it is still more probable than that this particular combination be produced by blind chance. Also, when we say "given $K$, the appearance of the poem had high probability," we are only speaking relatively. Even if $K$ is assumed to be true, there are myriad different meaningful texts with which a trickster could have achieved the same stunning effects. Still, meaningful passages constitute only a small subset of collections of symbols and any one of them is therefore more probable on $K$ than on the denial of $K$. Thus we introduce the explanation postulating a practical joker, since otherwise we would be faced with an immensely improbable event which justifiably would be regarded as stupefying by virtue of the applicability of (a) and (b). On the other hand, if we were presented with a page filled with nothing meaningful, then in spite of the equally improbable configuration of characters we would not be surprised since condition (b) is not satisfied.

Unfortunately, however, there are numerous examples which indicate that the Good–Horwich explication of the notion of an extraordinary, surprising event is inadequate. Consider the following example. A tornado touches down in three widely separated spots in a city consisting of 10,000 buildings, destroying three buildings. Given that the city is in the midwest, there is nothing particularly surprising about a destructive tornado. Suppose, however, that Fred owns exactly three buildings in the city and they were just those which happened to be flattened by the twister. Surely we would find such an occurrence quite astonishing. Most people would rule out the possibility that some powerful supernatural agent bent upon wrecking vengeance on Fred willed this disaster. But if not, then there seems to be no suggestion that is not wildly unlikely, and on which it is probable that a devastating tornado will destroy nothing except Fred's scattered buildings. We can find no clue in the accounts of Good or Horwich that would help explain why nevertheless such an event would be regarded as extremely surprising.

Another example is provided by our earlier story where I pulled a banknote from my wallet and observed its serial number to be B820586281M. As pointed out before, the prior probability of observing this particular serial number was less than 1 in 10,000, yet my observing occasions no surprise. Now let us modify that story. Instead of having a student across the hall, a few moments later I receive an overseas telephone call from an Australian friend. Apropos something he mentions I ask him what his account number is with the local telephone company, and he replies "B820586281M." I should certainly feel flabbergasted by such an incredible coincidence. But assuming that all account numbers in that company consist of eight digits and two letters, the prior probability of my friend giving me the number he mentioned was precisely the prior probability of my banknote having that serial number; why then is the first event of no consequence and the second a cause of mystification? Once again it is hard to think of any tolerably tame hypothesis which would render the coincidence probable and hence help us see why on the Good–Horwich thesis there is a fundamental difference between the two events.

Apart from the existence of any number of counterexamples, the Good–Horwich thesis does not as it stands sound very plausible. Why should the absence of a not-too-unlikely $K$ that could account for a given phenomenon make it less of a surprise? A firm believer in the efficacy of psychokinesis, who when told that the explanation for the tornado's wrecking all three buildings belonging to Fred is that a disgruntled tenant of Fred's with high extrasensory powers fervently wished on him such a catastrophe, may accept this as a reasonable explanation. Consequently, to such an adherent of parapsychology the destruction of Fred's property will no longer be such a source of amazement. Skeptics, on the other hand, would find the explanation preposterous and continue to regard Fred's case as an incredibly astonishing mishap. The very fact that we are unable to conceive any alternative hypothesis which could serve as a tolerably acceptable explanation of what we have observed, should, if anything, make it appear more incredible to us and increase our consternation.

### 3. Improbable Events and Improbable Kinds of Events

I should like to advance a somewhat different explication of the notion of an uncommon, genuinely astonishing event, and shall begin with an example involving everyday reasoning, an example which may render the explication more compelling. The names of the fifty students in one of my courses are listed alphabetically, and I find that the birthday of the first person listed is March 17, of the second August 7, and of the next February 11, and so on. Clearly, the prior probability of this particular sequence of fifty dates is exceedingly small, less than $50^{-365}$. Yet no one has found anything peculiar with the list. After all, it was obvious to anyone even before looking at it that listing the birthdates would generate some sequence, and none of the possible particular sequences had greater prior probability than the actual one.

On the other hand, if we found the birthdate of the first student on the list to be March 17, of the next, March 18, and then March 19, 20, and so on, that would strike us as quite amazing. Note, however, that the last sequence is no less improbable than the first, yet it seems so conspicuously anomalous that we would be convinced that there was some special explanation for it. Should we fail to come up with a reasonable explanation we would not cease to be puzzled.

It is reasonable to say that an occurrence, no matter how exceed-ingly unlikely, as long as it is an instance of a common type that was in any case bound (or highly probable) to take place, will not surprise us and does not prompt us to search for an explanation. However, when it is not just the event or a series of events that is improbable, but the very *kind* of event it instantiates is also of a rare sort, we demand an explanation.

The second list of birthdays was of a notable, orderly kind. Let us suppose $E_1, E_2, \ldots E_n$ form a class of events and it is certain or highly probable that some member of the class is going to occur. If $n$ is very large then the probability of a particular event $E_i$ is very small, nevertheless its occurrence will not constitute a surprise. The materialization of $E_i$ is not going to astonish us, essentially because it is not the *sort* of event that is highly improbable, since we have assumed all along that if not $E_i$, then some other equally improbable event of its kind was bound to, or at least was likely to, happen. On the other hand, when it is highly improbable that even a single member of a given kind of events should take place, then the occurrence of any member of that kind is an occasion for surprise.

Thus suppose I am standing blindfolded 250 feet away from a large board with twenty-five different circles painted on it, and am asked to shoot twenty-five times in its direction. If I should end up hitting precisely the center of each circle (or, say, the lowest point on the circumference of each circle), that would surely startle all the onlookers. But why? Was it not absolutely certain from the very beginning that there was going to be some extremely improbable configuration of bullet holes? But once again, if the final result was a random configuration, its improbability would not engage our at-tention: all outcomes were equally improbable, and one of them had to materialize. On the other hand, if each of my shots hit a bull's-eye (or the lowest point on the circumference of the various circles) then we are faced with an improbable *kind* of event: normally, twenty-five sets of coordinates would have to be given in order to describe the position of each bullet hole; in this case it is sufficient to say that each bullet hit the center (or the lowest point on the circumference) of a circle.

Returning to the tornado story, an event involving three differ-ent buildings, all belonging to the same person, is the sort of event that stands apart from occurrences relating to just any three build-ings. Items having a single owner are grouped together for many purposes (e.g., tax assessment); damaging them causes cumulative loss to someone in a way damage to three buildings with different proprietors does not, and so on. Consequently, a tornado hitting all three of Fred's buildings constitutes a special, extraordinary kind of event.

## 4. Some Notable Scientific Examples

An appreciation of the vital distinction between the two kinds of improbable events discussed above is indispensable for a correct understanding of the process of confirmation in the empirical sciences. Working scientists have no difficulty recognizing at once whether a given event belongs to one or the other type (without ever having attempted to articulate the vital distinction between them), and acting accordingly. Let me begin with some of the more spectacular examples, in which the recognition that we are confronted not with merely the improbable but also with an extraordinary event has led to some major scientific advances.

(I) Until the twentieth century everybody took it for granted that waves require some material medium to travel in. A falling stone when it hits the water generates waves we can observe and these waves are propagated through the water; sound waves must have air to travel in, and so on. The great physicist Clerk Maxwell suggested that the light waves we receive from outer space are transmitted through the material medium, the "luminiferous ether." His hypothesis implied that the earth, which is orbiting the sun and is also dragged along with the sun in its wanderings through the Milky Way, must be moving at a considerable speed relative to the ether. Two American scientists, A. A. Michelson and E. W. Morley, devised an ingenious experiment to measure the speed of the ether wind, by sending light signals in directions perpendicular to each other and attending to the slight difference in the time required to make their two-way journeys. The result, which was announced in 1887, was absolutely negative: the earth did not appear to be in motion at all! The outcome of the Michelson–Morley experiment stunned the scientific community. Since scientists at that time refused to entertain the suggestion that the earth was actually stationary, they were for a while at a loss how to account for the negative result. Eventually the physicist Fitzgerald put forward a hypothesis, that subsequently was refined and put in exact mathematical form by Lorenz, postulating that the earth's movement is masked by the contraction of our measuring instruments in the direction of our planet's motion.

The significant aspect of this episode for our purposes is that many scientists were reluctant to accept the Fitzgerald–Lorenz contraction hypothesis, which they found outlandish (the astronomer A. S. Eddington even compared it to something out of Lewis Carroll's *Through the Looking Glass*). It is not immediately obvious why the hypothesis should have been rejected out of hand. Fitzgerald and Lorenz had not made it entirely out of thin air; the hypothesis was based on the recent discovery of the electric structure of atoms. Given that matter was held together by electric forces and assuming that it is the ether that transmits these forces, it should not have seemed too implausible that the ether wind caused by the earth's movement through that medium affects the size of the instrument's arm in the direction of the movement.

The correct explanation, I believe, is that what struck people as astonishingly unlikely was mainly that of all the infinitely many possible effects the ether wind could have had it just "happened" to produce the unique kind of shrinking that is neither less nor more required for the observable effects to be such as if the earth were at complete rest relative to it. It seems fairly obvious that if the Michelson–Morley experiment had any one of the indefinitely many possible outcomes which, however strange, were different from what it actually had, scientists would not have been too disconcerted. If, for instance, the experiment required the postulation of a drastic amount of contraction or expansion in order to explain why the earth seems to move so slowly that it should require a century to complete its orbit around the sun, or so fast that a year should be shorter than a day, scientists would probably not have felt too uncomfortable to do so. But surely any proposition that the ether wind affects the size of a material body to a specific degree, is as improbable as every other. It is evident, however, that one particular change, though precisely as improbable as any of the indefinitely many other possible changes, is regarded an extraordinary kind of change; namely, the one which counteracts the motion to exactly the degree that engenders the illusion of motionlessness. That the ether wind should hit upon this extraordinary sort of interference that creates the appearance of a pre–Copernican earth at the unmoved center of the universe, is an astonishing kind of phenomenon which calls for a unique explanation. Scientists were only satisfied when Einstein advanced his special theory of relativity, according to which we are bound to fail to detect any movement relative to the ether, as there is no such thing as the ether.

(II) In the sixteenth century the mathematician Stevinus dropped objects of unequal weight from the same height, demonstrating that they hit the ground approximately at the same time. For a long time after Galileo, who formalized these results, scientists believed that a large lump of lead and a light feather accelerate at an equal rate, when in the absence of air resistance they are subjected to the same force. Now the pull of gravity on the heavy sample of lead is many times greater than on the light feather, but to counteract this the feather has the advantage that it offers appropriately less inertial resistance to acceleration than the massive lead.

Subsequently, Newton experimented with pendulums of the same length made of different materials, observing that they had equal periods. Thus he established the principle of the equivalence of inertial and gravitational masses to an accurate 1 part in $10^3$. In 1827 Friedrich Bessel continued the experiments with pendulums and showed that inertial and gravitational masses are equal to within 2 parts in $10^5$. These results were in turn vastly improved in 1890 by Roland von Eötvös, who with the aid of a torsion balance determined the validity of the principle to within a few parts in $10^{10}$, and with further refinements physicists later achieved an accuracy within a few parts in $10^{13}$.[5]

Neither Newton nor his followers had an explanation why the two types of masses, the gravitational and the inertial, should be precisely equal. They had to reconcile themselves to the idea that the equivalence between these two different features of a physical body is certainly to be marveled at, but may possibly be an unaccountable coincidence. Eventually Einstein came along with his revolutionary general theory of relativity, which led to a notable amount of simplification and unification in physics. Among that theory's great achievements was to provide a compelling reason why the two masses coincide in magnitude. Gravity and inertia were reduced to one and the same phenomenon; as Einstein said, the grounds for puzzlement at the "coincidence" disappear through explaining the numerical equality of inertia and gravitation by the unity of their nature.

Let us consider now a somewhat different situation. Imagine that Galileo, Newton, and others discovered that gravitational and inertial masses were not equivalent, but the first was precisely 3.17

---

[5] E. R. Harrison, *Cosmology* (Cambridge, 1981), p. 164.

times greater than the other. I believe it is safe to assert that in that case few scientists would have been stupefied at seeing that the ratio assumes the infinitely improbable number 3.17. It is unlikely that much energy and time would have been spent by physicists such as Bessel and Eötvös to attain results that confirmed with accuracies of the order of one in a billion or one in a trillion that the ratio between the two type of masses was neither more or less than 3.17.

Nor is it likely that many would have felt an irresistible urge to search for a theory that would have explained why the incredibly rare number 3.17 had to represent the ratio between the two masses. However, since the ratio was unity, the issue became a source of acute concern and the subject of intense investigation. As is known, Einstein worked for many years with great tenacity to develop general relativity, driven on by the profound conviction that such a theory—the outlines of which he had conceived at an early stage—must be true, and that he would eventually be able to iron out its remaining wrinkles. The main factor sustaining him in his efforts was his firm belief that it simple could not be a coincidence that the values of the two masses are exactly the same.

We might ask once more: The number 3.17 is no less rare among the values a ration may have between two physical quantities than the number 1, so why is it that the (supposed) discovery of the former to be the correct value would have most likely left everyone, including Einstein, indifferent? Why is it that one number may play a major role in initiating one of the important revolutions in science, while another may perhaps merely be recorded and then practically forgotten?

I suggest that the explanation lies in that while the probability of the ratio being 3.17 is infinitesimal, finding it to be the actual value would present us with a result, which although exceedingly improbable, is commonplace and "uninteresting." The value was bound to be *some* number. The number one is however not just some number; it has a special significance in the context of measuring the ratio between physical quantities. For example, the ratio between the number of animals that are featherless bipeds and the number of those that are sentient beings is one. The set of featherless bipeds is identical with the set of sentient beings. It often happens that when the ratio between two magnitudes is one, we find that we are not really measuring two distinct things but the manifestations of one and the same thing. Thus it was reasonable for many physicists of the last couple of centuries to regard the observed value of the ratio between the two masses as extraordinary enough either to require an explanation or to be shown to be inaccurate, and it was reasonable for Einstein to suspect right from the beginning that he was confronted with the manifestations of what ultimately is a single property.

(III) Around the year 1600 different physicists gave different accounts for why unsupported bodies near the surface of the earth move vertically to the ground (instead of moving upward, or horizontally, or at this or that angle to the horizontal, or just stay put), and why planets move along closed curves symmetrically about at least two axes. Conservative scientists held that all terrestrial bodies have the propensity to reach the center of the earth which was their innately preferred place. On the other hand, the movements of celestial bodies they explained by assuming them to be embedded in rotating crystal spheres. Others, such as Kepler, thought that the force of gravity between material bodies is what explains both types of movements. Terrestrial objects are subject to the earth's gravity and therefore fall towards it. The movement of planets, on the other hand, is a compromise result between their initial velocity away from the sun and the attractive force exerted on them by the sun.

Even though Kepler did not know much about the nature of gravity, not knowing how, or with what, its magnitude varied, all would now readily concede that his position was superior to the position of the Aristotelian scientists. The reason why is fairly simple. The Aristotelians were not trying to explain something truly surprising: there is nothing extraordinary in finding one group of bodies moving in one particular way and a second group in another, even though each particular way had an exceedingly small prior probability to be chosen as the path to be traversed by any set of physical objects. After all, whatever moves is bound to move along *some* curve. Kepler, however, *could* see himself being confronted with a remarkable, because extraordinary, conjunction of the behavior of two different classes of objects: the movements of terrestrial bodies as well as those pulled towards the most massive body in the vicinity. Thus Kepler's hypothesis was designed to explain what could otherwise be legitimately regarded as a puzzling phenomenon. It was therefore thought to be better confirmed by the data than that of Aristotle's followers.

## 5. What, in General, Calls for a Scientific Explanation

So far we have referred to rather special episodes which stand out in the history of science as notable cases in which the extraordinary is unmistakably calling attention to itself, demanding an explanation. Now we shall look at some representative routine cases of confirmation, and shall see that even in the most commonplace instances the essence of hypothesis construction is the attempt to transform what is extraordinary and surprising into the inevitable consequences of nature's laws.

Suppose a scientist decides to investigate the co-variation of two physical magnitudes $x$ and $y$, which have hitherto been assumed to be quite unrelated to one another. He performs 250 relevant experiments, obtaining values for $x$ and corresponding values for $y$. He finds that the 250 pairs of values can be accounted for by no simpler an equation than $y = f(x)$, which consists of 250 terms. Virtually nobody would wish to say that here we have experimental evidence that $y = f(x)$ represents the law governing the correlation between $x$ and $y$. The scientific community would continue to view the properties involved in this case as being independent of one another and regard the mathematical expression as a mere record of a long sequence of random occurrences.

One might be wondering just why this is so. After all, we have before us a list of an unusually high number of data and we find that of the infinitely many mathematical equations with two variables, none other but the considerably complex $y = f(x)$ is the one that fits them all with the maximum adequacy (i.e., it seems to be the simplest of all the equations satisfied by all 250 results). The prior probability that this should turn out to be the case was surely exceedingly low. Does it not stand to reason that it is not by just an incredibly rare coincidence that the uncommon expression is capable of accommodating the data, but because it was bound to do so; because the expression $y = f(x)$ represents a law of nature which determined what the observed values *had* to be?

The answer is that we refuse to treat $y = f(x)$ as representing a law because of the absence of positive grounds for doing so: laws of nature are as a rule posited in response to a demand for an explanation, a demand generated by our encountering an extraordinary, surprising phenomenon. Our scientist is not confronted with a remarkable phenomenon that cries out for an explanation. His list of results proves nothing special about itself by virtue of its capacity to satisfy an exceedingly rare expression, since in any case a finite number of data are bound to fit *some* expression. That $y = f(x)$ can accommodate all 250 results is—though an improbable instance— still an instance of an entirely common, indeed inevitable, kind of occurrence.

It is useful to mention that if prior to the series of experiments someone came along and predicted that all the 250 results the scientist was about to obtain would fit the equation $y = f(x)$, we would find that of course exceedingly astonishing. We would certainly seek an explanation, but not by suggesting that the phenomenon in question is after all governed by the law represented by the complex equation. For the source of the surprise would not be the phenomenon under investigation but the remarkable ability of the predictor. Thus we will want to find an explanation of how he managed to predict such a long series of random events.

On the other hand, if we found that all the results satisfied the equation $(\alpha)$: $y = 7x^2$, we would regard $(\alpha)$ as representing a genuine law of nature. The reason is that $(\alpha)$ would not be just any equation but an instance of a rare *kind* of equation, exemplifying several notable features. It is not merely considerably shorter than the list of data it embodies, it is the simplest equation satisfied by all 250 results and it is also the simplest to be satisfied by the first 249, 248, etc. results. In the previous case (where $y = f(x)$ was the simplest expression all the results fitted) given only 249 results there exists a different expression—still very long but somewhat shorter than $y = f(x)$—capable of accommodating all of them, and for 248 yet a simpler expression, and so on. In the proposed context $(\alpha)$ is a remarkable sort of equation, in that it sustains its maximum adequacy with respect to various sets having different numbers of results. It is surprising to find that our data have this peculiar feature of best satisfying $(\alpha)$ at many successive stages of experimentation. It calls out for an explanation, and we offer one, by postulating that there exists a law which ensures that the data exemplifies this remarkable feature.

We are to be reminded that the surprising phenomena in our first two examples also had the characteristic that different subsets of the final set of data lent themselves to the same description. The description "the first date on the list is March 17, and it is followed by a series of consecutive dates" would remain the simplest even if the list did not contain the last ten or twenty names. Similarly, if there were less than twenty-five shots, the best description of the configuration of the bullet holes would still be what it is now. Series of results possessing this unique kind of feature, whether in

the course of our everyday business or in the course of scientific
research, draw special attention and demand an explanation.

## 6. Revising Nicod's Criteria

A similar account may be given for elementary, enumerative induction. When the first bird of a certain species we observe is brown,
and the next yellow, and then a grey bird comes along followed by
a red striped bird and so on, we are not astonished, even though it
was exceedingly improbable that we were going to observe just this
sequence of colors. But when every raven appears to be black, then
we are confronted with an unusual kind of phenomenon. We thus
postulate that the uncommon sort of conformity is not a result of
accident but required by the law "All ravens are black."

Now consider an assortment of nonblack objects consisting, for
example, of a white pair of shoes, a green scarf, several yellow pages,
a blue ribbon, and a red carpet. Is there anything remarkable about
this collection of articles, in the sense that we should want to offer an explanatory hypothesis for their being collected together?
Virtually everybody would agree that no such hypothesis is called
for. We have to remember that given any finite number of particulars there will always be indefinitely many negative predicates (i.e.,
terms applying to a true vacuum are compatible with all other predicates of their kind, and which indicate the absence, rather than the
presence, of a specific property) correctly applying to them. Hence
when we find a number of nonblack things that are also nonravens,
we are not confronted with any remarkable kind of phenomenon.
No explanation is called for, and we would reject it if presented
with one.

These considerations provide us with a ready-made solution to
the famous Hempel's paradox. As will be recalled Hempel starts
out with three innocuous assumptions:

    (1) If two hypotheses are logically equivalent, then whatever
        confirms one also confirms (precisely to the same degree)
        the other.
    (2) "All ravens are black" is logically equivalent to "All non-
        black things are nonravens."
    (3) Generalizations are confirmed through the observation
        of their instances.

It follows from (3) that the observation of a white shoe, which is
an instance of "All nonblack things are nonravens," confirms that

hypothesis. But since by (2) that generalization is equivalent to "All ravens are black," it follows from (1) that "All ravens are black" is confirmed by observing the white shoe. This, however, sounds unbelievable.

Many solutions to this puzzle have been suggested during the last forty-five years and a number of these are remarkably ingenious. Some of the solutions propose to make use of the differences in our linguistic practices vis-à-vis ravens, for which we have a special name, and nonravens, whose name is parasitically formed through negation. Others employ the probability calculus and argue from the acknowledged vast difference between the number of ravens and nonravens in the universe. The present solution may be said to have existed long before this particular problem was thought of, since the basis on which it rests lies at the very heart of scientific method. "All ravens are black" is certainly logically equivalent to "All nonblack things are nonravens," and as we said before an assortment of nonblack things confirms neither. Thus principles (1) and (2) are undoubtedly correct, but (3) needs to be amended.

According to principle (3), which is a component of Nicod's famous confirmation criteria, generalizations are confirmed through the observation of their instances. If this principle were indeed valid it would have very odd consequences: any set of instances, regardless how greatly diverse, would confirm an indefinite number of unrelated generalizations. Consider the following multifarious bunch of items: a nuclear submarine, the Ohio Turnpike, an omelet, an iguana, Buffalo Bill, the snows of Kilimanjaro, the Republican Party, the Magna Carta, the Peruvian National Anthem. Immensely varied as the members of this set are, they have indefinitely many common aspects, for indefinitely many negative predicates apply to them all, e.g., 'nonraven' and 'nonblack'. If principle (3) were valid they could serve to support any number of the most far-fetched generalizations. They would, for instance, support "All objects outside our solar system contain gold," which is equivalent to "Everything that contains no gold is not an object outside our solar system." Nuclear submarines, the Ohio Turnpike, etc., are all instances devoid of gold and are not located outside our solar system.

We should therefore formulate a more restricted version of (3):

> (3) Generalizations are confirmed by the observation of a set of instances *the presence of which is surprising*.

In view of the fact that any finite number of particulars resemble one another (as well as does an absolute void), in that indefinitely many negative predicates apply to them, there is no occasion for surprise when we find a large group, each member of which is a nonraven, nonblack, lacking in gold, or is not situated outside the solar system. Hence our observing this to be the case does not make us want to look for an explanation why they all exemplify the same negative feature.

On the other hand, consider the nine particulars enumerated in the last paragraph: it will not be easy to find many positive predicates that correctly apply to each one of them. The same goes for any randomly selected group of particulars. Consequently, when we are presented with a considerable number of individuals that do resemble each other, in that the same two positive terms apply to each of them, we find the matter surprising, and feel justified in proposing a general law to account for the unexpected phenomenon.

Thus consider a profoundly ignorant individual who was uncertain whether a raven was a fish or fowl and knew no more than it had some property such as weight (which is clearly not something exemplified by a perfect void, and thus 'having weight' is a positive predicate), and who was similarly unsure of the meaning of 'blackness', and hence was certainly devoid of any idea of the scarcity or plentifulness of ravens or black things (something most philosophers thought was indispensable to the solution of Hempel's paradox). Such an individual would nevertheless be able to conclude that observing a good number of ravens and finding them all black confirmed "All ravens are black," since that generalization explains what otherwise would be an astonishing set of phenomena.

Also, without further relevant knowledge one may infer that the observation of any number of items among which the only feature we find in common is their nonblackness and nonravenness, presents us with nothing remarkable, nothing that cries out for, or warrants, an explanatory hypothesis.

## 7. The Bayesian Approach

Is the thesis we have developed in this chapter compatible with the Bayesian approach, according to which a rational person's degree of belief in a scientific hypothesis accurately reflects the mathematical principles of probability theory? According to the adherents of that approach the central role in determining the credibility of hypotheses is played by the inverse theorem of probability, which directly follows from the Conjunctive Axiom and is named after Bayes. It may seem that the thesis I am defending is at variance with the Bayesian approach, since the latter regards as factors relevant to the status of a hypothesis given certain evidence only the prior probabilities of the hypothesis and that of the evidence (i.e., $P(H)$ and $P(E)$ plus the probability of the evidence conditioned on the hypothesis (i.e., $P(E/H)$), and no role whatsoever is assigned to anything like the degree of extraordinariness or of surprise.

The correct answer, however, is that the view described in this chapter also makes full use of the calculus of probability, including Bayes's Theorem, except that the proposition '$E$' stands for is more circumscribed than in many texts on the topic. Let us begin by reminding ourselves that '$H$' generally asserts the existence of a law which implies the truth of $E$ as well as the claim that yet unobserved instances will continue to be governed by the same law. Invariably there is an immediate alternative to $H$, $H^*$, which more modestly asserts only the existence of a law implying the truth of $E$ and makes no claim concerning the unobserved. It stands to reason that $P(H^*/E)$ is greater than $P(H/E)$, and it may clearly be exhibited to be so by Bayes's Theorem. In the denominator of the fraction that equals $P(H/E)$ we have: $P(E/H) \cdot P(H) + P(E/{\sim}H) \cdot P({\sim}H)$. Since there are uncountably many contraries to $H$ which also imply $E$, $P({\sim}H)$ may be of considerable value, and the larger it is the smaller the value of $P(H/E)$. On the other hand, in the denominator of the fraction that equals $P(H^*/E)$ we have: $P(E/H^*)P(H^*) + P(E/{\sim}H^*) \cdot P({\sim}H^*)$. $P({\sim}H^*)$ equals zero, though there may be alternative hypotheses which say more than $H^*$ asserts. Thus $P(H^*/E)$ is equal to a fraction in which the numerator is identical to the denominator, i.e., it equals one.

There is however an obvious objection to $H^*$: it is surely not a proper explanation of $E$, as it says no more than $E$. Though $H^*$ asserts the existence of a law, its empirical import is precisely the same as that of $E$. Regardless of what the correct account of the nature of scientific explanations may be, this much is clear: $E$ cannot constitute an explanation for $E$. But this objection is effective only as long as we have to deal with a set of observations that are clamoring for an explanation. Thus Bayes's Theorem is not to be used to measure the credibility of $H$ in just any situation where it implies $E$, but only where $H^*$ cannot take its place, since the latter fails to explain what legitimately calls for an explanation. The following is then a detailed statement of what $E$ stands for in the equation that correctly reflects the credibility a putative law of nature has achieved through $E$:

> $E$ = The set of $n$ data we have collected is of a notable kind. It belongs to a relatively rare species of sets, namely, to those which exhibit the following conspicuous pattern: any subset of our data, consisting of $n-1$, or $n-2, \ldots$, or $n-m$, elements, resembles the final set in the significant aspect of lending themselves to be accounted for in the simplest manner by the same hypothesis.

The higher the value of $m$, the rarer the kind of peculiarity $E$ is referring to. By increasing our set of observations, that is, by increasing $n$, we increase also the value of $m$ and thus decrease the value of $P(E)$, which raises the credibility of $H$.

# VI

# FORESIGHT AND HINDSIGHT

## 1. Two Kinds of Evidence

Supporting evidence for an hypothesis falls into two classes. The first consists of evidence that suggested the hypothesis in the first place, that is, evidence gathered earlier which our hypothesis was devised to account for. The other is the novel kind of evidence, obtained after our hypothesis has been postulated—evidence predicted on its basis. In this chapter we shall look at the important issue of the comparative effects of the prediction of novel results on the one hand, and the accommodation of existing data on the other, vis-à-vis the credibility of a given hypothesis. We shall also have the opportunity to see the ways in which elementary probability theory is made use of in the course of the debate around this important issue.

Most philosophers who have expressed their view on this issue have held that to verify a prediction made on the basis of a hypothesis is to provide much more support for it than to use it in explaining what is already known or in accommodating data it was designed to account for. In 1678, for example, Leibniz wrote:

> Those hypotheses deserve the highest praise (next to truth), however, by whose aid prediction can be made, even about phenomena or observations which have not been tested before.

Nearer to our time we have the often quoted statement by P. Duhem:

> the highest test...of our holding a classification as a natural one is to ask it to indicate in advance things which the future alone reveals. And when the experiment is made and confirms the prediction obtained from our theory, we feel strengthened in our conviction.[1]

---

[1] P. Duhem, *The Aim and Structure of Physical Theory* (New York, 1962), p. 28.

On a commonsense level, it should appear reasonable to hold that one is unlikely to succeed consistently in making correct predictions unless one is guided by the truth. On the other hand, to accommodate already known results these facts confine us to a limited choice from among the hypotheses which suit them, regardless of whether any of them is true or not. Several philosophers have argued in this vein, among them R. N. Giere, who not so long ago said:

> The probability of fit between model and observation is not influenced if the observations play no role in the selection of the model. But it is exceedingly difficult to be confident that no such selection pressure existed when the result was known to the developer of the model. One can always be more confident of the goodness of a test if the result was not previously known.[2]

Giere appears to be suggesting that when the scientist already possesses the data to be accounted for, he is liable to put forward a conjecture devoid of the intrinsic characteristics of the law actually governing the situation, just so as to conform to the data. Consequently some philosophers, who have come to disapprove of conjectures made after the fact, occupy a position that reflects Homer's saying in the *Iliad*, "After the event even a fool is wise." Some, however, have gone even further and maintained not merely that prediction is superior to retrodiction, but that wisdom offered after the event is to be declined altogether.

A strong skeptical attitude toward a theory that has done no more than explain already existing data seems manifestly justified when contemplating the pronouncements of applied economists, political pundits, armchair strategists, and in general social scientists who venture to make their predictions available to the public. Often these predictions are wrong. Nevertheless, in retrospect few seem to hesitate to come forward with an explanation for why everything happened the way it did. Thus, one is naturally reluctant to attribute too much weight to an *ex post facto* explanation of an event offered by those who were unable to anticipate it.

On the other hand, a very positive attitude toward theories that merely accommodate data we possess seems to be justified in other contexts. For example, in crime detection it is quite common for the investigator to collect first the relevant clues, which are then seen as pointing toward the hypothesis that $X$ is the perpetrator

---

[2] R. N. Giere, *Understanding Scientific Reasoning* (New York, 1984), p. 286.

of the crime. Sometimes the accused is arrested, indicted, and even convicted solely on the basis of that evidence, without the detective's hypothesis yielding a single prediction. This suggests that not only is it permissible to let the evidence provide "selection pressure" upon the investigator's choice, but it may even constitute the one and only reason for it to be made, as in its absence not the slightest suspicion would have fallen on $X$. This may lead to the conjecture that while one will always be able to come up with some hypothesis accounting for what we already know, we may not invariably be able to produce a compelling hypothesis that has something unique to recommend it and which is preferable to all other hypotheses complying with the data.

In order to gain a more solid grip on this issue, it will be necessary to subject the relevant aspects of the process of confirmation to a more detailed and closer scrutiny. This, as I shall argue, is properly done by extending and applying the thesis introduced in the previous chapter, which stated that the status of a hypothesis is determined by the degree to which it alleviates our legitimate puzzlement generated by a unique sort of phenomenon. The reader who wants to get to the point may safely skip the next two sections, which represent a detour whose only purpose is to provide some picture of the wide range of opinions expressed on this topic and some of the ingenuity with which diametrically opposed views have been defended.

### 2. Attempts to Prove That Accommodation and Prediction Have Precisely the Same Effect

I first propose to examine two remarkable arguments advanced by Paul Horwich, who in his widely discussed book *Probability and Evidence* takes an extreme stand on the matter, contending that chronology in the present context is of no consequence whatever, and that accommodation is precisely as effective in providing confirmation as prediction. In his first argument he uses the following notation: $H_T$ = hypothesis $H$ is true; $H_R$ = $H$ was required to fit the data $D$; $F = D$ fits $H$. His argument goes thus:

> If we know of our theory that it was required to fit data $D$, this *does* provide us with more reason than we would otherwise have had to believe that this theory is true. Thus, $P(H_T/H_R) \neq P(H_T) \cdots$ what is relevant to the probability of $H_T$, in the information $H_R$, is precisely that our theory fits the data $D$. Therefore, $P(H_T/H_R) = P(H_T/F)$ and so $P(H_T/F \& H_R) = P(H_T/F)$. Thus, the capacity of

our theory to accommodate the data $D$ provides just as much reason to believe it as its ability in context $P$ to predict those data.[3]

The first thing to note is that Horwich takes it for granted that a theory's mere ability to conform with the pre-existing data recommends it to some (however small) degree. This is a fairly innocuous claim, and most of those philosophers who play down the significance of the capacity to accommodate what is already known, would concede that such a theory is still somewhat more credible than one which cannot even be made to harmonize with already available results. Thus Horwich begins with the claim, which we should not want to dispute, that $P(H_T/H_R)$ is not precisely equal to $P(H_T)$. In the next bold step of his argument he contends that once we concede that $H_R$ raises the probability of $H_T$ to any degree, we are forced to admit that it raises its probability to exactly the same degree as $H_C$ (where $H_C = H$ was postulated earlier and was used to predict the data D), i.e., $P(H_T/H_R) = P(H_T/H_C)$. In other words, Horwich maintains that if accommodation confirms (or raises the probability of) a hypothesis at all, then it confirms it to the same degree as does prediction.

Horwich's argument is perhaps somewhat more condensed than it should be and it may be easier to follow if I expand it slightly. He points out that the statement $H_R$ is equivalent to the conjunction of three other statements:

$D_{t1} =$ The data was obtained at $t_1$;

$H_2 =$ Someone happened to formulate $H$ at time $t_2$, and $t_1$ is earlier than $t_2$;

$F =$ The data fit $H$.

Thus, when we conceded that $H_R$ raises the probability of $H_T$ we conceded that $D_{t_1}$ and $H_2$ & $F$ raises the probability of $H_T$. It is clear however that the truth or falsity of $H$ is not in any way affected by the truth of $D_{t_1}$ or of $H_2$, that the probability of $H$ is independent of both these conjuncts, and the only relevant thing is that $F$ happens to be true. It follows therefore that $P(H_T/D_{t_1}$ & $H_2$ & $F) = P(H_T/F)$. But then in a similar fashion $H_C$ could be represented as the conjunction $D_{t_3}$ & $H_2$ & $F$, leading to the result that $P(H_T/C)$ is also equal to $P(H_T/F)$. Hence there is absolutely no difference in the amount of support a hypothesis receives from data obtained either before or after it was postulated.

---

[3] Paul Horwich, *Probability and Evidence* (Cambridge, 1982), p. 116.

It seems obvious that Horwich's brief argument leading to his sweeping conclusion is wrong. To see this, it should be sufficient to point out that he commits an elementary error when he claims that since $H_T$ is probabilistically independent of $D_{t_1}$ and of $H_2$, it follows therefore that $H_T$ is also independent of the conjunction of $D_{t_1}$ and $H_2$. Figure 14 illustrates clearly that this is not necessarily true. Since three of the six squares are $H_T$-squares, $P(H_T) = 1/2$. Also one of the two $D_{t_1}$'s is an $H_T$-square, and therefore $P(H_T/D_{t_1}) = 1/2$. Thus we see that $P(H_T) = P(H_T/D_{t_1})$, which means that $H_T$ is independent of $D_{t_1}$. In precisely the same way Figure 14 also shows that $H_T$ is independent of $H_2$. At the same time we see that

**Figure 14**

the only square which is both $D_{t_1}$ and $H_2$ is also an $H_T$-square. In other words, $P(H_T/D_{t_1} \& H_2) = 1$ and not $1/2$, which means that $H_T$ is not independent of the conjunction of the two statements although it is independent of both singly.

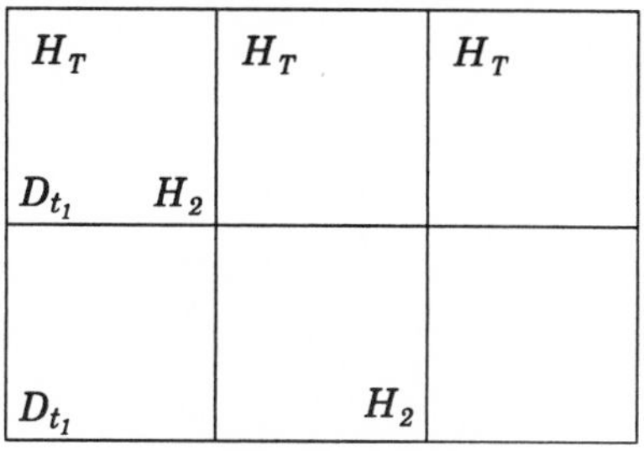

Horwich advances an additional argument in support of his view that data fitting a theory confirm it to the same degree regardless of when they were obtained. The strategy he adopts in this case is to describe explicitly the assumption that would be required for maintaining the superiority of prediction over accommodation, and then claims that such an assumption is unwarranted. Horwich begins his argument by asking us to assume that theory $T$ entails the data $E \& D$, and that we do not know whether $D$ has been predicted or merely accommodated like $E$. The following propositions are then stated:

(B) $T$ was formulated to account for $E$, further consequences $D$ were deduced from $T$, an experiment was performed and $D$ was found to be true;

(A) $T$ was formulated to account for $E \& D$.

Horwich's argument may then be presented as follows. Let us suppose we are given the inequality

$$P(B/T) > P(B). \qquad (\alpha)$$

Then from Bayes's Theorem we have

$$\frac{P(B/T)}{P(B)} = \frac{P(T/B)}{P(T)}$$

which together with $(\gamma)$ implies that

$$P(T/B) > P(T). \qquad (\beta)$$

Clearly $A$ is the denial of $B$ and therefore $P(A)+P(B) = 1$ as well as $P(B/T) + P(A/T) = 1$, i.e., $P(B/T) - P(B) = P(A) - P(A/T)$. Given $(\beta)$ it follows that the left-hand side of this last equation is positive and thus so is the right-hand side. We may conclude therefore that

$$P(A/T) < P(A). \qquad (\gamma)$$

Bearing in mind that from Bayes's Theorem we have

$$\frac{P(A/T)}{P(A)} = \frac{P(T/A)}{P(T)}$$

we can see that $(\gamma)$ entails that $P(T/A) < P(T)$. In view of $(\beta)$, therefore, $P(T/B) > P(T/A)$. All this amounts to saying that if we begin with assuming $(\alpha)$ to be true, then we are led to the conclusion that $B$ provides stronger confirmation for $T$ than does $A$, i.e., prediction is preferable to accommodation.

Thus Horwich claims that everything hinges on the question: Is it reasonable to assume $(\alpha)$, i.e., that given $T$ is true a scientist is more likely to formulate it prior to the availability of any supporting evidence than when $T$ is false? The reason why such an assumption might appear credible, Horwich explains, is because some of us believe we possess an innate propensity to recognize a true theory upon seeing one, that is, if a theory is true then on its own (even in the complete absence of relevant evidence) it is likely to recommend itself to us, by being intrinsically more plausible, than if it were false. In other words, $P(B/T) > P(B)$, or $(\alpha)$ would be the case if the truth of $T$ were likely, as it were, to stare the scientist in the face. Horwich rejects any such thought by insisting that we are not endowed with a special ability to recognize true theories on sight:

> it is not the case that supposing the truth of $T$ will modify our estimate of its plausibility. Thus $P(B/T) = P(B)$, and therefore $P(T/B) = P(T)$. It is of no consequence that the data were predicted.[4]

This seems a rather shaky piece of reasoning. I am not sure I understand why Horwich entertained the belief in the first place that

---

[4] Ibid., p. 117.

if we agreed that scientists had a natural tendency to gravitate toward true theories then there may be grounds for holding that $P(B/T) > P(B)$. Be that as it may, all that he does through his argument is to point out that there is no basis for such a belief. It is, however, very hard to see how merely discrediting the belief in the existence of an innate human aptitude to recognize a true theory on sight is sufficient for settling once and for all the question of the relative merits of prediction and accommodation. No argument has been produced why $P(B/T) > P(B)$ may not follow from some other assumption, that could be made on reasonable grounds. Indeed, those who set a higher value on data predicted through an already existing theory than on data used in the construction of a theory, do so on the basis of an assumption that has nothing to do with the human capacity for smelling out the truth. The assumption relevant to their position is that unless $T$ were true, it would be highly unlikely to predict correctly data yet to be produced.

### 3. An Attempt to Demonstrate the Utter Worthlessness of Accommodation

To cite an example from among those philosophers who are diametrically opposed to the view just discussed we shall look at a paper by Richmond Campbell and Thomas Vinci published in 1982. In that paper they claimed not merely that accounting for known facts provides less support for a given theory than making successful predictions with its aid, but that it provides no support at all. They advanced a very clear argument to show why explaining already existing data can be of no help to any theory. To reproduce their argument I shall be using their notation:

$T =$ Hypothesis $H$ is true;
$F =$ The evidence fits $H$;
$D =$ The investigator deliberately designed $H$ to entail the evidence.

They then produce the more detailed version of Bayes's Theorem:

$$P(T \& D/F) = \frac{P(T \& D) \times P(F/T \& D)}{P(T \& D) \times P(F/T \& D) + P(\sim T \& D) \times P(F/\sim T \& D)}.$$

The probability of $T$ is very small, and the authors ascribe the value .01 to it. Since they assume $D$ as given, they put $P(T \& D) = .01$. It follows that $P(\sim T \& D) = .99$. They also assume that if $D$ is given then regardless of whether $T$ is true or false, $F$ is assured to be true. Thus, $P(F/T \& D) = 1$. Substituting:

$$P(T \& D/F) = \frac{0.01 \times 1}{0.01 \times 1 + .99 \times 1} = .01.$$

This result clearly shows that the probability of $H$ (which the investigator has postulated after having obtained all the experimental data) has not risen at all as a result of all the data fitting it; with or without $F$, $H$'s probability is .01.[5]

This argument is instructive as it goes to the heart of the whole issue. First let us note that, provided their presuppositions are granted, the authors are so obviously right that the introduction of formal considerations was quite unnecessary; an appeal to plain common sense would have been sufficient. Suppose we are baffled by all the promises that hundreds of different political candidates are making and we are looking for some guidance who among them is to be believed and who is not. We interview candidate $A$ and ask him what he would do if elected. After listening to (and recording) his answer, we switch on our cassette player and hear a line from Shakespeare,

>    His heart as far from fraud as heaven from earth.

I do not believe that hearing this line loudly declaimed by the machine would convince anyone of the candidate's honesty. In fact it would be ruled to be totally irrelevant to that issue if for no other reason than that the recorder's utterance is entirely independent of the character of the politician, and it would assuredly emit precisely the same phonation in any context. Plain common sense dictates that no data can serve as confirming evidence for a given hypothesis if it is known to be not less likely to be forthcoming when the hypothesis is false than when it is true. Now Campbell and Vinci hold that (once $D$ is given) $F$ is guaranteed to be true not only when $T$ is true but also when it is false. Thus they are obviously right that $F$ cannot serve as evidence in support of $T$.

It is quite clear therefore that anyone who wishes to query the authors' conclusion that there is a radical difference between prediction and accommodation should question their contention that if $D$ guarantees the truth of $F$ regardless of whether $T$ is true or false, then $F$ is incapable of raising $T$'s credibility. The question

---

[5] Richmond Campbell and Thomas Vinci, "Why Are Novel Predictions Important?," *Pacific Philosophical Quarterly* (1982): 118.

we should raise—the question which lies at the core of the entire issue—is whether it is invariably the case that once we have gathered a collection of data we are bound to be able to formulate a hypothesis that smoothly accounts for the data. Admittedly it is always possible to come up with some hypothesis, and if scientific methods permit the introduction of just any hypothesis regardless of its form or shape as a legitimate candidate for accounting for the data, then the matter would indeed be settled along the lines suggested by these authors. If however there are additional conditions of adequacy other than the mere capacity to be satisfied by all the observational results then their argument is clearly irrelevant.

## 4. The Irrelevance of the Time At Which a Hypothesis Is Advanced

Now we come to the main point of this chapter, which is to show that in fact the time at which it is advanced makes absolutely no difference to the credibility of a hypothesis. Certain kinds of hypotheses are confirmed by a series of favorable experimental results, regardless of whether they are proposed before the series began, are in the middle of it, or are proposed only after the very last member of the series has become available; others are not confirmed no matter how early or how late they have been advanced.

As we shall see, what scientists do insist upon is having hypotheses with predictive power, that is, hypotheses with a favorable feature commending it to us for adoption already at the early part of the data-producing sequence, a characteristic feature which facilitates the prediction of the later parts of that sequence, regardless of whether this facility has in fact been made use of. The extent to which a given postulate is confirmed by the evidence at hand is a function of the precise contents of that postulate and the nature of that evidence, and definitely not of such fortuitous factors as the time at which someone happened to hit upon the idea of formulating that postulate, or the stage at which it has in practice been employed or for what purpose it has been employed. It is only its prior predictive power, or the capacity to have served as a means for prediction, that is relevant to determining the objective degree of credibility of a hypothesis; the actual use scientists happen to make of it indicates only the ingenuity and insight of the members of the scientific community.

Once we have obtained a description of the significant feature that marks adoptable hypotheses it will become evident why to so many philosophers, basing their judgment on what actually goes on in science, it seemed so natural that the chronology of theory and evidence was of crucial importance. We shall see that hypotheses lacking the required hallmark are very unlikely to suggest themselves to the investigator prior to his obtaining all the data he wishes to account for. Thus, as a matter of practice, such hypotheses have usually been employed merely to accommodate existing data. On the other hand, an alert scientist is likely to spot the hypothesis manifesting the required characteristic before completing the data-gathering process, adopt it, and as a rule make use of it in predicting further experimental results.

## 5. The Importance of Being Fit To Serve As an Instrument for Prediction

—oddHdTHE IMPORTANCE OF BEING FIT

In Chapter 5 I introduced equation $(\alpha)$ as representing a genuine law governing the co-variation of $x$ and $y$. Now I will develop my thesis with a specific example, namely, Galileo's law of free fall near the earth's surface, $(G)$. As we know, it states that the correlation between $s$, the distance covered by the body, and $t$, the time required to cover that distance, is given by $s = 1/2gt^2$. Imagine, for example, that all we were told was that the expression $(G)$ was found by a fair number of competent experimenters to hold when a hundred different values of $t$ were substituted in it, i.e., it was satisfied for $1/4, 1/2, \cdots 24\frac{1}{2}, 24\frac{3}{4}, 25$ seconds. We should find this information highly reassuring and believe in its consequence that Galileo's law was firmly established. None of us would find it essential to inquire: At what precise stage was $(G)$ formulated, i.e., how many of the results were predicted and how many were merely accommodated? It is safe to state that a scientist feels that there is no substantial difference between a situation in which $(G)$ is formulated right after the first half dozen observations, and thus the next ninety-four results are all correctly predicted on its basis, and one in which that equation was not formulated before all the hundred results became available.

I believe that in the context of the present example it is not too hard to see that the working scientist is justified in his attitude, and that there are no grounds for dismissing $(G)$ as being devoid of much significance, even if it has not occurred to anyone to advance it before all the results were available. After all, regardless of when $(G)$ was in fact thought of, there is something inherently unique about it: not only has it turned out to be the simplest expression to fit all the data, but it has also been the simplest that fitted the first five or six results. The great attraction of $(G)$ is not merely that it is a remarkably simple expression that accounts for the initial data, but that it remains the simplest accounting for the results obtained at many successive stages of our experimental investigations. The situation would be quite different if someone were, for instance, to measure at two minute intervals the number of words I have managed to put down on paper from the time I began writing and the time it has taken me to do so. It is most unlikely that the simplest mathematical expression to accommodate the first five results should also be able to accommodate the first ten results, or that the simplest to fit these would still fit the first fifteen results. Thus someone who had assumed this phenomenon to be law governed, and in compliance with the common methodological rule postulated the simplest suitable expression as the one to be adopted, would be forced to discard at every stage of the series of experiments the one he had subscribed to at the previous stage. On the other hand, in Galileo's case $(G)$ would have been the equation entitled to be trusted as truly representing the correlation between $s$ and $t$ at the very beginning, regardless of whether or not it had been actually thought of by anybody. It was therefore the expression which the early sets of results required us to adopt, at which time it was available as a means for the prediction of results yet to be obtained.

## 6. The Condition of Sustained Maximum Adequacy

The point I am trying to make may perhaps be more compellingly stated by utilizing the distinction drawn in the last chapter between an improbable phenomenon that calls no special attention to itself, and one that demands an explanation because it is an unusual, and thus a genuinely astonishing, type of phenomenon. Whether the construction of a hypothesis has easily been accomplished through the benefit of hindsight, or whether it required a great effort of foresight, as a rule has no bearing on its credibility. The relevant question is: Does the hypothesis meet a real need by showing that some seemingly extraordinary and thus surprising phenomenon is actually required by the laws of nature and the initial conditions? Thus, for example, Galileo's law of free fall strongly recommends itself to us, since without it we would be left in a baffling situation, where for every value of the distance traveled the corresponding value of the elapsed time fits a rare *sort* of expression, an expression which satisfies the vital condition which may be called the Condition of Sustained Maximum Adequacy, $C_{SMA}$, defined as follows:

> The hypothesis that is maximally adequate to account for the first few results, remains so in the context of increasingly larger sets of results.

On the other hand, the (very long) simplest expression that is satisfied by, say, a hundred results obtained by measuring the co-variation of the number of words I have written since the beginning of this year and the number of two-minute intervals that have passed since then, is most likely to be devoid of any indication that we are confronted with a phenomenon that cries out for an explanation. Though the expression is bound to be so rare as possibly never to have been seen in any context before, it should excite no genuine interest. It was after all inevitable that the results (regardless of how many, as long as they are of a finite number) were going to fit this or that expression.

In our first example involving Galileo's experiment, it does not matter how early or late his famous hypothesis was offered. In that experiment the data exhibit a unique pattern through conforming to the $C_{SMA}$, and thus demand, and will keep on demanding, an explanation until we declare Galileo's expression to be a law governing falling bodies. In our second example timing does not matter either: we have discovered nothing surprising, and thus no explanation is called for, and no grounds exist for accepting one if it were offered.

It should be quite obvious that the fact that we are in possession of all the results that need to be accounted for, and are free to tailor our hypothesis whichever way it suits these results, does not make it any more probable that the unique hypothesis which was the simplest at the beginning of our series of observations will remain so even in the context of the final situation. In other words, our being in a position in which we know exactly what theory is required by the relevant data gives us no advantage at all, since no amount of skillful manipulation will have an effect on $C_{SMA}$. The question of $C_{SMA}$'s truth is an entirely objective question, independent of the scientist's aims and his determination or skill in pursuing them. For this reason the credibility of $(G)$ is not in the least related to the time at which it happened to be advanced.

The upshot of all this is that what is essential in a hypothesis is its capacity to serve as the best account of the data available at different stages of our experimental investigations. The greater the number of such stages the higher the amount of confirmation conferred upon that hypothesis. Hypotheses which, though they are the best among those satisfied by all the data at hand, but were not so at any earlier stage, will of course always present themselves, but will have nothing to recommend themselves.

I should mention that Michael Gardner in a recent paper points out that the demand for novel evidence—evidence unknown at the time of a theory's construction and thus predicted rather than retrospectively explained or accommodated—belongs to "a lengthy tradition—not to say consensus—in the philosophy of science." He is quite right, there exists near unanimity concerning that demand. It is, however, not rationally warranted. All that we are entitled to expect from an acceptable hypothesis is that it should, prior to the data we now have, possess the appropriate feature which would have made it a suitable vehicle for predicting them.

### 7. An Illustration from Mathematical Sequences

The importance of the notion of Sustained Maximum Adequacy is likely to impress itself on our minds upon seeing the wide diversity of its application. The following is a brief example of its use in the construction of mathematical series. The noted physicist Heinz Pagels says, "Mathematicians have never succeeded in giving a precise definition of randomness." Most philosophers (e.g., N. Rescher,[6] H. Kyburg[7] )have adopted the view that there is simply no such thing as an absolutely random collection, for the concept of randomness is knowledge-dependent; all sequences are ordered relative to some rule and may be treated as random only with respect to place selection that makes no use of that rule.

Pagels, who also holds that absolute randomness is beyond definition, believes the explanation of it lies in the unique nature of randomness. He says:

> if you succeed in giving an exact definition [of a random sequence] the sequence may no longer be random. Being able to say precisely what randomness is denies the very nature of randomness, which is utter chaos—how can you be precise about chaos?[8]

I am not sure that Pagels meant this argument to be taken as much more than a rhetorical flourish. After all, a definition need not have

---

[6] N. Rescher, *Probability Statistics and Truth* (London, 1957), pp. 39–57.

[7] H. E. Kyburg, *Probability & Inductive Logic* (London, 1970), p. 79.

[8] H. R. Pagels, *The Cosmic Code* (New York, 1984), p. 85.

the characteristics of the definiens; the definition of 'circular' need not be circular, of 'inadequate' need not be inadequate, nor needs the definition of 'surprising' be surprising. Also, since apparently Pagels sees no reason why a full definition of an *ordered* sequence should be impossible, we are left with no explanation why a random sequence could not simply be defined as one that lacked an ordered series' characteristics.

One of the leading philosophers of probability, P. Suppes, recently advocated a more moderate position. Suppes favors the view that there is no sharp distinction between disorganized and deterministic phenomena, or between random and orderly sequences. Consequently, the best we can do, in his opinion, is to settle for a criterion with the aid of which we may be able to compare any two sequences and determine their relative randomness through comparing the degrees of their formation rules' complexity. Suppes says,

> I think it is satisfactory to think of randomness in terms of high complexity and to take the position that there is no absolute dichotomy between determinism and randomness. It is philosophically too artificial to have a totally sharp dichotomy.[9]

We shall not question the assumption that relative degrees of complexity of different rules can be determined. Still, Suppes's thesis is untenable since it claims that of any two sequences the one generated by the more complex rule exemplifies the higher degree of randomness. The fact is that there are any number of sequence pairs where the one which is generated by a very complex rule will be thought of as exhibiting a high degree if regularity, while the other, generated by a relatively simple rule, will be deemed an irregular succession of digits.

Consider a sequence 1, 4, 9, 22, for which one may devise a formation rule (R), namely, $a_n - n^3 = 5n^2 + 11n - 6$. Yet we would intuitively reject the idea that the sequence is a regularity-obeying, organized sequence, if for no other reason than because it is harder to remember the rule than the sequence it yields.

Consider now a sequence consisting of 4,000 rather than 4 digits. Suppose the entire sequence can be generated by a rule somewhat more complex than R, involving a polynomial to the fourth, instead of merely to the third degree. Unquestionably, we should regard this vast sequence as tightly ordered. Thus, though R was markedly simpler than the rule governing the second sequence, nevertheless

---

[9] P. Suppes, *Probabilistic Metaphysics* (Oxford, 1984), p. 32.

the comparative randomness of the first sequence is far greater than that of the second. This tends to show that the relative complexities of the organizing principle underlying the sequences as such, is not what determines their comparative degrees of randomness.

Yet, I do believe Suppes is right that randomness and orderliness come in degrees, but the answer to the question, to what extent is a given sequence orderly, is to be settled quite differently from what he had suggested. Essentially, the explication of the notion of randomness (and the absence of it) is also based on the Condition of Sustained Maximum Adequacy, the condition through which it acquires pattern repetition. A sequence is genuinely law governed to a degree that is determined by how much repetition of a given pattern it contains. Let us start with the following definition:

> The sequence $a_1, a_2, \cdots a_{n-1}. a_n$ is *perfectly* ordered iff the simplest formation rule needed to generate it, is also the simplest to generate the subsequence $a_1. a_2. \cdots a_{n-1}$ as well as the subsequence $a_1, a_2, \cdots a_{n-2}$ and so on, all the way down to $a_1$.

Thus, for example, the series: 1, 2, 3, 4, 5, 6, 7, 8, 9, is perfectly non-random. It should be hard to imagine that a simpler rule than $a_n = n$, is available to generate this sequence. At the same time, the same rule is also the simplest to generate the eight consecutive subsequences, including the shortest, 1. We thus may say that in this case the same pattern is repeated throughout the entire sequence, namely, that the simplest rule to generate the successive subsequences is always, $a_n = n$. Now consider the sequence,

$$S_7 : 1, 4, 9, 22, 49, 96, 169.$$

Each term of this sequence may be generated by the rule (R):

$$a_n = n^3 - 5n^2 + 11n - 6$$

R seems to be simplest needed to generate $S_7$. It is also the simplest to generate the subsequence, $S_6 : 1, \cdots, 49, 96$, and this in itself would make $S_7$ to *some* extent ordered. The fact that R is also the simplest in the context of : $1, \cdots 22, 49$, and perhaps even in the context of $S_4 : 1, \cdots 9, 22$, lends $S_7$ a considerably high measure of orderliness. $S_7$ is however not maximally ordered, since to form $S_3$, a rule much simpler than R is available, namely, $a_n = n^2$. However, even $S_3$ is not perfectly ordered since its subsequence S may be generated by the simpler rule, $a_n = n$.

$S_7$ being ordered (to a considerable degree) enables us after observing the first four of its terms, to predict its later terms through inductive reasoning and the use of $C_{SMA}$.

In view of the foregoing, it is natural to suggest that the measure of a sequence's orderliness (or the measure of its lack of randomness) is essentially bound up with the degree of the predictability of new terms, which in turn is a function of the amount of inductive grounds existing upon which prediction may be based. This is to say, that if R is the simplest rule whereby, for instance, sequence $S_n, S_{n-1}$, as well as $S_{n-2}$ may be generated, then $S_n$ may be said to be a genuine, regularity exhibiting sequence; it displays a pattern consisting of a recurrent feature. Further terms may be then predicted on the assumption that the same feature (of having R as the simplest generating rule), which is already repeatedly present in a small part of the series before us, will continue to be exemplified by the expanded sequence.

Clearly, if the simplest rule, R, by which $S_n$ is formed is also the maximally adequate rule with respect to subsequences that go further back than $S_{n-2}$, then we have before us a stronger inductive basis upon which to anticipate new terms, and thus the sequence may be said to enjoy greater measure of orderliness.

### 8. Legitimate Hypotheses Are Likely To Be Proposed at an Early Stage

Now it should be apparent that the "lengthy tradition" Gardner refers to, according to which hypotheses that have been successful in making correct predictions are preferable to those which merely manage to retrodict known results, is by no means unfounded. In fact it has a considerable degree of verisimilitude. Admittedly, the phrases "$h$ has actually been used to predict a good number of the results we have obtained" and "$h$ has the features that qualify it to be an instrument for prediction" have substantially different meanings. Nevertheless, they have nearly the same extension: if we restrict our universe of discourse to those hypotheses we regard as actually confirmed, then the two sets determined by these phrases are almost identical. After all, it is exceedingly improbable that when $h$ is not the hypothesis called for by the collection of our results until we have obtained the very last of them that $h$ will be picked by anyone, at an earlier stage, out of the infinitely many other possible hypotheses. Unless $h$ stands out among its alternatives by virtue of its repeated maximum adequacy in accounting for the growing set of data, it is almost certain to be passed over and not advanced before the last result is obtained. This means that it is virtually certain that a hypothesis that fails to comply with the $C_{SMA}$ will actually be employed only to accommodate and not to predict. Should however someone be able to produce it as a means for prediction, we should find this very surprising. The source of surprise would be the seeming wizardry involved in such an achievement, namely predicting such a large set of data not exhibiting any discernible pattern. On the other hand, it is quite probable that a generalization such as $(G)$, which so conspicuously satisfies the $C_{SMA}$ should occur to someone before all the feasible values of $s$ have been tested. Thus it may be employed as a means of prediction.

## 9. Attempts To Meet the History of Science Halfway

The many philosophers who hold that credibility is not determined just by the nature of a hypothesis and of the supporting evidence but that it also depends on the time of their production are not entirely unaware of the discordance between their position and the actual practices of scientists. A widely discussed example involves the confirmation of Newton's theory of gravity by the already well-known results of Galileo's experiments. Other cited examples include: the outcome of the experiments of Michelson and Morley published in 1887 that were nevertheless thought to confirm the theory of special relativity constructed in 1905, and the procession of Mercury's perihelion, known long before the advent of general relativity, and yet regarded as confirming evidence for that theory.

In view of these seeming counterexamples, it is generally assumed that the notion of 'novelty' required for the purpose of confirmation has to be defined in some special manner; however, it has by no means been obvious in what manner. Imre Lakatos, for example, at one stage held that the correct definition of 'novel' in our context is "improbable or even impossible in the light of previous knowledge."[10] However, E. Zahar has argued that a considerably more liberalized criterion is required, and first suggested the weaker definition "previously unknown to the scientific world," only to conclude that even this rules out much evidence that scientists

---

[10] Imre Lakatos "Falsification and the Methodology of Scientific Research Programmes" in *Criticism and the Growth of Knowledge*, ed. I. Lakatos and A. Musgrave (Cambridge, 1970), p. 118.

would in practice regard as legitimate. Subsequently he proposed that data are to qualify as novel with respect to a given hypothesis "if [they] did not belong to the problem situation which governed the construction of the hypothesis," that is, it was not "specifically designed to deal with"[11] that data.

A few years later Gardner argued that Zahar failed to realize that he had advanced not one but two independent definitions; the first involved problem-novelty, while the other (more permissive definition) involved use-novelty. A phenomenon may, for example, be part of the "problem situation," i.e., the class of problems a given theory was designed to solve, without ever having been referred to in the course of the theory construction. In any case, Gardner has claimed that both criteria are too restrictive. His own suggestion was, he thought, "perhaps the simplest and most obvious criterion of novelty with respect to a given theory: [that it be] not known to the person who constructed the theory at the time he did so," thus permitting it to be known by everybody else.

I shall not describe any additional positions people have adopted in their attempts to avoid standing in brazen opposition to the lessons of history. By now it should be fairly obvious to the dispassionate reader that there is no halfway retreat and the only correct position is to recognize that novelty *per se* does not in any of its suggested senses add any weight to the evidence. And it should seem just as obvious even to someone who does not wish to embrace any of the positive theses I have advanced in connection with this topic.

Here is a simple thought experiment one might ponder. Suppose that stunning historical evidence comes to light that establishes to everyone's satisfaction that before constructing any part of his theory, Newton was fully aware of all the evidence nowadays normally regarded as confirming those laws. In other words, not only did he know Galileo's laws and Kepler's laws but even the results of Cavendish's experiment and the precise orbit of Neptune. Would any of these philosophers seriously suggest that this would be the end of the science of mechanics, all of which would now be regarded as based on illegitimate evidence and hence completely unconfirmed?

Plainly, the circumstances of scientific discovery are of no interest when determining its trustworthiness. Instead of considering

---

[11] E. Zahar, "Why Did Einstein's Programme Supersede Lorentz's?" *British Journal for Philosophy of Science* (1973): 98–123.

any counterfactuals about what might have happened in the course of the history of science let me cite the everyday experiences of editors of scientific journals who are constantly called upon to evaluate the merit of pieces of scientific work. Suppose an editor receives a paper in which the author claims to have performed a great number of experiments, obtaining a hundred or so different values for a given physical magnitude and the corresponding values for another magnitude—something hitherto not regarded profitable to do—and shows that all of them may be accounted for by a startlingly simple mathematical expression. Now the editor, before coming to a decision, will sometimes want to check the veracity of the results by repeating some of the experiments mentioned in the paper, or to check the mathematics, or try to find out whether these results are really new, but surely it will never occur to him to query the author by saying: "This is all very good, but can you assure me that you did not construct your hypothesis after you had already known all these results?" The time at which a hypothesis was advanced has no relevance to its credibility.

Let us, however, allow the skeptic to speak his mind once more. "When all the facts are in"—he might say—"it is a trivial matter, requiring hardly any great skill or experience, to concoct a hypothesis which adequately accounts for them. If this were really permitted, then the common view that doing science requires brilliant skill would have to be revised. But more seriously, scientific conjectures would no longer be required to pass the crucial test of making successful predictions; we would then have given up our most important means for validating hypotheses." A brief answer should suffice. A set of data does not lend credibility to any lawlike statement merely by virtue of their compliance with that statement. A hypothesis is confirmed only if it is an account of a set of observations which demand an explanation. The ingenuity required in this context is the ability to recognize the legitimacy of that demand. To accomplish this, the skillful scientist will have to detect the recurring pattern manifested by the accumulated data which renders them unique. And, of course, the universal test for the validation of our theories has not been waived; we insist that the set of our experimental results have proper subsets exhibiting the characteristic features of what is appropriately accounted for by a theory. Such a theory could thus fittingly serve as a valid means of predicting the elements of the remainder of the set.

An important point, which by now will be pretty obvious, is the following. A hypothesis which satisfies the condition that it have its maximum adequacy sustained throughout a substantial part of the process of data accumulation is necessarily also a hypothesis that accounts for a set of results which constitutes a special kind of set and hence genuinely requires an explanation.

All this need not be taken to imply the futility of the numerous papers dealing with the question whether Einstein was aware of the result of the Michelson–Morley experiment, and if so, did he specifically have it in mind when constructing his theory. True, from the point of view of determining the amount of confirmation conferred upon his theory by that result, what Einstein knew, when he knew what he knew, and what he wished to accomplish through his theory, are of no consequence whatever. However, these questions are of interest when assessing the magnitude of his achievement; the less relevant data he was aware of, the greater his genius in sensing what theory was a likely candidate to represent the truth.

### 10. What Exactly Is an Ad Hoc Hypothesis?

What has been said concerning the notion of accommodation is also relevant to the notion of ad hocness. The term 'ad hoc' has as a rule been applied to a hypothesis regarded as inferior because it was formulated specifically to accommodate data already available, and therefore has not actually stood the test of experience that could confer confirmation on it. The accounts of ad hocness offered by different philosophers differ somewhat in detail, but in outline they more or less agree on a definition offered by E. Zahar:

> A theory is ad hoc if none of its novel predictions have been verified.[12]

In the light of our previous discussion it should be sufficiently clear that a theory (or a hypothesis) may be advanced at a given time, and subsequently not a single test is performed to verify any one of the indefinitely many predictions that can be worked out on its basis (for values of the parameters involved that have not yet experimentally been reproduced), and nevertheless that hypothesis may be regarded as well confirmed by all of the existing data it has managed to accommodate.

It is apparent that the fundamental point that Zahar's definition overlooks is that it is of no real importance what any scientist has

---

[12] Ibid.

done, or failed to do, with a given hypothesis; it does not affect the status of a hypothesis that in practice no one has happened to employ it to predict future results. These are extrinsic matters that in no way indicate the true nature of a hypothesis; what matters is the potential capacity of a hypothesis to be confirmed. If it has the suitable form, and thus the inherent capacity, to serve as a means for predicting results we have already obtained but neglected to predict, that is sufficient to confer upon it the required amount of confirmation.

C. G. Hempel's often cited account of ad hoc hypotheses is also imprecise. One of the historical examples he uses to present his views is the phenomenon of a liquid's rise in a tube emptied of air. Before Torricelli introduced his thesis that this is due to the pressure of the air that is not counteracted by any pressure inside the tube, the phenomenon was explained as a result of nature's abhorrence of a vacuum. Torricelli's hypothesis entailed that the height of a mercury column should be less on top of a mountain than at its base, since the amount of air pressure decreases with an increase in altitude. The old hypothesis of course has no such consequences, since there does not seem to be any reason why nature should abhor a vacuum more at the foot of a mountain than at its summit. Consequently, when it was observed that the height of the mercury column does indeed decrease with an increase in altitude, it was taken as a decisive confirmation of Torricelli's hypothesis.

Now Hempel points out that surely the old hypothesis could have been easily saved by introducing the auxiliary hypothesis that nature's abhorrence of a vacuum does happen to decrease with increasing altitude. This auxiliary hypothesis is by no means logically absurd, nor could anyone have claimed at the time to have empirical evidence that it is false. Yet it was regarded as objectionable, as it would have been a typical ad hoc hypothesis. Hempel explains that the reason is because it would have been produced,

> for the sole purpose of saving a hypothesis seriously threatened by adverse evidence; it would not be called for by other findings and roughly speaking, it leads to no additional test implications.[13]

Once more we should point out that it does not matter what the purpose, reason, or intention was of those who would propose the

---

[13] Hempel, *Philosophy of Natural Science* (Englewood Cliffs, N.J., 1966), p. 29.

hypothesis about nature's abhorrence of a vacuum varying with altitude. The status of a hypothesis does not depend on why, how, or when it is advanced. Furthermore, if matters had turned out differently, and the decrease of the height of a mercury column in a vacuum tube had not been anticipated on the basis of Torricelli's hypothesis, and in fact that hypothesis had been advanced only after this phenomenon became known, it would have made no difference.

The significant difference between the two hypotheses is this: Torricelli addresses himself to a unique aspect of the set of results associated with the behavior of the mercury column, by virtue of which it appears to be a rare *kind* of set consisting of elements that exemplify a common feature. The observations for which he is offering an account are the values of the height of the column, which vary according to a single fixed pattern. It is truly astonishing that the changes in the height of the mercury column should always take place in conformity with the rate of change in the magnitude of the air pressure surrounding the open portion of the liquid. Torricelli's hypothesis has the vital characteristic of an adequate scientific hypothesis: it explains that it is not an accident (and thus not puzzling) that a simple correlation exists between air pressure and the height of the mercury in the vacuum tube; it is nomically necessary for it to be so, as it is the air pressure which counteracts the fall of the mercury.

It is different with the postulate held by the conservatives who clung to Aristotle's opinion that nature abhors a vacuum. That postulate was in fact entitled to a hearing before the discovery of the variation of the mercury level's height with changes in altitude above sea level: vacuous regions are not easily found in nature, and their existence would (according to Aristotelian mechanics) imply the possibility of the infinite magnitude of entirely unimpeded motion, which seemed absurd—thus positing the natural tendency to fill all empty places had prima facie plausibility. But with the extra proviso (concerning nature's varying distaste for vacuums) this hypothesis does not qualify as one that has been called for by anything surprising, in the required sense. For if there is a variation in the height of the mercury column, then it could take place in indefinitely many ways: it could rise or fall with altitude and have any one of myriads of different functional relations to the latter, it could vary with latitude rather than with altitude, with its position relative to the moon, with the number of mesons in the surrounding air, and so on. In each of these cases we would be confronted with a specific variation of infinitesimally small prior probability. The situation recalls those we dealt with in the previous chapter where we were presented with incredibly improbable specific sequences of events, but where it was inevitable that some incredibly improbable sequence or other was going to take place.

It should be clear that if the precise variations in the height of the mercury column had happened to be fully predicted by Aristotelians that would have been astounding. It would have prompted us to seek an explanation for how they managed to accomplish such a feat. But it would have left it nevertheless just as flawed an explanation as it was in the light of the actual turn of events. Toricelli's hypothesis is inherently superior to it, regardless of how late his hypothesis might have been put forward.

Thus the evidential support provided by the data for a given hypothesis is not in any way weakened by the fortuitous fact that it occurred to no one before the very last result was obtained, as long as it is adequate (e.g., not needlessly encumbered) not only in the context of all the data we end up with, but also in the context of the smaller set of data at some earlier stage of our series of experimentations. When this condition is fulfilled, that hypothesis is available at that stage to be postulated by anyone adhering to the principles of scientific method who would have given the matter sufficient amount of thought. If, for whatever reason, we have not come round to formulating it earlier, that does not mean that the hypothesis did not exist as a potential, legitimate means for predicting some of the results we neglected to predict. It is the capacity of hypotheses to serve as readily available tools for prediction—regardless of whether or not that capacity is capitalized on—which confers upon them the susceptibility to confirmation by the data satisfying them.

Clearly the refusal to admit an ad hoc hypothesis is not to be interpreted as some sort of penalty, imposed upon the scientists advancing it, for their failure to display greater alertness or resourcefulness. Such a hypothesis is inadmissible because it is intrinsically inferior to those we normally regard as having received evidential support. But if we were to reject a hypothesis simply because no more has been done with it than to employ it to accommodate existing data, then surely we would reject it on account of some shortcoming—such as slow-wittedness—displayed by the relevant scientist. In truth, however, we disqualify ad hoc hypotheses because we judge them to be inherently flawed; because they lack the potential for facilitating the prediction of any of the results we have obtained, and since they could not have legitimately been advanced as a candidate for an acceptable account of previous data.

## 11. Right Hypotheses Based on Wrong Assumptions

Throughout this chapter the emphasis has been on the physical sciences. In the behavioral sciences we seem often to permit hypotheses which not only lack sustained maximum adequacy but lack adequacy altogether. Indeed, in many cases we just do not have any criterion—formal or intuitive—to determine which hypothesis is to be regarded as the simplest relative to the data. Suppose, for instance, that the unpopular Governor written off by all the political experts is re-elected to office. Which newspaper's account for the unexpected result most tightly fits the data: (i) "Since the other candidate was an obscure newcomer, the electorate must have reasoned 'better the devil you know than the devil you do not know'" or (ii) "Most people became convinced that the Governor, who is basically a sincere person, has at last seen the errors of his former policies which he is not going to repeat"? The answer in this case, of course, is that nobody would claim to have a solid criterion by which to determine the relative simplicity of the competing hypotheses, and thus unless further investigation into the facts of the matter is made the issue will remain undecided.

Let us look at a different, fairly common kind (though somewhat simplified) of example. At the time of Hitler's fateful attack on Russia in June 1941, quite a number of respected commentators predicted the imminent collapse of the Red Army. When these forecasts proved wrong there was hardly an expert who was not able to offer a convincing explanation for why the final outcome was inevitable. The USSR covered such a vast area, the winter cold was so harsh, Stalin had so much greater manpower at his disposal and could draw on America's almost inexhaustible resources. Only an insane megalomaniac could have expected to win against such odds.

Why then had so many respected experts made the wrong prediction at the beginning of the conflict? As Paul Johnson explains in his highly acclaimed *A History of the Modern World*, one of the major factors that was assumed by such experts to bring about the speedy undoing of the Soviet Union was the expectation that millions of its subjugated people would see the occasion of Hitler's assault as a long-awaited opportunity to seize their own freedom, and destroy the regime which had brought such an immense amount of misery.

It stood to reason that the Nazis would be smart enough to exploit these sentiments and come as liberators, helping the oppressed masses rise up against their tormentors. However, Hitler committed the unforeseeably foolish mistake of showing clearly from the very beginning that he was not in the business of liberation but in the business of the worst form of slavery. Only a short few weeks after the invasion,

> the Russian nation as a whole began to grasp the horrifying fact that they faced what appeared to be a war of extermination.

> The result was the salvation of Stalin and his regime. By the time Stalin finally brought himself to speak to the Russian people on 3 July, it was clear that he could turn the struggle into the Great Patriotic War.[14]

Let us assume that those commentators who initially regarded the evidence warranting their prediction of the Russian army's doom now embrace Johnson's explanation why it was bound to be victorious. Are they entitled to do so? Is theirs not a paradigmatic ad hoc hypothesis, not simply because the errant pundits happened to offer it at the wrong time, but because by their own testimony rationality did not require the postulation of Johnson's thesis at the beginning of the war? Or else, if it is not, does this not imply that sustained maximum adequacy is not required even when the set of relevant facts increases with time, and that one may keep adjusting one's hypothesis to suit the changing evidence?

I believe that this example, which typifies the situation where there is an explanation that was hard to anticipate before the event and which heavily relies on the benefit of hindsight but is nevertheless acceptable, raises no objection to the approach we have developed. Here we are plainly confronted with basically different circumstances from those obtaining in an inquiry such as the one aimed at discovering the regularity displayed by the free fall of a physical object. It is an essential characteristic of a law-governed sequence (e.g., a sequence formed by the values of the duration of the fall and the distance fallen) that its early part provides enough clues to enable the scientist to anticipate its later parts. Thus, in the context of a series of events where the repetition of a regularity has not been discerned, there is no warrant for regarding as a genuine law of nature the hypothesis through which we are capable of accounting for the data which now have been obtained. In

---

[14] Paul Johnson, *A History of the Modern World* (London, 1983), p. 382.

the case discussed by Johnson, on the other hand, the commentators were not trying to discover a law of nature. They took certain commonsense generalizations for granted and were attempting to predict a future event on the basis of the relevant initial conditions, of which they thought they had sufficient information. It turned out, however, that they were mistaken: they took it for granted that Hitler was a cool calculator who would rationally weigh the factors he needed for assuring victory. If we accept Johnson's thesis, the pessimistic commentators made their gloomy forecasts on ascribing a less deviant psychopathic personality to Hitler than the facts warranted. Their hypothesis was as a matter of fact the best suited one to the set of assumptions they were working with. Only later events revealed the depth of Hitler's irrationality, in the context of which the explanation involving the alienation of the conquered people and the vastly superior resources of the allies became highly adequate.

In other words, the disputants had not necessarily subscribed at the start of the invasion to different laws of sociology, economics, military science, and the like that were relevant to the issue. It was a prediction that they simply disagreed with because they assumed different initial conditions to prevail. The explanation of those pundits who changed their views concerning the final outcome of the war and adopted Johnson's thesis may well be compared to the explanation that might be offered when, for instance, Galileo's law of free fall has already been universally accepted, we observe the descent of a ball from the top of a tall building and find that it lands much sooner than we calculated it would. Later we discover that the ball was not merely released at the beginning of its fall but was hit with a racket and given a considerable impetus. Given this information we postulate that the ball had a specific initial velocity, and combining this assumption with Galileo's law we show that it landed precisely at the moment these considerations would have led us to expect it to land. It do not believe that this account would be rejected as ad hoc, even though Condition $C_{SMA}$ has not been satisfied, since we are not postulating here a law of nature, but merely revising our description of the initial conditions.

We raise no objections to the ex post facto explanation of the final outcome of World War II offered by those who initially held hypotheses implying a contrary outcome as best fitting the data, because what prevented them from making the right predictions was—as is typically the case in the context of large scale social phenomena—not their unfamiliarity with a relevant universal hypothesis, but their ignorance of some particular fact, in this case one concerning the psychopathological makeup of a given individual who was to play a crucial role in shaping the course of events. The greatest obstacle to making correct military, political, or economic predictions is the vast amount of relevant initial conditions, which no one is able to ascertain. The experts in the field are forced to foretell the future on a basis they are forced to assume to be true. Even if they turn out to be wrong, as so often they do, relative to the assumed initial conditions their hypotheses may have had maximum adequacy.

# VII

# COMBINED EVIDENCE

## 1. Hypotheses That Do Not Imply Their Evidence

So far we have been dealing with hypotheses while taking it for granted that when a certain kind of evidence provides them with support then two or more instances of the same kind provide them increased support. It may quickly be shown why this was so. As will be remembered, in the first two chapters we dealt only with cases where the evidence ($e_1$ or $e_2$) was logically implied by the hypothesis ($h$), and consequently both $P(e_1/h) = P(e_2/h) = P(e_1 \& e_2/h) = 1$. To say that $e_1$ confirms $h$ means that $P(h/e_1) > P(h)$, which from Bayes's theorem can be seen to be equivalent to saying that $1 > P(e_1)$. Also, the degree to which $e_1$ confirms $h$ may be said to depend on how much the probability of $h$ increases by virtue of $e_1$ from what it was when $e_1$ was not given. In other words, the degree of confirmation may be said to equal the ratio $1/P(e_1)$. But then, by the same reasoning the degree to which $e_1 \& e_2$ confirms $h$ is given by the ratio $1/P(e_1 \& e_2)$. Clearly, as long as $P(e_2/e_1) < 1$, i.e., as long as $e_1$ does not logically imply $e_2$, $P(e_1) > P(e_2/e_1)$. That is, as long as $1/P(e_1) < (1/P(e_1 \& e_2)$, the degree of confirmation provided by the joint evidence of $e_1$ and $e_2$ is higher than that provided by either on its own.

It cases where $h$ does not logically imply the evidence but merely raises its probability, matters are more complicated. In such cases in order to be able to compare degrees of confirmation we have to take into account two further expressions, namely $P(e_1/h)$ and $P(e_1 \& e_2/h)$, as there are many instances where the combination of the confirming evidence reduces the credibility of a hypothesis.

The following is an example that demonstrates how conjoining evidence that supports a certain hypothesis may not only fail to increase its credibility but in fact decrease it.

$H =$     Fred is a perfectly honest card player and is a genius at quickly figuring out probabilities,

$W_1 =$ Fred wins the first poker game,

$W_n =$ Fred wins each game from the first to the $n$th game.

Let us assume that our background information strongly supports our belief in Fred's honesty. Then if we observe $W_1$, we may well treat it as supporting $H$, since an expertise in probabilities can be of considerable help in poker. But if $n$ is of considerable magnitude we shall not want to say that $P(H/W_n)$ is much greater than $P(H/W_1)$, since Fred's mastery of probability theory is unlikely to do more than increase the frequency of his winning. There is really only one way of ensuring a *constant* win, namely, by cheating. Thus given $W_n$ the credibility of $H$ is actually lowered, since now rather than postulating that Fred is a math wiz, we shall be more inclined to suspect that he is a cardsharp.

Another illustrative example involves a state prosecutor. Suppose we are told of several cases he had won. We would naturally think of these as instances supporting the hypothesis that he is a very accomplished attorney. Suppose, however, that we hear of a chain of several hundreds of his victories at court, without ever losing a single case. We know that even the best of prosecutors do not in general succeed in all their cases. So in the light of too many successes we begin to suspect that the stories we have heard refer to a lawyer in one of those totalitarian countries where attorneys play hardly any role, and all the accused are virtually automatically convicted. Thus while a few cases of rulings in his favor support the hypothesis that he is a very skillful advocate, too many such rulings support it less.

An interesting topic for study is the question of the relative power of different numbers of witnesses testifying in court. By common intuition, the words of two witnesses carry more weight than those of a single attestant. The source of the principle that gives more credence to corroborated than uncorroborated testimony is, however, by no means obvious. For suppose,

$S$ = The defendant did do whatever he is charged with,

$R_1 = A$ testifies that $S$,

$R_2 = B$ testifies that $S$.

Clearly neither $P(R_1/S)$ nor $P(R_2/S)$ equal 1, though each is of higher value than $P(R_1)$ and $P(R_2)$ respectively. Consequently, as explained earlier, from the assumption that a story is confirmed to a certain degree through being affirmed by witness $A$ alone or by $B$ alone, it is impossible to derive logically that their joint affirmation confirms it to a higher degree. In addition, we must also keep it in mind that it is not unreasonable to believe that what a given witness is likely to say depends not only on the facts of the matter but also on his awareness that there are (or are not) other witnesses. As we shall see, under certain circumstances it may be reasonable to ascribe a higher value to $P(R_2/R_1)$ than to $P(R_2)$, since the second witness may be afraid to give uncorroborated testimony and might not be able to summon up enough courage to make an accusation unless he is reassured of the support of another witness. Then again, under other circumstances, the contrary may be the case and there could be grounds for ascribing a lower value to $P(R_2/R_1)$ than to $P(R_2)$. There could be reasons why a person should be more likely to be willing to testify when knowing there are no other witnesses.

Jonathan Cohen has over the years done much important work on the problem of precisely formulating the premises that are sufficient and necessary for the rigorous demonstration that corroborated testimony increases the support for a conclusion, above what it would have had owing to either piece of evidence on its own. He has claimed on a number of occasions, most recently in *Mind*, October 1986, that six premises are required for accomplishing the task. Cohen represents the required conclusion (for the above case) as $P(S/R_2 \& R_1) > P(S/R_1)$. He has demonstrated that the conclusion follows logically from the following suppositions:

(1)   $P(S/R_1) > P(S)$,
(2)   $P(S/R_2) > P(S)$,
(3)   $P(R_1 \& R_2) > 0$,
(4)   $P(R_2/S) < P(R_2/R_1 \& S)$,
(5)   $P(R_2/{\sim}S) > P(R_2/R_1 \& {\sim}S)$, and
(6)   $1 > P(S/R_1)$.

There has been a great deal of discussion of these suppositions in the philosophical literature. It seems that neither Cohen nor those who have raised objections to his argument have realized that the above six independent premises are not required for the derivation of the desired conclusion. As we shall see, it is possible to replace Cohen's premises (3), (4), and (5) by a single premise, to be denoted $(\phi)$, as well as replace (1) and (2) by two weaker premises, and still arrive at that conclusion (see Section 5). Our new set of premises are weaker than Cohen's since they do not entail his (1)–(6), but are entailed by them.

## 2. The Case of the Timid Witness

We shall look first at premise (4) and begin by inquiring whether common sense requires it as indispensable for the thesis of the corroboration of testimonies.

It seems that there are a number of people to whom the very thought of appearing as witnesses in a court of law makes uncomfortable, and who would try to avoid it, if possible. Such individuals may well be more likely to come forward to testify about a crime they had observed when they believe that no one besides themselves was going to testify, than otherwise. Suppose, for example, that $B$ has observed a criminal act and is rather anxious that the perpetrator should not get away with it. At the same time $B$ happens to be a tongue-tied person who dreads the prospect of being subjected to public cross-examination by a skillful and hostile attorney. Still, his desire to see justice done may be strong enough to make him want to reconcile himself to the thought of going through the ordeal of being grilled and browbeaten by the defendant's lawyer. But when he is aware that there is going to be another witness $A$, $B$ may well say to himself: The accused is most likely to receive his just deserts through the testimony of $A$ alone; why then should I have to go through the painful process in which I would be called upon to defend my memory and integrity?

Another situation, in which $B$ may also be more willing to give testimony when unaccompanied by other witnesses, might arise in case he is a very avid publicity-seeking individual. Suppose $B$ is not so much concerned whether justice is or is not done but is very eager to have his name mentioned in the local newspaper. He reckons that there is a fair chance that if he testifies in court then after the trial the paper will send a reporter to interview him. Given, however, that there is a second witness, $B$ may conclude that his chances for receiving the desired publicity have been halved, and it is not worth his while to spend the time and effort involved in testifying. It should be clear that it would be possible to concoct any number of further circumstances in which $R_2$ is less probable when $R_1$ is given than when it is not.

Let me point out that it is not essential for our purposes to maintain that relevant empirical investigations would prove the correctness of the psychological postulates underlying the previous two examples, and that the considerations I have ascribed to the potential witnesses do actually play a role in the thinking of many individuals. Let us assume that in fact they never do. Still we should consider the following: imagine—and it is undeniably at least imaginable—there *is* adequate evidence that a considerable number of people are prepared to give testimony when they assume to be the sole witnesses, but for whatever reason they are reluctant to do so when aware that there are others to testify. The question we must ask ourselves is, would it then be the case that we would no longer ascribe greater credibility to corroborated than to uncorroborated testimony? The answer appears to be that if there are people who have a strong inclination to refrain from testifying when other witnesses are available, then if they nevertheless do testify, surely that should be interpreted as indicating the presence of considerable motivating factors. It is a reasonable conjecture that what jolts such individuals out of their reticence is the shock of having observed a criminal act which they then desire to see punished.

It seems, therefore, that the commonsense principle to place higher trust in the deposition of two attestants than in that of one seems not to depend on the validity of (4). In fact, the argument of the last paragraph indicates possible circumstances under which the violation of (4) strengthens the reason why we should regard two witnesses more believable than merely one. We thus see that Cohen's (4) is not merely expendable but positively constitutes an obstacle: in some cases where the violation of (4) enhances the credibility of the witnesses, premise (4) would enjoin us to disregard their testimony.

### 3. Diseases and Their Symptoms

Before introducing any formal arguments let us take a brief look at Cohen's discussion of the nature of medical evidence available to the physician, in his paper "Bayesianism versus Baconianism in Evaluation of Medical Diagnoses." All would agree that he is correct in treating the manifestations of diseases in a parallel fashion to the treatment of testimony submitted by witnesses at a trial, as long as those manifestations are not inevitably present in all instances of a given disease. The reason that the forensic situation essentially differs from those obtaining in typical scientific generalizations such as "All $F$'s are $G$'s" is that the latter has, at least in principle, individual falsifying instances: a single $F$ observed to be lacking $G$—unless explained away—refutes such a generalization. On the other hand, a witness who does not testify that $S$, or even explicitly denies that $S$, does not refute $S$. In this fundamental aspect cases of symptoms and signs of most diseases are similar: their absence does not amount to a solid proof for the absence of the disease. And all this, of course, follows from what we have said in section 1. The fact that here, unlike in classical physics, the hypothesis does not logically imply the evidence, entails that discovering the absence of evidence does not necessarily falsify the hypothesis.

Also, most would agree with Cohen's assertion that a physician should regard two symptoms or signs as more strongly suggestive of an illness than the presence of merely one. Cohen, however, argues that here, too, in order to be able to derive this conclusion it is necessary to postulate a premise parallel to (4). In other words, he insists that we cannot do without assuming that a characteristic symptom or sign of a given disease is not made less probable by the fact that the patient displays another symptom or sign. He says:

> given the *presence* of the disease, the existence of the symptom, sign or other evidential fact $E_2$ is not rendered *less* probable by the existence of $E_1$. After all, in a disease where two symptoms characteristically *exclude* one another, their co-occurrence can hardly *reinforce* the diagnosis of the disease in question.[1]

On the surface this argument looks quite reasonable until we realize that a distinction between two different circumstances has been overlooked. In one kind of situation there is nothing in the nature of $E_1$ to impede the occurrence of $E_2$ as well; but when disease $D$ discloses its presence through $E_1$ it will not to do so through $E_2$. In other words, while there is no incompatibility as such between $E_1$ and $E_2$, it is an essential characteristic of $D$ to produce either one or the other, but not both. In this case we have to agree with Cohen that the appearance of $E_2$ together with $E_1$ could not reinforce our belief in the patient's having $D$, since these two conditions never occur jointly as manifestations of that disease.

There is however another situation in which there exists an intrinsic incompatibility between $E_2$ and $E_1$, so that when one of these conditions is present it tends to prevent the occurrence of the other. In such a case, it stands to reason that the two symptoms or signs should reinforce the diagnosis—in fact to a higher degree than in normal cases. The presence of $E_1$ as such prevents the emergence of $E_2$. If, in spite of $E_1$, $E_2$ has appeared, that suggests

---

[1] L. Jonathan Cohen, "Bayesianism versus Baconianism in the Evaluation of Medical Diagnoses," *British Journal for the Philosophy of Science* (1980): 50.

strongly that the patient has disease $D$, which produced a more powerful opposite propensity overcoming the forces tending to fight off $E_2$.

A concrete example may be provided by behavior occasionally accompanying strong alcohol addiction. It is reported that some chronic drunks find alcohol deprivation so intolerable that, in the absence of anything better, they will drink methylated spirit (that is, alcohol made deliberately undrinkable). Denatured alcohol tastes awful and most people feel sick immediately after taking the first sip. Usually, therefore, even those with a very strong craving for alcohol will feel so nauseated that they will not want to ingest anymore. There are some individuals, however, for whom the need to alleviate their withdrawal pain conquers the aversion to methylated spirit and go on drinking until relieved. Thus let

$D$ = The patient is strongly addicted to alcohol,
$E_1$ = The patient gulps down jigger 1 of methylated
　　　 spirits,
$E_2$ = The patient gulps down jigger 2 of methylated
　　　 spirits.

It should seem highly reasonable that (4) does not hold, and that instead

$$P(E_2/D) > P(E_2/E_1 \,\&\, D)$$

holds, since although $D$ tends to generate in the patient a strong craving for alcohol it is likely to be curbed through the aversion caused by $E_1$. At the same time, if we observe a person swallowing a jigger of denatured alcohol, even though he had just felt the highly unpleasant taste of the first one, we should justifiably take it to be a sign of strong addiction (much stronger than if after having drunk one he had stopped). Clearly then, $P(D/E_2 \,\&\, E_1) > P(D/E_1)$, even though (4) is false.

Indeed it may be mentioned that there exists a limiting case where the repulsive force between the two symptoms is so great that under healthy conditions they never occur jointly. It is only $D$ that it is capable of overcoming that force and bring about the co-occurrence of $E_1$ and $E_2$. Under these circumstances $P(D/E_2 \,\&\, E_1)$ = 1, and observing the two symptoms exemplified simultaneously amounts to *conclusive* evidence for the presence of $D$.

### 4. The Case of the Witness Who Has
### a Grudge Against the Defendant

If all this is not sufficiently convincing, let me offer a conclusive formal proof that, in cases of indirect indicators such as the testimony of witnesses to a crime or the display of signs and symptoms by a patient, two pieces of evidence may raise the relevant probabilities to a higher degree than would either of them on its own, even when (4) is violated. In other words it is decidedly false that (4) is a necessary condition for corroborative evidence to provide stronger support than uncorroborated evidence.

The easiest way to do this is once more with the aid of our usual square-diagrams. In Figure 15 we see that three of the squares are $S$-squares and thus $P(S) = 1/2$. Two out of the three $R_1$-squares are also $S$-squares and thus $P(S/R_1) = 2/3$. For the same reason $P(S/R_2) = 2/3$. (Hence both $P(S/R_1)$ and $P(S/R_2)$ are greater than $P(S)$, which inciden-tally satisfies premises (1) and

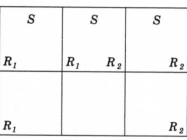

**Figure 15**

(2).) We also see that there are three $S$-squares out of which two are $R_2$, hence $P(R_2/S) = 2/3$, and there are two squares that are both $S$ and $R_1$ and only one of these is in addition an $R_2$-square, thus $P(R_2/R_1 \& S) = 1/2$. Thus Figure 15 represents a case where $P(R_2/S) > P(R_2/R_1 \& S)$, which violates premise (4). Nevertheless we see that the only square which is both $R_1$ and $R_2$ is also $S$, which means that $P(S/R_1 \& R_2) = 1$. In practice, of course, it is hard to imagine a situation in which two witnesses should have such a powerful effect as to remove all doubt concerning their truthfulness, but this is a definite counterexample to Cohen's claim, showing that the violation of (4) may not in principle prevent even the probability of $S$ rising from 2/3 to absolute certainty.

Now we move on to (5). Let us once more begin with an informal objection to the claim that it is an indispensable premise. Consider $B$, who bears such a grudge against the accused that he would feel no compunction in bringing about his conviction on trumped up charges. At the same time, $B$ is aware of the severe penalty for per-jury. Consequently, if he has to face the court on his own, $B$ will not dare to bear false testimony; he would fear failure resulting either from the jury's not accepting his word against that of the accused, or worse, he may be found out and punished for his fraudulence. However, if he was aware of the likelihood of being supported by a second witness, $B$ may feel confident enough that in collusion with him it would be possible to secure his enemy's conviction for at least two reasons. First, $B$ is more likely to feel assured of the success of his scheme, for even if the accused happens to be a model citizen, given two witnesses the jury will tend to place confidence in their story in spite of the defendant's protestations of innocence. Secondly, $B$ is justified in feeling more confident that the perjury will remain undetected. There may exist potential witnesses who have good reasons to suspect that the accusations are mere fabrications, but these people should be more hesitant to come forward and make charges against two witnesses than against one.

It is also possible to think of cases where, though the testimony is false, the witness is not consciously lying, and where again the contrary of Cohen's (5) holds, i.e., $P(R_2/R_1 \& \sim S) > P(R_2/\sim S)$; in other words, a case where the witness is more inclined to assert what he mistakenly believes to have observed when he knows his statement will be corroborated, than otherwise. This is likely to be so when an alleged observation concerns phenomena commonly regarded to be too fantastic to be credible, e.g., the sighting of extraterrestrial creatures. There have been many people who have come to believe quite sincerely that they have observed vehicles from outer space, and had a strong urge to tell others of their experiences but were afraid of being disbelieved, and even ridiculed. However, when joined by others claiming to have had similar experiences, they were prepared to come forward, fearing being distrusted less. In spite of this it is clear that regardless of how bizarre their testimony is, given a large number of witnesses assuring us of its veracity our reluctance to credit it tends to lessen. It seems clear enough that no matter how absurd a story may sound, given a sufficient number of different witnesses we shall eventually be prepared to believe it. Thus even though (5) may be false, in certain contexts the conclusion $P(S/R_1 \& R_2) > P(S/R_1)$ is nevertheless true. Thus this is another example showing that, contrary to Cohen, (5) is not a necessary condition for his conclusion.

Once more it is not important to know how many—if any—people are motivated by the psychological factors just described. What is relevant is the answer to the question: What would our attitude be if (conceivably if never actually) more than 50% of those who are unscrupulous enough to deliver false testimony against an innocent person were willing to do so only when assured of support, but not when they would have to face the court by themselves? It should be obvious that as long as more people were actually guilty in instances of corroborated testimonies than in uncorroborated ones, we should give greater credence to two witnesses than to one. The same can be said of stories that seem intrinsically unbelievable. It should not matter that in case the witness is a victim of self-delusion his confidence may be boosted by the presence of another witness; it may still well be possible that a second witness should be less likely to be available unless the event in question actually took place, and therefore $P(S/R_1 \& R_2/S) > P(S/R_1)$.

As before with premise (4), there exist concrete examples that decisively demonstrate that (5) is not a necessary premise for the derivation of the result we are after; the probability of $S$ may increase with the number of witnesses even when (5) is false. In Figure 16 there are four squares that are not-$S$-squares and two of these are also $R_2$-squares. Thus $P(R_2/\sim S) = 1/2$. There are two squares that are both non-$S$ and $R_1$ and only one of these is also an $R_2$-square. Thus $P(R_2/R_1 \& \sim S) = 1/2$. So the inequality stipulated by (5) does not hold here. At the same time, there are five $R_1$-squares of which three are $S$-squares, thus $P(S/R_1) = 3/5$, while of the three squares that are both $R_1$ and $R_2$ two are $S$ and therefore $P(S/R_1 \& R_2) = 2/3 > P(S/R_2)$. Thus the desired inequality holds without satisfying condition (5)!

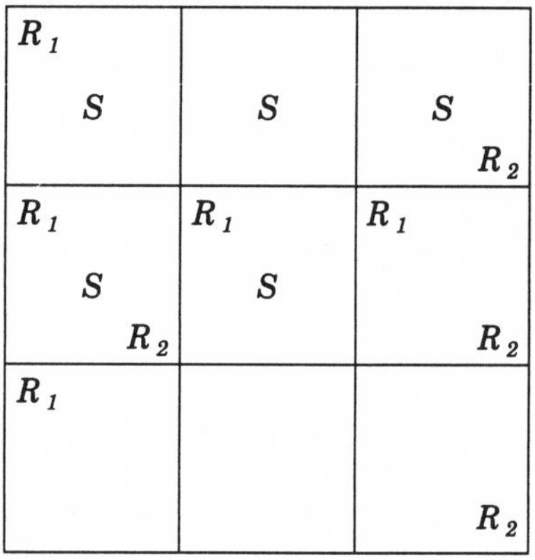

**Figure 16**

## 5. An Informal Discussion of the Relationship Between One of the Premises and Our Conclusion

I now propose to show that it is possible to derive Cohen's conclusion from fewer and weaker premises. First of all we shall replace his (1) and (2) by the weaker,

(1*)  $P(S/R_1) > 0$,
(2*)  $P(S/R_2) > 0$.

More importantly, however, we may dispense with his (3), (4), and (5) and replace them with the single expression,

(o)  $P(R_2/R_1 \& S) > P(R_2/R_1 \& \sim S)$.

Before continuing it will be useful to mention possible circumstances under which ($\phi$) would not hold, which may provide us with an informal—and therefore a more easily grasped—way of showing how (o) is connected to the conclusion concerning the higher credibility of joint affirmations. Imagine a situation where the defendant is charged with being a member of a powerful crime syndicate. If the charge is true then—regardless of whether there is another witness or not—$B$ may be unwilling to come forward in fear of the omnipresent threat of the syndicate's reprisal. Thus $P(R_2/R_1 \& S)$ may be very small. On the other hand, when the charge is false and the witnesses are likely to be motivated by personal grudges against the accused who is not protected by a mighty organization, $B$ need not fear retaliation from any associates of the defendant. There is, of course, in the latter case the possible penalty for perjury. We may postulate that $B$ is considerably more afraid of the almost certain and merciless retribution meted out by the syndicate than the much less probable and less harsh legal troubles he might get into for testifying falsely. Regardless of how uncommon such circumstances might be, it is clear that these are circumstances under which $P(R_2/R_1 \& \sim S)$ is not that small and thus the inequality ($\phi$) does not hold. It also seems fairly obvious that, prior to any formal proof, in such a context (where there is considerable extraneous motivation for the witnesses to claim that $S$, a motivation that is not rooted in the truth of $S$, and where the truth of $S$ in fact constitutes a deterrent against making that claim) the words of two witnesses should not carry more weight than that of a single witness.

## 6. The Formal Derivation of the Conclusion

I shall begin by showing formally that

$$P(R_2/R_1 \& S) > P(R_2/S) \tag{$\alpha$}$$

can be derived from our premises.

*Proof:* By the Rule of Elimination,

$$P(R_2/R_1) = P(S/R_1) \cdot P(R_2/R_1 \& S) + P(\sim S/R_1) \cdot P(R_2/R_1 \& \sim S)$$

$< P(S/R_1) \cdot P(R_2/R_1 \& S) + P(\sim S/R_1) \cdot P(R_2/R_1 \& S)$
(substituting the left-hand side of $(o)$ into the second term of the right-hand side of the expression above, i.e., replacing $P(R_2/R_1 \& \sim S)$ by $P(R_2/R_1 \& S)$, the latter having according to $(o)$ a higher value than the former. Also, $P(\sim S/R_1) > 0$ follows from (6): $P(S/R_1) < 1$.)
$= [P(S/R_1) + P(\sim S/R_1)] \cdot P(R_2/R_1 \& S)$ (by moving the common factor outside square brackets)
$= P(R_2/R_1 \& S)$           $(a)$

Now we are in a position to derive Cohen's (3). Given the inequality $(a)$, it follows that

$$P(R_2/R_1 \& S) > 0.$$

This together with (1*) yields:

$P(S/R_1) \cdot P(R_2/R_1 \& S) > 0.$ i.e.,
$P(R_2/R_1) \cdot P(S/R_2 \& R_1) > 0.$ i.e.,
$P(R_2/R_1) > 0.$

But this means that $P(R_1 \& R_2) > 0$, since

$$P(R_2/R_1) = \frac{P(R_1 \& R_2)}{P(R_1)}.$$

Next we employ Bayes's theorem,

$$P(S/R_1 \& R_2) = \frac{P(R_1 \& R_2/S) \cdot P(S)}{P(R_1 \& R_2)}$$
$$= \frac{P(R_1/S) \cdot P(R_2/R_1 \& S) \cdot P(S)}{P(R_1) \cdot P(R_2/R_1)} \quad \text{and}$$
$$P(S/R_1) = \frac{P(R_1/S) \cdot P(S)}{P(R_1)}.$$

Dividing the last two equations, which is permissible given that $P(S/R_1) > 0$,

$$\frac{P(S/R_2 \& R_1)}{P(S/R_1)} = \frac{P(R_2/R_1 \& S)}{P(R_2/R_1)} \qquad (\beta)$$

i.e., $P(S/R_1 \& R_2) > P(S/R_1)$ by $(a)$.

Obviously in similar fashion we can also prove that

$$P(S/R_1 \& R_2) > P(S/R_2).$$

Thus we see how the thesis that corroborated testimony is superior to uncorroborated ones can be derived without assuming premises (3), (4), or (5) to be true.

It is easily seen how one may prove formally that, as we have claimed earlier, the inequality $(o)$ is also a necessary condition. Let us assume that it is not, and thus,

$$P(R_2/R_1 \,\&\, S) < P(R_2/R_1 \,\&\, {\sim}S).$$

We simply go through the same steps as before and get, instead of $(\alpha)$:

$$P(R_2/R_1) > P(R_2/R_1 \,\&\, S).$$

Substituting this into $(3)$ we end up with

$$P(S/R_1 \,\&\, R_2) < P(S/R_1).$$

Let us consider briefly an objection. Suppose we are dealing with a situation where the hypothesis does not entail but only renders the evidence probable; however, if the hypothesis is true, then once $\epsilon_1$ is true $\epsilon_2$ inevitably follows. Thus we are given that $P(\epsilon_2/\epsilon_1 \,\&\, h) = 1$, while $P(\epsilon_2/\epsilon_1 \,\&\, {\sim}h) < 1$, i.e., that $(o)$ is satisfied. It has been given however that $P(\epsilon_1/h) = P(\epsilon_1 \,\&\, \epsilon_2/h)$ (or that once $\epsilon_1$ is given $\epsilon_2$ may be taken for granted). In that case adding $\epsilon_2$ to $\epsilon_1$ should not increase the credibility of $h$, contrary to the conclusion we have derived from $(\phi)$.

It is fairly obvious however that there is no difficulty here. Since $(o)$ is true so is the conclusion that $P(h/\epsilon_1 \,\&\, \epsilon_2) > P(h/\epsilon_1)$. After all, we could have observed what is definitely incompatible with $h$, namely $\epsilon_1$ and ${\sim}\epsilon_2$, in which case we would have had conclusive evidence that ${\sim}h$. The fact that such refuting evidence does not exist as indicated by $\epsilon_2$, should indeed raise the credibility of $h$.

Finally, let us ask what happens in a situation where for some reason either $R_1$ on its own or $R_2$ on its own holds with the same probability irrespective of whether $S$ is true or not, but it is much less likely for both of them to hold at the same time when $S$ is false than when it is true. I believe it will appear obvious to everyone that $R_1$ combined with $R_2$ should then raise the credibility of $S$ from what it was before, when only one of them or neither of them was true. It is clear that Cohen's demonstration fails to yield this elementary result: given his premises (1) $P(S/R_1) > P(S)$ and (2) $P(S/R_2) > P(S)$, it follows that the conclusion has been demonstrated to apply only where both $R_1$ and $R_2$ on their own raise the probability of $S$, which of course is incompatible with the probability of $R_1$ and $R_2$ by themselves being independent of $S$.

We, on the other hand, postulated merely (1*) and (2*), which state that both $P(S/R_1)$ and $P(S/R_2)$ are greater than zero, which is compatible with both being equal to $P(S)$. Thus our premises do not exclude the case where the truth or falsity of $S$ has no effect on the probability that one of $R_1$ or $R_2$ is true. The conclusion that corroborated evidence provides greater support to a hypothesis than uncorroborated evidence applies therefore also to the special case where uncorroborated evidence provides no support whatever.

## 7. The Case of the Bribed Witness

It is worth remarking that Cohen, in a note published in 1981, explicitly mentions condition ($\phi$)—which he denotes by (II) — and claims it to be insufficient to establish his conclusion. He says:

> We can interpret (II)...to state that witness $B$ is more likely to concur with witness $A$ when what $A$ testifies to obtains than when it does not obtain. And at first sight this looks like being all that is required for genuine corroboration in a forensic context. But in fact it is not all that is required. There is nothing in (II), thus interpreted, to exclude the possibility that $B$ has been bribed always to say the same as $A$ though he finds it somewhat easier to earn his bribe when $A$ is telling the truth than when $A$ is not. Hence there is nothing in (II) to exclude the possibility that in the present case $B$ is earning his bribe by stomaching his dislike of parroting $A$'s falsehoods.[2]

As we have seen, however, the inequality $P(S/R_1 \ \& \ R_2) > P(S/R_1)$ can definitely be derived from a set of premises that includes ($\phi$), instead of Cohen's more substantial premises, a set which in particular does not include his (4) and (5). It is thus clear that, contrary to Cohen, ($\phi$)—or what he calls (II)—plus a few other obvious premises, is all that is required for genuine corroboration in a forensic context.

I should mention that even before providing a strict proof for the validity of our conclusion, merely from an informal point of view we shall find Cohen's reasoning faulty. After all, he asks us to take into consideration the possibility that we are facing a special situation where $B$ has been bribed always to say the same thing as $A$. But then he immediately adds that even in this strange context

---

[2] L. Jonathan Cohen, "What Is Necessary for Testimonial Corroboration?" *British Journal for the Philosophy of Science* (1981): 163.

we are to assume that the second witness is more inclined to testify when he has been paid to say the truth than when bribed to testify falsely. Thus, even under the conditions postulated by Cohen, in the majority of cases the additional witness, even though he may be bribed, is not going to lie. Contrary to his own intentions, therefore, he seems to have provided a reason why $S$ is more likely to be true when $R_2$ is given than when it is not given.

## 8. Diagnostic Evidence That Reinforce Each Other

Expression $(\phi)$ is relevant to a claim made in the course of their arguments about the integration of evidence by A. Tversky and D. Kahaneman. In their highly influential "Causal Thinking in Judgment Under Uncertainty" they cite the following example as illustrative of their views:

> PROBLEM 10   Bill has been referred by his physician to the hospital with suspicion of a malignant tumor. Following the examination the following data were obtained.
> (i) The chance of malignant tumor is 5% among patients referred to the hospital for such examinations.
> (ii) The hematologist who examined Bill's blood test estimated the chance of malignancy to be 10%.
> (iii) The radiologist who examined Bill's X-ray estimated the chance of a malignancy to be 45%.
> Question: What is the probability that Bill has a malignant tumor?[3]

They contend that the two pieces of diagnostic evidence reinforce each other, and in an endnote they offer a formal demonstration in the following manner:

> in Problem 10, conditional independence i.e. $P(D_1 \text{ and } D_2/H) = P(D_1/H) \cdot (D_2/H)$ [$H$ =Bill has cancer; $D_1$ and $D_2$ refer to the two items of diagnostic evidence] may be expected to hold, at least as a reasonable approximation.[4]

It so happens, however, that it is entirely superfluous to assume the independence of $D_1$ and $D_2$. Furthermore, cases where they

---

[3] A. Tversky and D. Kahaneman, "Causal Thinking in Judgment Under Uncertainty," *Basic Problems in Methodology and Linguistics*, ed. R. E. Butts and J. Hintikka (D. Reidel, 1977), p. 185.
[4] Ibid., p. 189.

are actually interdependent are easily conceived and it seems that even there we would intuitively regard two symptoms to reinforce one another. Let us look at such cases.

For the sake of greater clarity let us remind ourselves that conditional independence may also be represented as the assertion that $P(D_2/H) = P(D_2/D_1 \mathbin{\&} H)$. This condition may be violated in two different ways:

*Case I:* $P(D_2/H) < P(D_2/D_1 \mathbin{\&} H)$.

Such a situation obtains where $H$ may be represented as $E \vee A$, $E$ refers to cancer in its earlier stages (when symptoms are harder to detect), and $A$ to its advanced stage. When both $H$ and $D_1$ are true then it is more likely that $A$ holds because when $A$ holds symptoms are more readily observed. But then it is also true that when $A$ is true, $D_2$ is more easily established. In other words, the inequality holds for $P(D_2/H)$—where there is nothing to differentiate between the chances that $H$ is true because of $E$ or because of $A$—which is of a smaller value than $P(D_2/D_1 \mathbin{\&} H)$, where $H$ is most likely to be true because of $A$.

At the same time, nothing that we said could be construed as even a remotely plausible reason why, in this case, the general principle that symptoms reinforce one another should not hold.

*Case II:* $P(D_2/H) > P(D_2/D_1 \mathbin{\&} H)$.

Such a situation could be envisaged to obtain where the cancer has limited potency, which can either be harnessed as a force to feed the local tumor and enlarge it, or to invade the whole body through the blood stream, but not both. Thus $D_2$ is more likely to be present when $D_1$ is not given than when it is. And it is reasonable to assume that in the absence of a malignancy $D_1$ and $D_2$ are even less likely to appear together, and therefore the inequality provides no reason for failing to treat two symptoms to be stronger evidence for cancer than either symptom on its own.

But without any of these illustrative examples, it must be obvious that the assumption postulated by the authors that $D_1$ and $D_2$ have to be independent is unnecessarily restrictive. Figure 16 in section 4 of this chapter shows clearly that even if $P(D_2/H)$ is greater than $P(D_2/D_1 \mathbin{\&} H)$ it is still possible that $P(H/D_1 \mathbin{\&} D_2)$ is greater than $P(H/D_2)$. To see this, all we need to do is change $R_1$, $R_2$ and $S$ to $D_1$, $D_2$, and $H$ respectively.

Then again, it is very simple to demonstrate that $D_2$ may be dependent on $D_1$ in the sense that $D_2$'s probability is higher when $D_1$ is given than when it is not, i.e., $P(D_2/H) < P(D_2/D_1 \& H)$, and at the same time their combined effect raises the credibility of $H$ more than each would on its own. Figure 17 provides an illustration of such a situation. Of the two $H$-squares only one is also a $D_2$-square and thus $P(D_2/H) = 1/2$. There is only one square that is both $D_1$ and $H$, and it happens to be also a $D_2$-square,

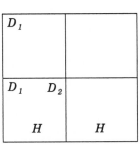

**Figure 17**

thus $P(D_2/D_1 \& H) = 1 > P(D_2/H)$. Yet $D_1$ and $D_2$ reinforce one another since $P(H/D_1 \& D_2) = 1$, which is greater than $P(H/D_1)$ (as only one of the two $D_1$-squares is also an $H$-square, and therefore $P(H/D_1) = 1/2$).

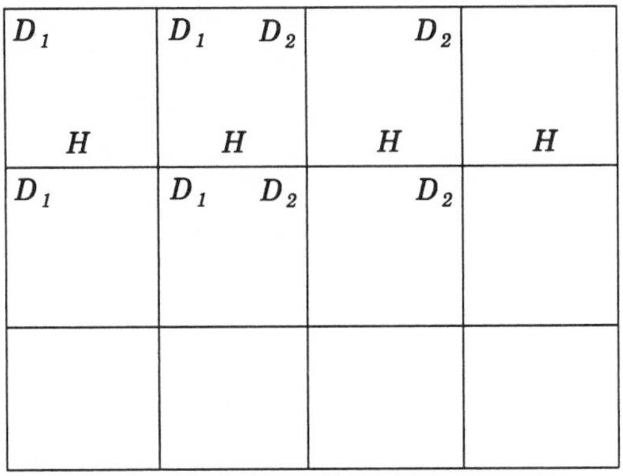

**Figure 18**

In fact, unlike Cohen's premises (4) and (5), which turned out to be unnecessary but still sufficient conditions, the condition of independence seems entirely irrelevant and it is not even a sufficient condition to ensure that $D_1$ and $D_2$ reinforce each other. This should be obvious from Figure 18, where both $P(D_2/H)$ and $P(D_2/H \& D_1)$ equal $1/2$ and thus $D_1$ and $D_2$ are independent, and yet $P(H/D_1 \& D_2)$ is not greater than $P(H/D_1)$ since these also equal $1/2$. (And of course $D_1$ and $D_2$ are both properly called symptoms, since each on its own raises the probability of $H$ from $1/3$ to $1/2$.)

But as we have shown earlier, the only relevant condition is

$$(\phi) \quad P(D_2/D_1 \mathbin{\&} H) > P(D_2/D_1 \mathbin{\&} \sim H).$$

If condition ($o$) is satisfied, and only if it is satisfied, then the combined evidential force of $D_1$ and $D_2$ is greater than the force of either by itself.

# VIII

# RELEVANCE

## 1. Prospective Evidence

There exist a number of different notions of 'relevance' that play an important role in the philosophy of science. The sense in which a sentence $A$ may be required to be pertinent to another sentence $B$, will depend on the task we expect $A$ to perform for $B$. For example, if $A$ is supposed to serve as a scientific explanation for $B$, then apart from the various criteria suggested by philosophers that need to be satisfied, it is obvious that $A$ cannot explain $B$ unless it is relevant to $B$ to a minimum degree. Similarly it is a necessary condition for $A$ to be relevant in some sense to $B$ in order to be able to serve as confirmatory evidence for the latter.

Since currently we are mainly interested in the various aspects and uses of elementary probability, we shall devote most of our discussion to one kind of relevance that is most tightly connected with probabilistic reasoning, namely the relevance associated with prospective evidence. This notion may be described roughly in the following manner. Suppose we are entertaining a hypothesis already supported by some evidence $e$, which however is insufficient to establish $r$'s credibility. There may be any number of propositions of unknown truth value of which we nevertheless know whether or not they are relevant to our inquiry. Clearly, a proposition $p$ is relevant to $r$ in the context of the already existing evidence $e$, if the discovery of $p$'s truth value is going to affect the probability of $r$. If we are able to foresee that introducing $p$ would neither raise nor lower $r$'s probability, then we should regard $p$ to be irrelevant for the purposes of our inquiry, and should make no effort to pursue the matter.

163

## 2. The Traditional Definition of the
## Relevance of Prospective Evidence

It is fairly obvious that apart from its philosophical significance the notion of relevance of prospective evidence has a considerable practical usefulness, playing a vital role in determining the direction the growth of science will take. A given area is likely to be opened up for exploration when it is believed to contain material that has a bearing on the problem at hand; others may be ignored because nothing relevant is expected to be found in them.

It is worth noting that the concept of relevance may be said to be more basic than that of confirmation, to which nevertheless much more attention has been paid during the last few decades. To mention but one reason for this: relevance can be established a priori, that is, we may know ahead of time whether establishing the truth value of $p$ will or will not confirm our hypothesis $r$.

It may also be said that relevance is a simpler concept than confirmation. Among other things, when it comes to confirmation we need a criterion for settling conflicts, as when there is evidence supporting incompatible hypotheses. But finding an adequate means for adjudicating among competing hypotheses is one of the thorniest problems of confirmation theory. Obviously there exists no generally applicable method for gauging the relative degree of confirmation received by the various hypotheses held by different scientists, hence the sometimes very protracted controversies in the history of science. There is, however, no such competition with respect to relevance among different hypotheses; no such problems seem to arise in that context. It is thus somewhat surprising to find that as soon as we attempt to formulate a rigorous definition of relevance some puzzling difficulties come into view.

Peter Gardenfors, who has recently written a highly instructive paper on the topic,[1] in discussing the deploring scarcity of pertinent literature on this topic declares, "... 'relevance' ought to be a central concept in the philosophy of science." Nevertheless, there were some pioneering attempts in the early parts of this century to give a precise characterization of relevance. Gardenfors first cites what he calls the "traditional" definition:

(D1) (a)   $p$ is relevant to $r$ on evidence $e$ iff

$$P(r/p \& e) \neq P(r/e).$$

---

[1] Peter Gardenfors, *Synthese* (1982): 351–367.

(b)   $p$ is irrelevant to $r$ on $\epsilon$ iff

$$P(r/p \,\&\, e) = P(r/e).$$

He then goes on to point out that (D1) was regarded as too weak by Keynes. It is after all possible to have a case where $P(r/p \,\&\, q) = P(r)$ even though $P(r/p) \neq P(r)$ and $P(r/q) \neq P(r)$. But according to (D1) $p \,\&\, q$ are irrelevant to $r$ even though $p$ and $q$ taken as separate pieces of evidence are relevant to $r$. Keynes, being of the opinion that evidence, part of which is favorable and part of which is unfavorable, is always relevant, believed that (D1) was inadequate.

Now Keynes went too far in insisting that as long as $p$ and $q$ on their own were relevant to $r$ then even if $p \,\&\, q$ does not affect the probability of $r$, that conjunction is *always* relevant to $r$. If he were right, we would have to accept the absurdity that everything was relevant to everything! For let $s$ be any sentence such that $P(r/s) = P(r)$, and let $p = r \lor s$ and $q = \sim r \lor s$. Then it can be shown that as long as $P(s) \neq 1$, $P(r/p) \neq P(r)$ and $P(r/q) \neq P(r)$, but of course $s \leftrightarrow (r \lor s) \,\&\, (\sim r \lor s)$, i.e., $s - p \,\&\, q$, and therefore $s$ is relevant to $r$.

Nevertheless, it seems correct to say that *sometimes* $p \,\&\, q$ is relevant to $r$ even though $P(r/p \,\&\, q) = P(r)$, by virtue of the fact that $p$ and q on their own are relevant to $r$. For suppose everyone is convinced that either Fred or Herb must be the murderer. Let

$p_1 =$ A very reliable witness testifies that Fred is the murderer,

$q_1 =$ A very reliable witness testifies that Herb is the murderer,

$r \;=$ Fred is the murderer.

Both $p_1$ and $q_1$ are of course relevant on their own to $r$. Let us suppose that the testimony of the two witnesses in question are precisely of equal weight, and consequently the probability of $r$ is no more and no less when $p_1 \,\&\, q_1$ is given than when neither of them is given. Surely, in spite of all this, all those who want to discover who the murderer is will greatly welcome the information that $p_1 \,\&\, q_1$. While that information does not affect the probability of $r$, it opens up a great number of avenues of inquiry that would otherwise not be available. Given the truth of $p_1 \,\&\, q_1$, then upon learning that one of the witnesses contradicts himself under extensive interrogation, or that his interest would be greatly harmed if Fred or if Herb were to be found guilty, or that lately he was for long periods under the influence of hallucinatory drugs, or that at the time of the murder he was in bed asleep, etc., we shall assign a different probability to

$r$ from what we assigned to it before. Without being given $p_1 \& q_1$ no such information exists that may lead to a reassessment of the probability of $r$ without being related to the accused and to his comings and goings.

### 3. A New Definition

After a thorough discussion of the various desirata for an adequate criterion for relevance Gardenfors proposes the following:

(D3)  (a)  $p$ is *irrelevant* to $r$ on evidence $\epsilon$ iff either (i)
$P(r/p \& \epsilon) = P(r/\epsilon)$ *and* for all sentences $q$, if
$P(r/q \& \epsilon) = P(r/\epsilon)$ and $P(p \& q \& \epsilon) \neq 0$, then
$P(r/p \& q \& \epsilon) = P(r/\epsilon)$, or (ii) $P(p/\epsilon) = 0$.
   (b)  $p$ is *relevant* to $r$ on $\epsilon$ iff $p$ is not irrelevant to $r$ on $\epsilon$.

(D3) can be seen to be superior to (D1) in a number of ways. For example, the objection involving $p_1$ and $q_1$ we just raised does not apply to (D3). For let $p^* = p_1 \& q_1$; then as we have already explained $P(r/p) = P(r)$. Now let

   $q =$ The witness referred to in $p_1$ bears a strong grudge against Fred.

Clearly, if $q$ is given then the two sets of witnesses are no longer of equal weight, since there are good reasons to suspect the motives of those trying to incriminate Fred. Thus, $P(r/p^* \& q) < P(r)$. It follows from (D3)(a)(i) that $p^*$ is, as we felt it should be, relevant to $r$, since $P(r/p^*) = P(r)$ as well as $P(r/q) = P(r)$, while it is not the case that $P(r/p^* \& q) = P(r)$.

Nevertheless, it seems that (D3) is subject to a variety of objections.

*Objection 1:* In general, a scientist will be interested in ascertaining the truth value of any proposition the discovery of which can aid him in achieving his objective of establishing the status of $r$. It is clear, however, that the magnitude of his interest will vary from proposition to proposition depending on the degree of hope he is justified in having that the proposition in question will serve his purpose. This point is not merely of philosophical but also of vital practical interest to the working scientist. Given the finitude of time and energy at the disposal of an investigator, he can as a rule pursue a small fraction of the lines of inquiry that may prove useful. Obviously when choosing the actual route of exploration he should be guided by the relative degrees of expectation of usefulness associated with these. He need not waste time on trying to discover the truth values of propositions that offer very little likelihood of proving useful, and should concentrate instead on probing propositions that are most likely to be of service.

It is reasonable to expect that an adequate definition will reflect the existence of different degrees of interest a scientist takes in different relevant propositions. This could be accomplished either by admitting different degrees of relevance, or allowing the probability that $p$ is relevant to $r$ to have different values. To be more concrete, we saw that according to (D3), if under appropriate conditions $P(r/p \,\&\, q \,\&\, e) \neq P(r/e)$, then $p$ is relevant to $r$. Clearly the working scientist's interest will be greater in $p$ the greater the probability of $q$. When the probability of $q$ is very small there is little to gain from discovering that $p$ is true. Ascertaining that $p$ is true will not affect $r$'s probability even when $P(r/p \,\&\, q \,\&\, e)$ differs greatly from $P(r/e)$ if $q$ turns out (as it is likely to turn out) false. There is nothing in (D3) that reflects this important variable-factor which determines the warranted interest an investigator may have in $p$ when attempting to confirm $r$ or its denial. (D3) does not mention degrees of relevance. Also, since no knowledge of any fact is required to determine relevance, an inspection of $p$, $q$, $r$, and $e$ will reveal either that $p$ is definitely relevant or definitely not, that is, no provisions are made for different likelihoods for $p$ to be relevant to $r$.

A further important point is that even in case $P(r/p \,\&\, q \,\&\, e)$ is a thousand times greater than $P(r/e)$, if $q$ is believed to be definitely false there is absolutely no point in finding out that $p$ is true, and therefore in this case $p$ ought to be regarded as completely devoid of relevance to $r$. Yet if (D3) is our criterion, $p$ is to count as relevant in this case precisely as much as when $q$ is to be true! To illustrate, let

$r =$ All Australian swans are black,

$e =$ No Australian swans have so far been sighted. All the thousands of swans that have been observed everywhere else were white,

$p =$ Everything stated in the diary exhibitied in the Museum of Bombay written 200 years ago by an Indian explorer is true. That diary contains the sentence "Kutah prunah grnato...,"

$q =$ "Kutah prunah grnato..." means in Sanskrit that all Australian swans are black.

$P(r/\epsilon)$ is clearly exceedingly small. Someone who understands no Sanskrit at all, and thus does not have a clue what the Sanskrit sentence mentioned in $p$ may mean, has absolutely no reason to suspect that $p$ has the slightest relevance to $r$. In the eyes of such a person, the addition of $p$ to $\epsilon$ will have no effect on the probability of $r$. Obviously, adding $q$ alone to $\epsilon$ makes no difference to the probability of $r$ either. Thus $P(r/\epsilon) = P(r/\epsilon \& q) \ll 1$, while of course $P(r/\epsilon \& p \& q) = 1$. It follows therefore that according to (D3) $p$ is to be regarded as relevant to $r$ even if $q$ is definitely false and even if everyone knows $q$ to be false. This does not seem to accord well with anybody's notion of relevance of prospective evidence.

*Objection 2:* The notion of relevance that scientists are concerned with is certainly such that it provides scope for error; it makes good sense to speak of someone believing that $p$ is completely irrelevant to $r$ when in fact it is highly relevant. For example, most scholars would agree that an investigation into a question such as, "What did Julius Caesar have for breakfast ten days before he crossed the Rubicon?" would be quite a hopeless undertaking. The reason for this is not that the truth value of any proposition relevant to that question is inaccessible to us at this late stage, since there are no firm grounds for asserting this to be the case. It is rather that even though there may be several relevant propositions that we would be able to confirm, we are not in the position to know that they *are* relevant.

Suppose an ancient letter has been preserved in which the author, writing in Latin, reveals that his cousin has vowed that for the next twelve months he is going to have eggs for breakfast. It could very well be that the classicists whose one burning interest in ancient history was to describe correctly the breakfast Caesar had on the particular morning we have mentioned would dismiss that letter as devoid of the slightest interest to them. This, however, could be an unavoidable mistake because they did not know, nor did they have the means of discovering, that the letter writer was the cousin of the Roman war lord, to whom he was referring in the letter, and the date of the letter was the same year in which he crossed the Rubicon.

It should be obvious that there is also scope for an opposite kind of error, namely that someone should be convinced that $p$ was relevant to $r$ when in fact it had no relevance at all.

Clearly, however, (D3) provides no scope for erroneous beliefs concerning the relevance of any proposition. As we have already indicated, according to that criterion no empirical knowledge of any kind is required in order to discover whether a certain statement is or is not relevant. In the context of our particular example it is of no importance whatever who the letter writer was or whom he was referring to, since the letter is definitely relevant to the question at hand. Whether the statement "Julius Caesar is the cousin referred to in the letter" is true or false is of no interest whatever, what matters is that it, together with the assertion made by the letter writer concerning his cousin's vow, imply an answer to our inquiry.

*Objection 3:* The first two objections implied that (D3) is too liberal, for it bestows full relevance on what is not certain to be so, or on what is not known to be so, and even on what should decidedly be regarded as irrelevant. This last objection points in the opposite direction, and charges that in another sense (D3) is too restrictive, since it rules out as irrelevant some things that seem to have sufficient qualifications for being relevant.

Now (D3) seems to imply that in case $P(r/e) = P(r/e \& p)$ then *even though there exists some sentence* $q^*$ such that $P(r/e \& p \& q^*) \gg P(r/e)$, as long as it is also the case that $P(r/e \& q^*) > P(r/e)$, as well as for every $q$ for which $P(r/e \& q) = P(r/e)$ it is also true that $P(r/e \& p \& q) = P(r/e)$, then $p$ is irrelevant to $r$. In view of this, let us consider the case where $P(r/e) = P(r/e \& p)$ and $q^* = p \supset r$ (and also where $P(r) < 1$ and $p$ does not logically entail $r$). It is easy to show that $P(r/e \& q^*) > P(r/e)$. We are of course free to stipulate that $p$ is such that for every $q$ for which $P(r/e \& q) = P(r/e)$, it is also the case that they both equal $P(r/e \& p \& q)$. Thus we are dealing here with an example where according to (D3) $p$ is irrelevant to $r$. But surely if $q^*$ happens to be true then it is of very great concern to find out whether $p$ is true as well, for if so $r$ may be inferred by Modus Ponens.

It might be argued in defense of (D3) that we should consider two situations: one in which we have evidence that $q^*$ is true or is likely to be true, the other in which there is no such evidence. In the first case the evidence is part of $e$, and it can no longer be the case that $P(r/e) = P(r/e \& q^*)$, since now adding $p$ to $e$ raises the probability of $r$. On the other hand, in case there is absolutely no evidence in favor of $q^*$, the scientist anxious to establish the truth value of $r$ will not be aware of any reason why he should be interested to find out whether $p$ was credible, as $p$ on its own has no bearing on the status of $r$.

Whether or not we find this defense satisfactory will depend on how we construe the notion of relevance. Someone who maintains that $p$ is relevant to $r$ as long as it is a fact—regardless of whether anyone is aware of it or not—that there exists some true proposition which when conjoined with $p$ alters the probability of $r$ would reject this defense as inadequate. Gardenfors might reasonably argue, however, that if we are concerned with a notion of relevance that is to serve as a guide for the practical scientist, then unknown factors should surely not be allowed to play any role in determining it. On that view, $p$ is relevant to $r$ iff a scientist is actually aware of reasons that provide him with rational grounds for wanting to discover the credibility of $p$, in the belief that it will aid him in his pursuit of the truth value of $r$.

## 4. An Amended New Definition

I should like to advance a new definition, one which seems to accomplish everything (D3) does but is not subject to the same objections:

(D*) (a)   $p$ is *irrelevant* as prospective evidence to $r$ on existing evidence $e$ iff either (i) $P(r/p \,\&\, e) = P(r/e)$ and there is no true sentence $q$ such that both $P(r/p) \neq P(r/p \,\&\, q)$ and $P(r/q) \neq P(r/p \,\&\, q)$, or (ii) $P(p/e) = 0$.

(b)   $p$ is *relevant*, etc.

Objection 1 can now be seen to be taken care of. Suppose we find that $P(r/p) = P(r)$ but $P(r/p) \neq P(r/p \,\&\, q)$, and $P(r/q) \neq P(r/p \,\&\, q)$. According to our criterion, this on its own does not yet ensure that $p$ is relevant to $r$; there is an additional requirement, namely that $q$ has to be true. It follows, therefore, that when $q$ is not certain to be true, the higher its probability the higher the probability that $p$ is relevant to $r$. We thus see that (D*) does reflect the fact that the scientist will be more interested in probing $p$ the higher the probability he assigns to $q$. Admittedly, even according to (D*) relevance does not come in degrees. However, according to (D3), when the specified conditions have not been fulfilled $p$ is definitely irrelevant to $r$, whereas as soon as they have been fulfilled $p$ is fully relevant, and it is always clearly decidable whether they have or have not been fulfilled. It is different with (D*). Owing to the fact that one of the requirements for $p$'s relevance is that $q$ be true, the answer to the question of whether the specified requirements have or have not been fulfilled is not always clear and admits of different probabilities. Consequently the probability of $p$ being relevant to $r$ is not invariably 0 or 1 but admits of any value in between. (D*) might thus be said to reflect faithfully scientific practice; the scientist's interest in discovering the truth value of $p$ will vary with the magnitude of the probability of $q$'s being true.

But matters are not as simple as that. Often there will be several auxiliary hypotheses, say $q_1$ and $q_2$, both of which render $p$ relevant to $r$ because of (D*)(a)(i), but where $q_1$ and $q_2$ are of unequal probability. Which one is then to determine $p$'s degree of relevance? The answer is by no means immediately evident. Some may wish to argue that of all such auxiliary hypotheses the one with the maximum probability is the one that plays the crucial role here. Others might suggest that we have to introduce a somewhat more complicated notion than the one we have taken to be adequate so far and talk about the relevance of $p$ to $r$ on evidence $\epsilon$ *in the context of* $q_1$, and so on.

Regarding Objection 2, it should be obvious that there are indefinitely many propositions that are relevant to the question of whether Julius Caesar had eggs for breakfast ten days prior to his crossing the Rubicon. Why is it then that no scientist would think it profitable to make the slightest effort to try and investigate such a question? The answer is because nobody is capable of identifying any of those propositions. It is important to realize that this answer is available on our definition but not on the definition offered by Gardenfors. He defined 'relevance' in terms of the logical relations that have to obtain among $e$, $p$, $q$, and $r$. As soon as we are given these propositions, without having to establish whether any facts obtain we are able to determine by inspecting them whether or not the required relation obtains among them. In our definition, however, there is also the requirement of truth for $q$. The question whether an empirical statement such as $q$ is true cannot be established by subjecting $q$ to any amount of careful scrutiny. Thus, according to (D*) it is possible that there are propositions of which we can never know whether they are relevant. According to (D3), however, if a proposition is relevant then we know it is relevant.

Finally, Objection 3 disappears, since given that $q = p \supset r$, $P(r/p \,\&\, q) = 1$, which is different from both $P(r/p)$ and $P(r/q)$.

## 5. The Need for Independent Ways of Investigating the Evidence and the Hypothesis

I do not wish to maintain that (D*) is fully adequate as it stands; in fact it needs to be qualified in a number of ways. First let us consider a relatively small point, with the aid of the following example. Let

> $r =$ In order to establish his hypothesis that different weights take the same amount of time to reach the ground, Galileo dropped pebbles of various masses from the top of the tower of Pisa.

As is known, many contemporary scholars doubt the authenticity of this story, and believe that most probably Galileo conducted no experiments at all while standing on the top of the tower of Pisa. Now let

> $p =$ The famous person to whom popular tradition attributes the uttering of the words "e pur si muove," after being compelled by the Inquisition to swear that the earth stood still, was dropping pebbles of various masses from the top of the tower of Pisa to verify that they take the same amount of time to reach the ground.

> $q =$ Galileo is the famous person who is believed to have uttered the words "e pur si muove" after being compelled, etc.

Clearly, in the present situation all the conditions laid down by (D\*) have been fulfilled since $P(r/p \,\&\, q) = 1$, while $P(r) = P(r/p) = P(r/q)$. Suppose there exists a contemporary scholar who is very keen in establishing once and for all whether $r$ was true, that is, whether the popular image of Galileo carefully timing the fall of rocks from the top of the tower of Pisa corresponds to reality. Is it then correct to maintain, as I have claimed in the previous section, that our historian's interest in $p$ will be proportional to the degree of credibility he ascribes to the crucial statement $q$—which reveals to us that the person who uttered certain famous words and the one named Galileo were one and the same individual? Surely the answer is that no matter how anxious our scholar may be to discover the truth value of $r$, and how eagerly he will grasp at even the most trivial bit of information that may seem relevant to his investigation, he will show no greater interest in finding out about $p$ when $q$'s probability is virtually sure than when it is almost nil.

The reason, of course, is that to a practical investigator $p$ will be of interest if he is unable to get directly to $r$ and believes that he may approach it in a roundabout way via the truth value of $p$. In the particular case before us, however, it appears that to the extent there are obstacles preventing us from establishing the truth value of $r$ in a straightforward manner, to that extent there are obstacles in the way leading to the discovery of $q$'s truth value. Thus $p$, which requires $q$ to raise $r$'s probability, is relevant to $r$ virtually in the sense in which $r$ is relevant to itself, and not in an interesting way that could enable it to serve as an aid in establishing $r$'s truth value in an indirect manner.

Thus an obvious proviso needs to be added to (D*), to the effect that $p$ cannot be regarded relevant to $r$ as prospective evidence that could help us in our investigation of the latter, unless there exists some route leading to establishing $p$'s credibility that is different from any of the routes directly leading to establishing $r$'s credibility.

## 6. The Different Senses of Relevance

So far we have dealt with the notion of relevance as a relation between a hypothesis $r$ and prospective evidence $p$. Here the central issue was whether there is any point in attempting to determine the truth value of $p$ as an aid to our inquiries into the status of $r$. In this context, $p$'s relevance to $r$ was essentially determined by whether or not there existed a certain probabilistic connection between the two propositions.

There is, however, a radically different notion of relevance, whose explication is indispensable to the understanding of a wide variety of topics. When we employ the notion of relevance in this second sense, $A$ is not regarded as relevant to $B$ unless $A$ makes a statement that has something specifically to do with what is conveyed by $B$, that is, the content of $A$ has a selective bearing on $B$—a bearing it does not have on any other proposition.

For example, the problem of formulating the sufficient and necessary conditions $A$ and $B$ must satisfy so that $A$ may function as a legitimate scientific explanations for $B$, has been a matter of dispute for more than half a century. Regardless of which of the many accounts is the most adequate, one thing is undeniable and has to be assumed by all parties, whether they have stated it explicitly or not: if $A$ is to serve as explanans for $B$ then it is indispensable that $A$ should be pertinent to $B$ in some minimal sense (soon to be explained), that is, $A$ has to assert something that has a unique bearing on the specific substance of $B$. In other words, explanatory relevance is a necessary condition for there to be an explanation. Similarly, $A$ has to have some bearing on the special content of $B$ in order to confirm it.

Thus, whatever else may be required for $A$ to be an explanation for $B$, at the very least it has to have some relevance to it, and this amounts to saying that the required relation must be content-dependent. The same goes for confirmation and several other relations in the context of which relevance is essential. A logical relation $R$ between two sets of sentences is not content-dependent if it does not depend on the specific denoting terms, that is, if $R$ continues to hold when any other denoting term is substituted for the denoting terms in the sets. A logical relation $R$ that is not content-dependent may also be called 'nondifferential', owing to the fact that since $R$ is not distinctively a function of what the relata are about, an arbitrary change in the components of the relata makes no difference to $R$.

The quickest and most convincing way to demonstrate the indispensability of content-dependence wherever relevance (in the second sense) is required is to consider the notion of understanding. Many philosophers hold that to understand a sentence a person must be able to recognize its truth conditions. Now, while some philosophers subscribe to a different definition of 'understanding', it is a matter of simple common sense and not subject to any philosophical controversy that a person's ability to recognize all the truth conditions of a statement $S$ is at least a fairly reliable *sign* that he understands it, while his inability to recognize a single one of those conditions is a strong indication of his failure to understand $S$. And if he is capable of recognizing some (but not most) of them, then very likely he partially (but not fully) understands $S$,

Let us consider a concrete example, where '$S$' stands for "The entropy of a closed physical system tends to increase." There are a good number of people who know no physics and have absolutely no idea what $S$ means. Such people would be at a total loss in recognizing any of the conditions a physicist would mention as affecting the truth value of $S$. Suppose Fred, who remembers some of the highschool physics he was taught, is capable of pointing out that if one half of a sample of gas which is isolated from its surroundings were spontaneously to rise in temperature, while the temperature of the other half dropped, that would make $S$ false. All would agree that it would be reasonable to assume that Fred had some idea of what $S$ meant; he at least partially understood $S$. On the other hand, suppose all that Fred is able to claim is that $S$ is true provided the conjunction "Fortune is blind" and "If fortune is blind then $S$" is true. No one would be prepared to grant that Fred's knowledge of this condition lent him the slightest understanding of $S$. I believe that it is quite transparently clear why the knowledge of the first truth condition provides Fred with some measure of understanding of $S$, while the knowledge of the second provides none. Only truth conditions relevant to $S$ can generate an understanding, or constitute a sign for an understanding, of $S$. The statement "If one half of a sample of gas . . . to rise in temperature etc." is relevant to $S$ since it constitutes a truth condition by virtue of its particular content. But if we were to change "rise in temperature" to "rise in courage" or "rise in compassion," the truth value of the conditions mentioned by Fred would no longer have an impact on the truth value of $S$. On the other hand, in the second case, in the sentence "Fortune is blind" we could substitute "Homer is blind" or indeed any word we wish for 'fortune,' as well as 'blond,' 'bland' or anything else instead of 'blind,' or indeed change any of the terms of $S$, and Modus Ponens will continue to ensure that the conditions Fred was able to mention imply the truth of $S$. Fred's knowledge that "Fortune etc." implies the truth of $S$, does not amount to a knowledge of conditions that guarantee the truth of $S$ by virtue of anything characteristic of the relata. Thus those conditions do not intimately touch upon the specific content of $S$; they are not particularly relevant to it. They therefore cannot generate any understanding or constitute any sign of an understanding of $S$.

## 7. Probabilistic Explanatory Relevance

We have illustrated through many examples how vital a role this notion of relevance plays in a remarkable variety of instances. I shall not repeat here any of those examples, but shall discuss one not mentioned before. It concerns Nagel's well-known conditions an explanation must have in order to ensure that it is not a trivial self-explanation: There must be more than one premise, each of which is essential to the derivation of the explanandum, and they do not follow logically, singly or conjointly, from the explanandum. Furthermore, the premises must be adequately supported by evidence independent of that on which the acceptance of the explicandum is based.

In a brief note, Roger Cooke has claimed that Nagel's account is untenable, and advanced a clever argument to support his claim, which shows that any statistical law lends itself to being explained in what is obviously a trivial way but which satisfies Nagel's conditions.

Cooke asks us to suppose that $P(H/G) = x$ represents some well-supported statistical law, where $x$ is slightly less than 1. Let $F$ be a statistically irrelevant property such that,

$$\text{(i)} \quad P(H/G \& F) = x. \quad \text{(ii)} \quad P(H/G \& {\sim}F) = x \qquad (\alpha)$$

Cooke then goes on to demonstrate that (i) and (ii) logically imply $P(H/G) = x$. This can very quickly be shown with the aid of equations $(\alpha)$:

$$\begin{aligned}
P(H/G) &= P(F/G) \cdot P(H/G \& F) + P({\sim}F/G) \cdot P(H/G \& {\sim}F) \\
&= P(F/G) \cdot x + P({\sim}F/G) \cdot x \\
&= [P(F/G) + P({\sim}F/G)] \cdot x = x.
\end{aligned}$$

The conclusion does not follow from either (i) or (ii) alone, and neither (i) nor (ii) can be derived from the explanandum. Thus, provided also that Nagel's other conditions are fulfilled, namely that there is sufficient evidence supporting both premises other than the evidence on which the credibility of the explicandum rests, our example is an instance of an adequate explanation. This, however, would show that something is seriously wrong with Nagel's criterion, since it is absurd that we should be able to explain why the probability of $H$ is high on $G$ with the help of statements having no relevance to $H$.

It is worth noting that Cooke focuses on statistical explanations rather than on explanations which fully imply the explanandum. The reason is that if $P(H/G) = 1$, then it logically follows that $P(H/G \& F) = P(H/G \& {\sim}F) = 1$, and Nagel would disqualify them from serving as explanans. However, as long as $P(H/G)$ does not quite equal 1, the probability of $H$ given $G$ conjoined with some other statement may have any value.

It might seem that Cooke's objection could be met by claiming that Nagel's last condition has been violated. In order to be able legitimately to maintain that $P(H/G) = x$, it is essential that the conclusion not be based on a biased sample class, which among other things means that one has observed that the frequency of $H$ among $G$ did not differ when the latter was accompanied by $F$ from cases where it was accompanied by ${\sim}F$. In other words, our observations cannot establish the explanandum unless they have first established (i) and (ii).

This however is not generally true. There are indefinitely many sentences $F$ such that our background knowledge has taught us they have nothing to do with $G$. For example, the law $P(H/G) = x$

may be a law concerning the probability of an individual suffering from a specific illness given $G$, i.e., given that the individual manifests certain symptoms, while $F$ stands for the statement that the same individual drives a foreign car. It would be taken for granted by everyone, before any investigation of the disease and its symptoms, that $F$ is utterly devoid of relevance to the inquiry concerning the occurrence of $H$, and its frequent presence or absence constitutes no bias. Thus, by observing the frequency of $H$ among $G$, while completely neglecting to note how many of these were accompanied by $F$, one could justifiably arrive at $P(H/G) = 1$.

It is important that we note how Cooke interprets Nagel's condition that the "premises must be adequately supported by evidence independent of that on which the acceptance of the explicandum is based." It is clear that Cooke does not take this condition to mean that our belief in the truth of the premises should not *in fact* be based on any evidence which supports the explicandum, but merely that it should in principle be possible to establish each premise by evidence other than that in which the credibility of the explicandum is grounded. It does indeed seem reasonable that we should not insist that the explanans and the explanandum be in fact supported by different evidence. All agree, for instance, that Newton's theory of gravity adequately explains Kepler's laws of planetary motions, even though the movements of the planets upon which Kepler's laws were based played an important role in supporting Newton's theory. But what matters is that Newton's laws, though based on planetary motions, could have been confirmed adequately without them, since there exist other phenomena relevant to his laws, e.g., the Cavendish experiment. In Cooke's example, we must remember that self-evident as it may seem to us, our belief that a car's country of origin can have no effect on its driver's state of health has not been established a priori. Thus in principle it would be possible to be in a situation in which we were ignorant of the empirical fact that $F$ is irrelevant to $H$. In that case we may observe that the frequency of $H$ among particulars that exemplify both $G$ and $F$ is $x$. Our observations would establish for us that $P(H/G \& F) = x$, without at the same time also establishing that $P(H/G)$, since we would not yet know that the presence of $F$ does not introduce a bias.

Before continuing let me mention that given his assumptions Cooke could have raised his objection in many different ways. Suppose, for example, that once more we are required to explain the statistical law $P(H/G) = x$. Let $F$ stand for some statement such that it should be possible to determine that it is true to say of a given individual that $H \lor F$ without determining that it is either $H$ or $F$. This is always the case when $H$ and $F$ have some property $P$ in common that is exemplified by nothing else, in which case by observing that an individual possesses $P$ we can conclude that it cannot be anything else but something that satisfies either $H$ or $F$ without being able to say which. For example, it is possible to know that an individual is an adult human without knowing whether that individual is a man or a woman; it is possible to know that a particular card is a face card without knowing whether it is a King, a Queen, or a Jack. We shall suppose that we have determined that $P(F/G) = y$, as well as that $P(H \lor F/G) = x + y$. And finally let us assume that $H$ and $F$ are incompatible. Then

$$P(H/G) = P(H \lor F/G) - P(F/G) = x + y - y = x$$

In other words, Nagel seems to permit that we should explain why $P(H/G) = x$, because $P(H \lor F/G) = x + y$, and $P(F/G) = y$.

Yet neither Cooke's objection, nor the objection just described, nor indeed any other similar objection will shake our conviction that nothing is basically wrong with Nagel's account. It is after all an account which can be seen to be faithfully reflected in any number of probabilistic explanations. Suppose we are wondering why the probability is $9/10$ that in the big city of Townsville a randomly selected adult will vote for the International Justice Party (when everywhere else only a small minority of voters have done so). The explanation that 95% of the inhabitants of Townsville are of Baltic origin, roughly 95% of whom passionately advocate the national interests of the Baltic states (which forms an important part of the Party's platform) would seem an impeccable explanation. And it is easy to see that there are indefinitely many other examples which conform to Nagel's rules, which is what makes them illuminating explanations. Thus one is bound to suspect that Nagel's schema is fundamentally sound, even though it may require an extra proviso to exclude those vacuous examples cited before.

The additional proviso stipulates that the premises implying the explanandum provide a genuine explanation only if the implication is content-dependent. As soon as Nagel's criterion is thus revised, it becomes immune to each of the two counterexamples cited above. In Cooke's example it makes absolutely no difference what $F$ is about since premises (i) and (ii) imply the explanandum, i.e., the implication does not depend at all on the specific content of $F$. In our example too, all we need to know is that $F$ is incompatible with

$H$ to be certain that the premises imply the explanandum regardless of what $F$ may stand for.

It is worth noting that Cooke's complaint against Nagel was precisely that it has the specific flaw of admitting entirely irrelevant explanans to serve in a legitimate explanation. As we know, when $P(H/G) = P(H/G \& F) = P(H/G \& \sim F)$ that *means* that $F$ is irrelevant to $G$, because $G$ is independent of $F$ (the denial or affirmation of $F$ has no effect on $G$'s probability). In fact, however, the complaint loses its basis once it is seen that $F$ has no effect on $G$'s probability. I am not suggesting that Nagel explicitly had the basic requirement of content-dependence in mind at the time he formulated his criterion, but it is quite likely that he would have adopted it had he been presented with it. And in that case he could have turned Cooke's counterexample into a positive, supporting example: it is *because F* is irrelevant that it must not be included among the premises that genuinely explain why $G$ is highly probable.

## 8. Catchall Explanations

Various philosophers have suggested further requirements that need to be satisfied by a set of sentences before they qualify as adequate explanans. Few, however, would disagree that content-dependence is at least a *necessary* condition for explanatory relevance and hence for adequacy. In a genuine explanation the explanans is supposed to illuminate the explanandum and a minimally necessary condition for it to do so is for it to imply something specific concerning the explanandum. Nothing specific is being implied when indefinitely many different terms may be substituted without there being any effect on the implication.

By way of a somewhat remote, though not entirely far-fetched analogy, we may cite Samuel Johnson's maxim, "He who praises everybody praises nobody." An indiscriminate encomiast's laudation of, say, a given author will not accomplish what genuine praise does; it will not commend that writer's book to us. His approval may well be said to be content-independent, not having been generated by the specific contents of the book, and hence irrelevant as a measure of its true merits. Similarly, and closer to our point, Coleridge in criticizing the psychological theories of his day, used the famous expression that "what explains everything explains nothing." To explain something is, according to Coleridge, a differential activity through which we are supposed to give reasons why "what is, is right," and thus why anything else would not be right. If our explanation is not selectively pertinent to what is to be explained, and could just as well account for the facts if something different from what actually happened took place, it would be relevant to nothing specific, and could throw no light on anything.

We have already come across an example which we recognized as an inadmissible explanation, essentially because of what we may call "Coleridge's Principle." It was discussed in chapter six and involved the two explanations why a mercury column of a certain height in any given vacuum tube is maintained. One was that of the Aristotelians, who applied the principle that nature abhors a vacuum, and the other was that of Torricelli who attributed it to the atmospheric pressure. When it was discovered how the height of the mercury column decreased as the altitude to which the instrument was taken increased, the Aristotelian hypothesis had to be abandoned. We pointed out that had the defenders of Aristotle's hypothesis introduced the auxiliary explanation that nature's abhorrence of a vacuum is not of constant intensity, and that in fact it varies with altitude in a precisely suitable manner, there would have been no observational results directly proving them wrong. The reason why such a defense would have nevertheless been deemed untenable was, we said, because it was an ad hoc explanation. Now we may elaborate slightly the point and add that the Aristotelian auxiliary explanation is a catchall explanation and violates Coleridge's Principle.

Had the mercury column dropped at twice the rate it actually did, or rose instead of dropped, or varied not with altitude but with the phases of the moon, the same kind of auxiliary explanation could have just as well been capable of accommodating those facts.

# IX

# INDIFFERENCE

## 1. Interpretation and Evaluation

We are about to examine what might be the most vital tool for all empirical investigations, the Principle of Indifference. Without this principle hardly any assertion about the unobserved could be made. First, we shall focus on its indispensable function in the context of probability statements, and subsequently direct our attention to its all-embracing role in the confirmation of any empirical hypothesis.

As indicated in the Introduction, the principle states that if we can see no grounds for distinguishing between alternatives we should ascribe equal probabilities to them. This has been made use of for two basically different purposes: (i) as an essential means for determining the numerical values of certain probabilities, and for the much less important purpose (ii) to serve as a definition of the notion probable. It is imperative to realize that using it for (i) does not commit us to using it also for (ii). As we shall see, when it comes to the evaluation of the probability of certain events (or of the truth of certain statements describing those events), it is impossible to get along without the principle. On the other hand, philosophers have argued in support of a considerable number of different interpretations of probability, and the one employing the Principle of Indifference at most represents one of many prima facie plausible interpretations.

Let me say a few words about the possible interpretive function of the principle, and then devote the rest of the chapter to examining its role in determining which events are to be treated as equiprobable.

Some writers who are often referred to as adherents of the classical interpretation of probability, and occasionally as Laplacians, have defined 'probable' as the "ratio of equipossible favorable outcomes to the total number of outcomes," where in turn 'equipossible outcomes' is defined as "outcomes relevant to which we have no

181

grounds to prefer one to the other." Thus when we are about to roll a standard die, we are to reason that the die has six sides and can land with any one of these facing upward. As we can see no grounds for preferring one particular side over any other, we ascribe equal probability, 1/6, to each side. Strictly speaking, by pronouncing the probability of, say, face two showing to equal 1/6, we are saying that the event in question is one among six practically indistinguishable possibilities.

At first one might want to object: how can the notion of equipossible alternatives have any application whatever? Where can we ever expect to find truly interchangeable events? In our own example: surely face $i$ is different from face $j$, since among other things it has a different number of dots painted on it! To this the Laplacian should reply: If I am to associate different probabilities with faces differently numbered, what precise amount should that difference be? Furthermore, am I to ascribe the higher probability to face $i$ or to face $j$? Any particular answer, in the absence of relevant evidence, is inevitably unjustified; to avoid unsupported assumptions about the nature of a putative difference, I postulate no differences. Thus, to the Laplacian 'equiprobable alternatives' means alternatives in the context of which the assignment of any specific difference to their probabilities would be wholly arbitrary.

A different objection contends that the classical interpretation is inapplicable when the relevant alternatives can definitely not be treated as indifferent, owing to the existence of evidence for their dissimilarity. Suppose we know for sure that the die we are about to throw is biased, as in the past during a long run of trials one of its sides turned up with markedly greater frequency than any other. We do not know, however, which way it is loaded. Those who rely on the Principle of Indifference would still say that the probability of any one face turning up is the same as that of any other. Henry Kyburg, in his influential book *Probability and Inductive Reasoning*, finds this rather odd:

> the probability of two is therefore 1/6. This is strange enough, considering that we know the die to be loaded.[1]

The conclusion Kyburg mentions goes back to Laplace, who considers not a die but a biased coin, but the argument is essentially the same. It is by no means clear why Laplace deserves to be censured.

---

[1] Henry Kyburg, *Probability and Inductive Reasoning* (London, 1970), p.33.

Admittedly, had he given the reason why the probability of two was 1/6, his assumption that there is no difference between that face and any of the other faces, that would have been not merely strange but inconsistent: it would contradict his explicit postulate that the die is not symmetrical. But Laplace claimed only that our *knowledge* concerning each face is the same, that we have absolutely no more reason to suspect the bias favoring face *i* rather than face j. Thus he applies the Principle of Indifference not to the die's faces but to our state of knowledge as it relates to those faces. He is right in observing that our information reveals only that the die is not fair and leaves us ignorant about the nature of the bias. Laplace is therefore entitled to regard our limited information as providing no reason for distinguishing between side two and any other side, and thus we ascribe the same probability to each.

Moreover, not only is it evident that Laplace can well defend himself against Kyburg's criticism, but in fact it is the latter's own position which seems hard to defend. Suppose Kyburg found himself in the situation just described and that he was compelled to bet on the roll of that biased die. Given that he was anxious to ensure fair betting conditions, what probability would he assign to face two coming up? Surely, it would be absurd to assign any other value than 1/6. But how would he justify the choice of this particular value? Conceivably he could vindicate his decision by invoking frequencies; Kyburg might claim that in the past, among loaded dice, the frequency of bias was observed to be evenly distributed over each of the six faces.

Let us not question whether it is realistic to suppose that Kyburg actually possesses this kind of data. Let us instead consider the situation in which almost all the dice in use throughout the world have been manufactured by the same method, and it is a peculiarity of that method that it produces a biased die once in every so many hundred cases and that the bias is always in favor of one particular number. We shall assume, however, that we do not know which of the six numbers this happens to be. Clearly, Laplace would handle this situation exactly the way he handled the original situation. But how could Kyburg fall back on the frequency interpretation in this case to justify assigning 1/6 to the probability of two coming up? We know for sure that in the past the frequency of imperfect dice being biased in favor of two was either zero or one, and definitely not one in six!

Let us now look at what may seem a more serious objection to Laplace's thesis. Suppose, over the course of a long sequence of throws, we saw the die landing with face two up twice as often as with each of the other five faces. An adherent of the classical interpretation will of course no longer wish to assign 1/6 to the probability of two, since there is evidence that it differs from the other faces, evidence which also indicates by how much it differs. He will agree with everybody else that we should assign 2/7 to the probability of the die showing two, and 1/7 to the probability of it showing any other specific face.

The trouble this seems to create for the Laplacian is: What does it *mean* to say that the probability of getting two is 2/7? While everyone else, subscribing to whatever interpretation, can without any difficulties attach the same meaning to the term 'probable,' whether speaking of a standard die or of a loaded die landing in a certain way, the Laplacian is unable to do so. The die, loaded though it may be, has still only six faces and not seven, of which no more than one displays two dots. How then can the assertion that the probability of two coming up is 2/7 mean that the ratio of favorable outcomes to the total number of equipossible alternatives is 2/7; what equipossible alternatives have we counted to reach this number?

This difficulty (that nothing is available for the Laplacian to count in order to arrive at the required ratio) arises in all contexts where evidence in support of the various alternatives is not symmetrical. It is one of the reasons, says Kyburg, why the classical approach had been discredited and abandoned:

> It was...observed long ago that in many uses of probability—
> particularly those associated with insurance, with vital statistics,
> with scientific experiments in biology and agriculture, as these be-
> gan to be performed in the nineteenth and twentieth centuries—
> the only way of arriving at probabilities was not to compute num-
> bers of equally likely alternatives, but to count instances and to
> take the probability of an event to be indicated by the relative fre-
> quency with which that event occurred among the instances
> counted. [2]

According to Kyburg, in view of the frequent absence of suitable alternatives which might be taken into account when assessing probabilities, the idea of defining probability in terms of equipos-sible alternatives is seen to be inadequate. This major defect of the classical interpretation is what was mainly responsible, Kyburg

---

[2] Ibid., p. 40.

informs us, for philosophers and reflective mathematicians ceasing to regard it any longer as a viable interpretation.

These difficulties may have forced many classical theorists themselves to abandon, at least unofficially, their own interpretation. Roy Weatherford, for example, writes:

> When they [the classical theorists] came to consider various problems in mortality and natural science, however, this [the classical] definition failed them, and they tended to abandon it. . . . But they did *not* replace the official with other terms of likelihood, relative frequency etc. Instead they just continued as if everyone understood its meaning, while actually employing methods and concepts which are clearly inconsistent with what they said 'probability' meant.[3]

On reflection, however, it appears that the Principle of Indifference may have a role in shaping the meaning of probability, even when the evidence unequally supports the various alternatives. In the case we have just been discussing, suppose that there was a large number, say $n$ of trials, and on $2/7$ of these occasions the outcome was two. It is essential that to our knowledge each of these trials took place under basically identical conditions. Had we known of any feature of the circumstances surrounding a particular trial that was absent from the others, and which could reasonably be suspected to affect the chances of one of the sides, we could not have—as we shall soon explain—included it in our sample class. Thus $n$ was the total number of instances of trials conducted under circumstances that are for practical purposes indistinguishable from one another (as well as from the circumstances prevailing now), and therefore the likelihood of every outcome was the same at each one of these trials. Among these a fraction of $2/7$ turned out to be landing with face two up. In other words, out of the total number of equipossible circumstances (i.e., circumstances that did not differ from one another in any relevant sense, and consequently the forces favoring each of them did not vary from instance to instance) $2n/7$ were observed to have been favorable. This means that the ratio of favorable outcomes (that is, outcomes in which the desired result was actually realized) to the total number of equipossible instances was $2/7$.

It is to be noted that the contention is not that in the context of each past trial the conditions tending to turn face two upward were

---

[3] Roy Weatherford, *Philosophical Foundations of Probability Theory* (London, 1982), p. 27.

indistinguishable from those tending to produce a given alternative. We have firm evidence that this is not so, and that certain forces favoring side two are constantly at work. What is being claimed is that, to the best of our knowledge, the factors tending to facilitate or hinder each outcome were the same throughout the entire sequence of past trials. And the crucial point is that Kyburg, or anyone else, whatever interpretation of probability he may be subscribing to, must assume this to be the case. For suppose we had reason to suspect that the conditions under which the various trials took place were not identical, and that the trial #$k$ occurred under circumstances which included a factor $F$ that might with some plausibility be thought of as having an influence on the die, while $F$ was absent from all the other trials. All would agree, then, that if the next trial is conducted under circumstances that lack $F$, then the sample class we are entitled to use for assessing the probability of getting two must not include trial #$k$. It is the essence of empirical arguments to maintain that like cases are alike, and therefore the sample class must not have members which are different in any relevant respect from the instance whose likelihood we are trying to evaluate. In brief, biased sample classes cannot serve as legitimate evidence for predictions.

It is thus a universally acknowledged principle that an assessment of probabilities is permitted only in a context where a favorable outcome in the next trial and in the sample class appear to be equipossible. We are of course not required to be certain that the sample class has no member differing significantly from the instance to be produced next, for in that case we would never be able to make any probability judgments at all. But we are required not to have any reason to believe that there is such a difference.

Thus, for example, in a situation dealing with insurance (with which Kyburg seems to be particularly concerned) the classical notion of probability can be conceived as making sense. Suppose a forty-year-old man with a hazardous occupation wishes to take out life insurance for a year. The company might deal with him on the basis of an ascription of a 92% probability of his surviving another year. They would do so if they found the ratio of favorable instances to the total number of, say, a thousand past instances of forty-year-old men similarly occupied, to equal $92/100$.

We may note briefly that some classical theorists have held views different from Laplace. For example, Bernoulli equated probability with degree of certainty. The gap between the two views may, however, not be so wide. An event is aptly regarded as having a small degree of certainty if it is rare, and a high degree of certainty if it is frequent. But an event is rare or frequent depending on whether the ratio of its actual materialization at instances with circumstances that render its occurrence equipossible is low or high.

My purpose in this section was not to defend the claim that the Laplacian interpretation of probability is the correct one. I doubt if there is such a thing as *the* correct interpretation at all. If the task were to discover what some historical figure had in mind when using the term 'probability,' then it would in principle be possible to find enough evidence to show that the view that he held this or that interpretation was correct. But the actual task of philosophers has been not that of providing a correct definition of 'probability' but merely an adequate definition in the sense that it is coherent, clear, comprehensive, and not too much out of line with the meaning somewhat vaguely ascribed to it by common sense. Naturally, therefore, there is room for a number of viable definitions with different degrees of adequacy.

As already indicated, I certainly believe that the Laplacian interpretation is viable, but I would go further and say that it may be even superior to some of the other known interpretations. A truly adequate definition might be said to be one that tells us what role the value we have assigned to a given probability has, or what practical purpose the assignment of that value has, as well as what made us assign that value, i.e., what the rational grounds upon which we make assessments of probabilities are. Now the well-known subjectivistic theory identifies probability with the degree of belief with which a given proposition is being held. According to the more extreme version of this theory, anyone can have his own opinion concerning the degree of belief that it is appropriate to have, with the sole constraint that the various values he assigns to different propositions must not violate the basic axioms of probability. The translation of the term 'probability' provided by this theory includes nothing about the rational grounds upon which probability values are assigned. But that cannot be held against it, since according to this theory such grounds simply do not exist as it is up to every individual to make the assessment he feels to be right. However, according to a more moderate version, degree of belief in this context does not mean just anybody's belief, which may be held on a whim, but degree of rational belief. This position has the obvious disadvantage that the term 'probable' suggests nothing about the basis for ascribing a given degree to a belief.

On the other hand, the classical interpretation does include reference to both of these fundamental aspects of probability assignments. It refers to the grounds on which probability is assigned a certain value, as it indicates that it is based on the ratio of favorable outcomes to the total number of outcomes. This ratio may be obtained by counting the number of equipossible outcomes, when we know of no difference by virtue of which we should not regard them as equipossible and thus equiprobable, and we know of no results of past trials; otherwise we count the number of trials that were conducted under essentially identical circumstances (and where each outcome was precisely as possible at any given trial as at any other) and where the sought after outcome did actually occur, and divide this number by the total number of such trials. The classical interpretation also refers to the practical purpose the assignment of probabilities may serve. On its basis we are able to predict the future; we are in a position to say that in the future when trials of a basically similar nature occur the ratio of favorable outcomes to the total number of outcomes will approximate to the fraction representing the relevant probability.

## 2. Does the Principle Lead to the Wrong Results?

The Principle of Indifference, in its role as a means for determining equipossible instances, which has been its central role from the earliest history of probability, has come under attack from a variety of directions. The greatest number of complaints that philosophers, as well as statisticians, physicists, and social scientists have made is that under certain circumstances the principle is bound to produce incorrect or even contradictory results. I shall select two of the many examples that may illustrate this point.

Our first example concerns a passage from Kyburg's book we referred to before, where he makes use (as have also others subsequently made use) of what is known as the Bertrand Box Paradox. A seeming incongruity arises in connection with a box fitted with three indistinguishable drawers, $a$, $b$, and $c$. Drawer $a$ contains two golden coins, $b$ one golden and one silver coin, $c$ two silver coins. A drawer is selected at random (by a method by which each drawer is equally likely to be selected) and a coin is chosen at random from that drawer. The selected coin turns out to be gold. What is the probability that the other coin in the drawer is also gold?

*Answer I*: Since the selected coin is gold it is certain that we have not picked drawer $c$. Now we have no more reason to believe that our drawer is $a$ rather than $b$ or vice versa, and therefore we apply the Principle of Indifference: there are two equiprobable alternatives one of which is favorable. Hence the probability is $1/2$ that the other coin is also gold.

*Answer II*: There are three ways in which the first (golden) coin may have been drawn. One way is that the selected coin is the one in drawer $b$ in which case the next coin must be silver. The other two ways are favorable. Thus, the probability that the remaining coin in the same drawer is gold in $2/3$.

Now, as Kyburg has complained:

> But the principle of indifference seems to lead to an alternative result. Merely examining the use of the principle in Answer I, it is impossible to see what went wrong.[4]

On reflection it becomes hard to see how the Principle of Indifference might mislead anyone into making him believe Answer I to be the correct answer. Admittedly, at the very beginning, before we have established what kind of coin turned up on our first selection, there was no reason to ascribe a greater chance to our having reached into drawer $a$ rather than into drawer $b$ or vice versa, as the drawers were explicitly stipulated to be indistinguishable. At that stage the Principle of Indifference was definitely applicable. But after that the situation has radically changed through a significant occurrence that distinctly points in the direction of $a$ rather than $b$: the coin we have selected has been observed to be a golden coin, which is more likely to be found in $a$ (the drawer containing no other kind of coin) than in $b$ which could have just as well yielded a silver coin. By definition, the principle does not apply to alternatives in the context of which there are good grounds to suspect them to be different. In the present case we have decisive reason to treat $a$ and $b$ differently, since we were explicitly told that the arrangement of the coins is such that the drawing of a golden coin is by no means neutral with respect to their relative probabilities, but in fact renders $a$ significantly more likely to have been its source than $b$.

There is even a stronger argument to vindicate the Laplacian approach in the present case. It is not merely the fear that by employing the Principle of Indifference we might arrive at the wrong answer, Answer I, but that the principle inevitably leads to the numerically precise, correct answer. For let,

---

[4] Kyburg, *Probability and Inductive Reasoning*, p. 34.

$A = $ The first coin was selected from $a$,
$B = $ The first coin was selected from $b$,
$G = $ The selected coin is gold.

Using Bayes's Theorem,

$$P(A/G) = \frac{P(G/A) \cdot P(A)}{P(G)}.$$

Obviously $P(G/A) = 1$. Given that it was distinctly stipulated that initially it was impossible to tell one drawer from the other two, the Principle of Indifference bids us to assign equal probability to reaching into any one of them. Thus $P(A) = P(B) = P(C) = 1/3$. Also, since the number of golden and silver coins is equal, and they are symmetrically distributed among the drawers, the Principle demands that we ascribe the same prior probability to selecting a silver or a golden coin. Thus $P(G) = 1/2$. Substituting these values in the above equation we get $P(A/G) = 2/3$. Thus, by scrupulously observing the Principle of Indifference in determining both the prior probabilities of $A$ and of $G$, we are inevitably led to the correct result.

Our second example originated in Keynes's writings. It has been repeatedly used by D. A. Gillies, who saw in it a demonstration that the Principle of Indifference "... leads us at once into a number of grave contradictions," and more recently by Michael Oakes. Suppose we have a mixture of wine and water and we are told that the ratio between the two liquids is at most 3 to 1, but not of which liquid there is more. Thus all we know is that the ratio between wine and water has a maximum 3 and a minimum $1/3$. That is, that the range of the equipossible values of that ratio is of magnitude $3 - 1/3 = 8/3$, and thus we should regard every point within that interval as equiprobable. Suppose now we wish to evaluate the probability of there being at most twice as much wine as water in the mixture. In other words, we wish to evaluate the probability of the ratio between wine and water being somewhere between 2 and $1/3$, that is, within an interval of magnitude $5/3$. Given that this probability equals the amount of favorable possibilities divided by the total amount of possibilities, we divide $5/3$ by $8/3$ and obtain $5/8$. Now the question concerning the probability of the ratio of wine to water being between 2 and $1/3$, is equivalent to asking about the probability of the ratio of water to wine being between $1/2$ and 3, that is, a question concerning that ratio being at some point in the interval of magnitude $3 - 1/2 = 5/2$. The answer to that has to be obtained by dividing $5/2$ by $8/3$, which gives us, not

5/8, but something quite different, 15/16. Thus, through the use of the Principle of Indifference we arrive at contrary answers to the same question.

It may be mentioned that Keynes could have gone further and made the difficulties more acute by showing that with the use of the principle one can obtain other values as well. He could have, for example, pointed out that the information given amounts to saying that at most 3/4 of the mixture is either wine or water. This means that the wine component is between 3/4 and 1/4 of the liquid before us, i.e., it has a magnitude that lies somewhere within a range of $3/4 - 1/4 = 1/2$. The question we were asked may then be reformulated as, "What is the probability that the blend consists of no more than 2/3 wine, i.e., that the value of the proportion of wine in the mixture lies in the interval $2/3 - 1/4 - 5/12$?" The answer is, 5/12 divided by 1/2, which is 5/6, a result different from either of the previous results. Then again we might concentrate on the fact that the wine in question consists of 10% pure alcohol, and thus if the maximum amount of wine is three times the amount of water the total percentage of alcohol in the whole blend is at most 7.5%, and so on. Thus it could have been claimed that through the use of the Principle of Indifference we may obtain any number of contrary answers to our question.

But all this presents to real difficulties to a follower of Laplace. He will, for example, not go along with the conclusion of the first argument that the value of the probability we are after is 5/8. Recall that that conclusion was reached with the aid of our assumption that every point in the interval $3 - 1/3$ was equiprobable, as we assumed there to be no reason to distinguish one point within that range from any other. But it is wrong to make such an assumption since, as we have seen, with the second and third and so on lines of arguments, equally reasonably looking assumptions lead to different results. The Laplacian will thus realize that the principle will be of no use here, and only on the basis of some further information will it be possible to arrive at an evaluation of the probability in question. That conclusion will leave him in no worse a position than others who take a different approach to probability.

## 3. An Objection from Bernoulli's Theorem

A different sort of objection against the classical interpretation has consisted in the claim that it is in conflict with one of the cardinal principles of the theory of probability, namely Bernoulli's Limit

Theorem. For our purposes it will be sufficient if we state the theorem as follows: If the occurrence of a given event in an individual trial is $p$, then the probability of its frequency of occurrence in a series of $N$ repeated, independent trials will be $p$, and can be made as close to one as we wish by making $N$ large enough. Although a rigorous proof of the theorem is somewhat complex, it says something rather simple and commonsensical: the greater the number of occasions in which conditions $C$ are recreated, the more nearly will the frequency of a given event (whose occurrence under $C$ has a probability of $p$) equal $p$.

Kyburg, considering the case where we know that a die is loaded but not in which way, and where Laplace assigned $1/6$ to the probability of it landing with side two facing upward, claims that,

> since there is no connection between what happens on one toss of a die and what happens on another, the outcomes of a sequence of rolls of the die are independent in the sense required by [Bernoulli's Theorem], and therefore the die is practically certain, in a long run of tosses, to yield a two about a sixth of the time. Yet in another sense, knowing that the die is loaded, we should be practically certain that in the long run it will not yield two about a sixth of the time, but should yield two either more than a sixth of the time (if it is loaded in favor of that side) or less than a sixth of the time (if it is loaded in favor of some other side).[5]

I believe that Kyburg's argument stems from a basic error, which will be easier to see if we look at a piece of reasoning of a similar but more transparent kind. Michael Oakes in his *Statistical Inference* declares that the Laplacian "classical conception of probability cannot withstand more than a casual examination." Subsequently, he claims that complying with the Principle of Indifference will inevitably lead us to estimate the value of an event's probability differently from its long-run frequency. He employs the following example:

> Suppose we are handed a pack of cards from which five cards, all of the same suit, have been removed. What is the probability of drawing a spade? We *know* the pack has been tampered with and surely feel this should affect our answer. But the principle asserts that we have no grounds for expecting one suit rather than another, so the

---

[5] Ibid., p. 33.

probability must remain $1/4$. And if this is so, the long-run frequency is certain to be very close to $1/4$, but that cannot be the case.[6]

Now we must remind ourselves that when in connection with Bernoulli's Theorem we talk about long-run frequencies of repeated trials, we are of course referring to a long sequence of recurrences accompanied by essentially the same conditions. 'Essentially the same' in the present context means that the conditions, though they may differ in some respects, do not differ in any which we have reason to believe may affect the probability of the event in question. Thus let us look at the first real trial of the series; it is the drawing of a card from a pack of forty-seven cards which contains either thirteen or eight spades. Suppose the card drawn turns out to be a spade. In that case the second trial consists in a card being drawn from a pack containing either twelve or seven spades. The second trial is thus significantly different from the first: the new conditions have lowered the probability of drawing a spade from what it was the first time, as there are definitely fewer spades now than before. The second trial would also substantially differ from the first, in case we drew a nonspade on that occasion: the changed conditions will have raised the probability of drawing a spade.

It should be evident therefore that we have no grounds for believing we were focusing on a series of tokens of the same kind of event, that is for believing to have assessed the long-run frequency of spades under comparable circumstances, if we have been concentrating on what happens when we continue to draw cards from one and the same diminishing pack. Thus, if we wish to talk correctly about a uniform series of events, we must consider a long series of recurrences of the same kind of situation, where we are repeatedly handed a pack from which five cards, all of the same suit, have been removed. We then should ask ourselves what the frequency of spades is likely to be in a large heap of cards we will have collected through reiterated first draws from different packs, each containing forty-seven cards. The answer clearly is that, given the existence of four different suits among which we have no reason to favor one more than any other, the frequency among these repeated actions with which we will have a pack lacking a full suit of spades is $1/4$, while that of one with some other suit being deficient is $3/4$. It follows, therefore, that the frequency of drawing a spade in the

[6] Michael Oakes, *Statistical Inference: A Commentary for the Social and Behavioral Sciences* (New York, 1986).

*relevant* long-run is to be estimated as $(1/4 \times 8/47) + (3/4 \times 13/47)$, which equals $1/4$. But $1/4$ is also the value we obtain, through the application of the Principle of Indifference, for the probability of a spade turning up on any particular occasion.

That Oakes did not get hold of the appropriate set of trials should also become obvious through the fact that Bernoulli speaks about the frequency of the favorable event getting as close to $p$ as we wish by suitably increasing $N$. The implication is that we can increase the number of trials indefinitely. The series I have just described permits a limitless number of trials. On the other hand, Oakes's series must come to an end after forty-seven trials.

Returning now to Kyburg's objection, the crucial question is: Has he been focusing on the appropriate series of events when he was considering what would likely happen if we rolled the *same* loaded die many times in succession? It does not appear so. After all, at the beginning of his series the prevailing conditions provided no clue whatever for determining on which side the die is loaded. Thus the first trial takes place under circumstances where the total evidence is symmetrically related to all six faces. This condition is more and more likely to change as the number of trials increases, since we are eventually going to observe one particular face (the one toward which the die is actually biased) turning up with decidedly greater frequency than any of the other five. After a considerable number of throws, evidence pointing to a bias favoring face two is increasingly more likely to emerge and to keep growing. Thus Kyburg, no less than Oakes, has failed to address himself to the relevant collection of trials, since as mentioned before in a Bernoulli series each trial is identical with every other trial with respect to those features that have a bearing on the outcome's probability.

Another way of showing that no incompatibility has been discovered between Laplace and Bernoulli is to draw attention to Bernoulli's demand that the trials that form his series be statistically independent of one another. Oakes in attempting to set up a series which he could use to refute Laplace, violated Bernoulli's condition: the probability of drawing a spade on the second trial is not independent of the outcome of the first trial (it is lower if the first trial produced a spade and higher if not). Strangely enough, Kyburg, who mentions Bernoulli's condition and explicitly claims that his series satisfies it, also happens to violate that condition. Recall that Kyburg said, "... there is no connection between what happens on one toss of a die and what happens on another, the outcomes of a sequence of rolls of the die are independent ..." He apparently had the impression that the fact that one toss of the die has no physical effect on another settles the issue of relevance in the required sense. This however is a mistake. As we have explained, because of the peculiar circumstances prevailing, namely that we know we are dealing with a loaded die but know no more, it is inevitable that over the course of successive trials the specific location of the bias becomes increasingly more evident, and that has an impact on the probability of a given outcome in the future. Consequently, the probability of getting a two on a given trial is dependent on the relative frequency of two's among the outcomes of the preceding trials. In other words, the outcomes of the rolls are definitely not evidentially independent in the required sense.

Thus, if Kyburg wanted to consider the genuine Bernoulli series relevant to his story, he should not have been thinking about a single die that is thrown repeatedly, but about an indefinitely large collection of dice every one of which is of the same kind (namely, in the context of each die we knew precisely the same thing, that it is biased in favor of one of its sides which it is twice as likely to show than any of the other five sides and we have no idea which the favored side is). If we roll each of these dice once (or for that matter each one twice, or simply each one the same number of times), then we will indeed find that the larger the number of dice the closer to 1/6 will be the frequency of instances where face two turns up.

## 4. The Principle of Indifference and Empiricism

The many objections that have been raised against the Principle of Indifference may all be said to be rooted in the common contemporary conviction that experience and not reason is the ultimate source of our knowledge of the world, and hence in the aversion to anything perceived as a tendency to impose upon reality empirically ungrounded hypotheses. In the Introduction we cited philosophers who have explicitly stated their opposition to the principle based on their belief that its use in every instance amounts to an a priori judgment of how the universe is bound to be. Any method that takes one beyond the evidence, any practice involving unwarranted assumptions such as an evidentially unsupported ascription of equal probabilities to certain alternatives, violates a cardinal tenet of modern science that all knowledge about the world is a posteriori.

My major contention is that everybody, including its harshest critics, knowingly or unknowingly use the Principle of Indifference and could not get anywhere without it. Before demonstrating this point I should like to emphasize that as a matter of fact it is the refusal to apply the principle rather than the willingness to apply it under the appropriate circumstances that would amount to making experimentally unsupported and hence unjustified assumptions. Admittedly, in the course of the history of philosophy the principle has been put to a great variety of uses (notably by Leibniz, who referred to it as the Principle of Insufficient Reason), among others to speculate about some far-reaching metaphysical questions that were entirely inaccessible to scientific inquiry. However, in the restricted context to which we have confined ourselves so far and shall confine ourselves in the rest of this chapter, namely where it is employed merely as a means of determining equiprobable alternatives, the principle serves not as a license granting free rein to the imagination, but on the contrary it provides a barrier against speculations that cross beyond what is grounded in evidence. Rather than permitting the introduction of extraneous hypotheses, it enforces maximum parsimony with respect to our assumptions.

Consider, for example, the Surgeon General's famous advice that cigarettes are hazardous for the smoker's health. That warning was not issued light-heartedly, but only after an extended period it became well established that the frequency of diseases, particularly lung cancer, is markedly higher among people who smoke than among nonsmokers. Thus medical scientists regarded it as verified beyond reasonable doubt that the intake of large amounts of nicotine and tar appreciably increases one's chances for developing cancer.

The Surgeon General's claim could conceivably be challenged— and some tobacco companies who have a large stake in the matter have toyed with the idea of doing so—through raising the possibility that we are facing here a more complex situation, one which involves two opposing causes. Cigarette smoking as such, it might be argued, in fact decreases, rather than increases, the chances of cancer. However, a considerable proportion of the population has a genetic factor that lowers their immunity to lung cancer and this very same factor happens also to generate a craving for tobacco. Thus the existing statistical results, instead of being interpreted as evidence that smoking is a probabilistic cause of cancer, should be taken as indication that it, as well as the development of cancer, are joint effects of a single genetic factor. Consequently, stopping smoking will accomplish nothing except create unnecessary discomfort; it will not modify the relevant genetic flaw and thus will fail to diminish the threat of cancer. Even if there is further statistical evidence which shows that heavy smokers who, after a given period (say, of ten years), have succeeded in giving up the habit, and though more likely to fall victim to cancer than nonsmokers, are yet less likely to do so than those who continue to smoke far beyond a ten-year period—the pro-smoking theoreticians could take care of that too. Smokers unable to break their habit inevitably have the cancer and tobacco-craving causing factor to a more accentuated degree than those who could stop, and it is this pathogenic condition, and not their continuing smoking, that makes them more vulnerable to disease.

Virtually everyone would recoil from this kind of defense of smoking. The reason underlying the common attitude is none other than the instinctive reluctance to violate the Principle of Indifference. It seems obvious that if we were to lend weight to the idea of a special genetic factor generating both a propensity for tobacco consumption and a weakening effect on the body's immune system, then there would be no reason why some other outlandish hypotheses could not be entertained, in particular one leading to the conclusion diametrically opposed to the tobacco defenders' conclusion, implying that in fact the danger from smoking is far greater than hitherto envisaged even by the most pessimistic researchers. According to that hypothesis, most people who have an innate need for tobacco are lucky enough to have in their genetic makeup a factor that lends them an unusually high immunity against malignant growth. Unfortunately, the toxic effects of tar and nicotine are so strong as to succeed very often in breaking down even an abnormally enhanced immune system. On this hypothesis the incentive to resist the urge to smoke is higher than it is normally thought to be. The stronger the urge, the more likely the existence of the beneficial, protective genetic factor and the less likely a person is to be a victim of cancer, should he only manage to resist the temptation to smoke.

There is precisely as much evidence for a cancer-related benign genetic factor as for a malign genetic factor among those addicted to smoking; there is no more reason to postulate the existence of the first kind rather the second kind. The basic empirical principle to minimize arbitrary assumptions surely bids us to postulate neither the one or the other. In other words, since the available statistical evidence is not differently related to the hypothesis that smokers harbor a harmful gene weakening the body's immune system than to the hypothesis that they have the innate advantage of possessing a special cancer-resisting gene, the Principle of Indifference instructs us to refrain from positing either.

This was but a particular instance of one of the fundamental guiding principles of scientific theorizing, namely Ockham's razor. A plausible way of interpreting Ockham's razor in general is as representing one of the important uses of the Principle of Indifference. The razor instructs us not to multiply entities beyond what is necessary. Newton's first rule of his four "Rules of Reasoning in Philosophy" printed in the third edition of the *Principia*, has been construed as one version of Ockham's razor. It says: We are to admit no more causes of natural things beyond those that are both true and sufficient to explain natural phenomena. The razor has sometimes been referred to as the principle of parsimony, telling us that other things being equal, and given the choice of theories, explanations, hypotheses or laws, the simplest one is to be preferred.

J. J. C. Smart has recently dealt illuminatingly and in considerable detail with the razor and explained that Ockham's central idea was that whenever we have two theories, one of the form $p$ and the other of the form $p \& q$, and these are precisely equal in their explanatory force, we should adopt the simpler theory $p$.[7] Smart also points out that originally the razor was interpreted to be an ontological claim about the way nature works. "Nature never works by more complex instruments than are necessary," said Sir William Hamilton. However, this is too bold an assertion, for among other things it is only if we know for certain what all the objectives of nature are that we are able to judge confidently what instruments are or are not the simplest for achieving them. Subsequently J. S. Mill changed the interpretation of Ockham's razor and turned it into a methodological rule about the way to make choices among competing hypotheses. A possible reading of that rule is, we are told, never to go beyond the evidence, not to make any arbitrary assumptions. Thus if $p$ is sufficient to account for our observations then we must resist positing $p \& q$, since we have no grounds to prefer that conjunction to $p \& r$, $p \& s$, etc., where $r$, $s$, etc., are contraries of $q$. The evidence is entirely indifferent concerning the question whether $p \& q$ or any of the innumerably many alternative conjunctions are to be preferred; it provides us with no more reason to adopt one rather that the other since whichever we were to adopt we would be making an arbitrary decision. We thus invoke the Principle of Indifference and decide to make no arbitrary decisions by not conjoining $p$ with anything.

---

[7] J. J. C. Smart, "Ockham's Razor" in *Principles of Philosophical Reasoning*, ed. J. H. Fetzer (Totowa, 1984), pp. 118–129.

## 5. A Fundamental Principle of Inductive Reasoning

The Principle of Indifference plays yet a more fundamental role in empirical reasoning in general, and even the most elementary kind of inductive argument could not get off the ground without its use.

Consider, for example, the case of the soldier who has volunteered for dangerous patrol duty, and is able to carry with him a single gun only, either gun $A$ or gun $B$. Both guns have been fired frequently before, and it was found that $A$ did not function properly 2% of the time, whereas $B$ misfired 5% of the time. The soldier is faced with a life-or-death choice: he is given no more than the information just described and there is no time left for a closer examination of the guns; which of the two should he take with him on his mission? Ruling out philosophical skepticism concerning the basic validity of inductive reasoning, I do not believe there exists a sane person who in a situation like this would prefer gun $B$ to gun $A$. Any minimally sensible person would surely argue that the large number of past outcomes provides strong evidence that the probability of gun $B$ failing to work properly is 2.5 times greater than $A$ misfiring, and therefore one should choose gun $A$.

Let us suppose that the soldier's CO, a former student of philosophy and hard-headed empiricist, before issuing the rifle questions the patrolman's decision: "Are you justified in making a priori assumptions and postulating that the sample classes consisting of the performances of the two guns provide evidence that is truly relevant to their future performance? Do you have any grounds for assuming that these sample classes were not inadmissable because biased? After all, you are going to patrol an area where many of the conditions are very different from those under which either of the guns have been put to extensive tests; among other things, the temperature, the humidity, the percentage of carbon dioxide in the air, and the amount of ultraviolet radiation are all different there than they were in the past. Do you have evidence that none of these differences has any bearing on the effectiveness of these weapons, and may thus be disregarded?"

Assuming that the soldier is no less fervent an empiricist than his commander, what should he reply? He could reasonably insist that he is selecting gun $A$ *because* of his commitment to a strict empiricist attitude and because he is determined to minimize the number of unsupported postulates he will allow himself to entertain. Ideally, the best thing to do would be to say that there is no assurance concerning the fairness of the sample classes, and refrain from drawing any inferences about the relative reliability of the two guns. This option however is not available, since he is determined to go on the mission and it would be suicidal to enter the danger zone entirely unarmed; it is to be taken for granted that one gun or the other must be chosen. Thus, given that a complete suspension of judgment is not permitted, how is one to make a decision that involves the minimum amount of unsupported assumptions? The rifleman readily concedes that the commander is right that all the instances of the sample class have features in common which the instances yet to be encountered fail to exemplify. Furthermore, he acknowledges the total absence of positive evidence that these differences are of no significance, and may be ignored. But if we are not to ignore them, how should they feature in our deliberations? Should we assume that the bias exemplified by the sample class is of the kind that creates a tendency to make gun $A$ more efficient than it would otherwise be? In that case the evidence at hand would have to be regarded as misleading concerning the future relative reliability of the guns under the conditions the soldier is about to encounter, in which gun $B$ may prove to be the more effective weapon. But then it may just as well be the case that the bias in the sample class worked in the opposite direction, and was such that were it not for it, $A$ would have performed far better, and $B$ far worse. Our mistake then would be that we thought that $B$ is merely 2.5 more likely to fail than $A$, when in fact the failure rate in the absence of the special conditions prevailing in the testing area is more than ten times greater for $B$ than for $A$.

Clearly, the evidence we have provides no clue as to the nature of the bias and the magnitude of the distortion (if any) it creates, and whether that distortion is in favor of $A$ or of $B$. Thus it would be entirely arbitrary to postulate the specific way and degree the conditions, which are present in the sample class and absent from the event about to materialize, interfere with the functioning of the guns. Thus, anyone anxious to avoid baseless conjectures will feel compelled to refrain from capriciously ascribing any specific bias to the available evidence relevant to the shooting capacities of the two guns, and will make a straightforward prediction of their future performance on the basis of their past records.

The Principle of Indifference plays a similar role in all cases of inductive reasoning, regardless of whether they lead to a singular or a general statement, to a probable conclusion or to the confident enunciation of a law of nature. For example, scientists believe they have overwhelming evidence that all electromagnetic radiation travels at the same velocity. But why? The whole body of evidence on which their belief is based, vast as it is, exemplifies several biases. For example, according to many cosmologists the density of matter throughout the universe constantly decreases, thus everything in the past has been observed in a universe more dense than it will be in the future. We have no assurance that a decrease in the average density of matter below a certain crucial value has no effect on the velocity of some type of electromagnetic radiation; are we then justified in asserting that in the future all electromagnetic radiation will continue to travel at the same speed?

But, of course, it is one of the most fundamental principles of scientific method to ignore the possibility of such a bias. Given that all finite sample classes are bound to have many common features that set them apart from future instances, scientists ignore them, unless they have positive evidence that they are likely to be relevant features. This does not just happen to be their unfailing practice but is imposed upon them as an unavoidable necessity. There exist only two alternatives to scientific method as it is actually practiced. One would be to insist that there be evidence testifying to the fairness of a sample class before one is entitled to make use of it. In that case one would never make a single prediction or advance a single generalization, since it is in principle impossible to produce evidence that would itself be above the suspicion of being biased. Thus, such an unbending empiricism would prohibit all conjectures concerning the future and rule out all planning and predictions. The only other alternative would be to consider the evidence and make arbitrary assumptions in each case as to the precise nature of the bias and adjust our inductive conclusions accordingly. Everyone would regard this as wildly irrational.

It should be evident that the charge we cited in the Introduction that the Principle of Indifference amounts to a rule for treating an absence of knowledge (of a difference) as if it were a knowledge of an absence of a difference, was unjust. A correct characterization of it would be that it is a rule requiring that, in the absence of a knowledge of a difference, we should not arbitrarily posit any specific difference. It is a rule against the introduction of groundless conjectures which is indispensable for preventing either all empirical reasoning coming to a full halt or turning it into a chaotic activity unguided by any restraint.

In fact, however, regardless of whether one is prepared to go along with my interpretation of the Principle of Indifference, as essentially a rule for minimizing the a priori assumptions we make concerning how things are, it is beyond any question that all those philosophers who have voiced their objections to it and denounced it as the *bête noire* of clear thinking or as the "most notorious principle in the whole history of probability theory" do not take a single step without it, and trust their very lives to it! It is not that they do so in a way explicitly contradictory to their professed beliefs; it is easy to follow the dictates of the principle without an awareness that one is doing so, for it is so ever-present in all our activities that we tend to become oblivious to it. We might for example ask these strict empiricists how they permit themselves to sit down on an ordinary chair, and why they are not afraid that it will sink into the ground, explode, go up in flames, pulverize, or evaporate? Obviously they do so without much thought, like everyone else, by relying on past experience that chairs under usual conditions are safe to sit on. But how can one rely on past experiences, which after all took place under circumstances not identical with those we are confronted with at present? Surely no chair has proven itself safe in the past under the unique circumstances surrounding the chair we are confronted with now, which among other things include the unprecedentedly high average global temperature over the surface of the earth owing to the global greenhouse effect. The only answer to this can be that they assume that these differences are of no consequence. It is not that they *know* that they are of no consequence—they cannot, since the set of novel circumstances in which they find themselves at this moment has never been experienced before. It is just that they do not know that these differences do matter, and thus following the Principle of Indifference they assume that they do not, and that they are therefore entitled to use the set of past experiences relevant to the present case as a legitimate sample class.

# X

# DEONTIC LOGIC

## 1. The Furthermost Reach of Elementary Probability

Arguably the most dramatic illustration of the wide-flung range of the basic concepts of the theory of probability is the strict parallel that exists between the logic of justified belief in the context of empirical hypotheses and the seemingly unrelated field of deontic logic. Once the close correspondence between these two branches of applied logic becomes apparent we are able to form a remarkably effective criterion by which to determine the status of any putative theorem in the logic of obligations.

Few would wish to deny that such a criterion should prove of vital importance. As is known, a number of philosophers have already expressed doubts about the future of deontic logic. Peter Geach begins his paper "Whatever Happened to Deontic Logic" by saying:

> A branch of human learning that is at first strong and healthy may early contract some malady that distorts its further growth...So it happened...with deontic logic...[1]

The malady Geach is referring to is the high number of recalcitrant puzzles and paradoxes that have plagued this branch of logic ever since its inception. It is not so surprising that on assuming the validity of theorems that are not valid, one should end up with all sorts of difficulties. Philosophers have advanced half a dozen or more contrary systems of theorems in the logic of moral obligations. Given that at most one of these may be correct, a sufficient number of invalid argument forms are in circulation, which provide the right conditions for paradoxes to arise.

Why has it been harder in the context of deontic logic to arrive at a general agreement on what is and what is not a theorem than in other contexts, such as, sentential logic or Euclidean geometry? The answer seems to lie in the relative unreliability of

---

[1] Peter Geach, "Whatever Happened to Deontic Logic," *Philosophia* (1982): 1–12.

203

the method which as a rule is being employed in the case of the former system for the selection of the basic axioms. When confronted with an axiom in sentential logic, such as the law of excluded middle, one can immediately see that its denial would lead to a breakdown of coherent thought. In Euclidian geometry we feel we can unmistakably see, through direct visualization, that (for instance) it is possible to describe any circle with any center. In the logic of obligations, on the other hand, most philosophers have felt that there is no such quick way to determine the status of putative theorem; the correct way to proceed is to substitute a large variety of values for the propositional forms featured in that theorem, and then check whether what the result says accords with our moral intuitions. If the theorem seems to apply in all the instances reviewed, then usually an attempt is made to formulate an argument why it is bound to apply in all conceivable cases. But moral situations are immensely variegated, and thus it may occasionally happen that the vast majority of the relevant situations are similar enough for the theorem in question to hold, yet there exists a radically different type of situation which does not present itself so readily to the investigator's mind, where the reason offered for the universal validity of the theorem fails to apply.

Let me offer a concrete illustration of how an argument form which applies in almost all cases we are likely to think of, and one which can be backed up by fairly persuasive reasoning, will be seen to be invalid in the light of an example found slightly off the beaten ground. David Lewis has advanced a system of deontic logic, which he claims to be both sound and complete, and which is based on thirteen axioms. One of his axioms is:

(a)  $O(A/B) \& O(A/C) \rightarrow O(A/B \vee C)$

which asserts that if it is morally obligatory to ensure the truth of $A$ when $B$ is given, and also when $C$ is given, then it is morally obligatory to make $A$ true when either $B$ or $C$ is given.[2] Axiom (a) appears too obvious for anyone to think of faulting it; simple reflection on the meaning of the antecedent and the consequent should place it beyond doubt that if $A$ is required when both $B$ on its own or $C$ on its own holds, then $A$ is required when either of the two holds.

---

[2] David Lewis, "Semantic Analyses for Dyadic Deontic Logic," in *Logical Theory and Semantic Analysis*, ed. S. Stenlund (Dordrecht, 1974).

Yet Lewis's axiom is bound to be invalid, since our general criterion (in section 3) shows it to be invalid. Here I shall confine myself
to citing a counterexample to (a). In the Australian outback there
used to be a Flying Doctor Service which provided emergency medical services for several widely separated tiny communities. In one
remote place the whole service in addition to a pilot consisted of
two physicians, one trained to deal with injuries, to mend broken
bones, treat badly burnt people and the like, while the other's expertise was confined to internal diseases. They had a small airplane
at their disposal which, in addition to the pilot, could carry only one
of the doctors and some of his equipment. We may then state that
$O(A/B)$, meaning that given a message that someone suffered serious injury has been received, the Flying Doctor #1 should take off
immediately in response to the call, as well as that $O(A/C)$, i.e.,
given a message concerning someone who has come down with a
dangerous contagious disease, the Flying Doctor #2 should rush to
the aid of the patient. Now one day a message arrives saying that in
such and such a place an emergency has arisen and the attention of
a Flying Doctor is urgently required. The message did not specify,
and we shall assume that at the moment it was impossible to find
out, what the nature of the trouble was, and hence the presence of
*which* of the two doctors is needed was also unspecified. Thus here
we are confronted with a situation where we know that $B \vee C$ is true,
without knowing whether $B$ or $C$ is true. It makes good sense to
claim that unless further information is received the Flying Doctor
should stay put, since only one of the two doctors would be able to
make the journey it may be as likely as not that the wrong one, who
can do little to help, will arrive at the place of emergency. Moreover,
during his absence another call which clearly requires his presence
might come in, which will have to go unanswered. Thus $A$ may not
be obligatory given the disjunction $B \vee C$; indeed it may be even
prohibited.

In what follows I propose a method which bypasses the source of
the difficulties that have inevitably arisen with other approaches.
The method is based on a single general criterion derived from a
fairly straightforward definition, through which the validity of any
putative deontic rule may be tested by employing the firmly established theorems of the calculus of probabilities. With the aid of our
criterion we are able to construct a system of theorems that are
bound to be immune to counterexamples, and will thus avoid all
the paradoxes generated through the use of incorrect theorems.

## 2. The Bridge Between the Logic of Probabilistically Justified Belief and That of Moral Obligations

As a practical project it might be absurd, but in principle we could grade the entire human population according to the amount of moral excellence they possess or lack. Let us imagine that we have a set which contains 10% or 15% of people who are morally superior to the rest of us. Let us assume that we have a full record of each member's behavior who belongs to this august body of individuals, and in particular we have noted what happened when over the course of the last five or fifteen years any one of them found himself in a situation in which $B$ obtained. Suppose we find that the substantial majority of these individuals have on all, or a great majority of all, such occasions, acted so as to ensure the truth of $A$ and in doing so they were at least partially motivated by moral considerations. 'Moral consideration' in this context does not have the limited implication of an action deriving from some sophisticated, systematic theory of ethics, but a wide spectrum of possible moral motivations. For example, doing $A$ was accompanied by sentiments of compassion; the agent felt shame when contemplating not doing $A$, or he decided to do $A$ after considering that it is how an acquaintance revered for his high moral standards would have acted under similar circumstances. I submit that it is very highly probable—and therefore one is rationally justified in asserting it—that when these conditions are fulfilled, $A$ amounts to a moral obligation, given that $B$. I would also maintain the converse, namely that whenever $O(A/B)$ holds it turns out that a substantial majority of the set of morally superior individuals acted almost invariably in accordance with $A$.

One comment before continuing. It will be preferable to speak of a substantial majority rather than a plain majority. Many will agree that there exist acts which, though they are morally desirable, are not obligatory, and those who fail to perform them are not to be condemned for moral laxity. Virtuous people are, however, likely to do more than what is strictly obligatory; they often go beyond the call of duty to perform acts of benevolence. But of course, even a greater majority may be relied upon to perform acts that are strictly obligatory. Since our objective is to set up a system of theorems involving not what is merely morally commendable but what is mandatory, we shall focus on what a substantial majority of right-minded people do. We may now assert the following equivalence, which may serve as a general criterion for determining what is and what is not a valid theorem of deontic logic:

($\delta$)   $O(A/B) \equiv (P(A/B) \geq n)$.

which means: Given $B$, $A$ is morally obligatory if and only if the probability that an individual picked at random from the set of righteous individuals who have ever found themselves in circumstances in which $B$ applied, acted in accordance with $A$ and for moral reasons, is greater than or equal to $n$. The fraction $n$ may equal some fraction between $1/2$ and $1$.

Definition ($\delta$), of course, flagrantly violates the standard rules for definitions. It does not provide a clue for someone lacking the concept of moral obligation, even to the extent of enabling him to assess whether the performance of a single act is a sacred duty or a heinous crime. But ($\delta$) is not intended to convey the meaning of something we are not already fully familiar with. Its function is to throw light on the parallel structure of probabilistic and deontic logic, and thus to provide a means for testing the validity of theorems in the latter.

### 3. The Application of Criterion ($\delta$)

We shall begin with rather simple examples to illustrate the uses of our criterion.

*Example 1*: Suppose it is given that $\sim O(A/C)$. Is it then also possible that $\sim O(\sim A/C)$? Recall that in Chapter Three we examined the epistemic counterpart of this question, and concluded that it is quite possible that there be insufficient justification for either the affirmation or the denial of a given proposition; that is, $\sim E(A/C)$ and $\sim E(\sim A/C)$ are compossible. (Recall: $E(A/C) \equiv (P(A/C) \geq n)$.)

Applying our principle it follows that $\sim O(A/C)$ and $\sim O(\sim A/C)$ may also be compossible. And this is only too obviously true. It used to be said ironically that under some totalitarian regimes very few things are permissible, and those which are are obligatory. In fact, however, even under the harshest tyranny there exist some neutral acts which people are neither obliged to perform nor obliged to refrain from performing.

*Example 2*: In our second example in Chapter Three we showed that $E(A/C)$ was compatible with $E(A/\sim C)$. Clearly the parallel holds here too: $O(A/C)$ is compatible with $O(A/\sim C)$. Regardless, for example, of whether today is Tuesday or not one is obliged to refrain from driving when intoxicated.

*Example 3*: Through the use of criterion ($\delta$) we see quickly that Lewis's theorem, $O(A/B) \& O(A/C) \equiv O(A/B \lor C)$, which we claimed earlier to be invalid, is indeed invalid.

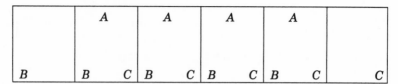

**Figure 19**

In Figure 19 four out of the five $B$-squares are also $A$-squares, thus $p(A/B) = 4/5$. Similarly $P(A/C) = 4/5$. At the same time, all six squares are $B$ or $C$, and thus $P(A/B \vee C) = 2/3$. Consequently, if for example $E(X/Y) \leftrightarrow (P(X/Y) \geq 3/4)$, then $E(A/B)$ as well as $E(A/C)$, and yet $\sim E(A/B \vee C)$. That is,

$$E(A/B) \,\&\, E(A/C) \rightarrow E(A/B \vee C)$$

is not valid, nor is Lewis's theorem valid.

*Example 4*: Let us consider whether a weaker claim than Lewis's, namely

(b)   $(O(A/B) \,\&\, O(A/C)) \rightarrow O(A/B \,\&\, C)$

is a valid theorem. Once more on the surface it looks like it is. Surely when both $B$ and $C$ are true $A$ has to be obligatory since we are told both that when it is true that $B$, $A$ is obligatory, and when it is true that $C$, $A$ is obligatory. For example, if it is morally obligatory to refrain from smoking in a room in which there are small babies and it is also morally wrong to smoke in a room where there is any person who is allergic to tobacco smoke, then it follows that it is even more strictly obligatory to refrain from smoking in a room where there are infants as well as people with an allergy to smoke.

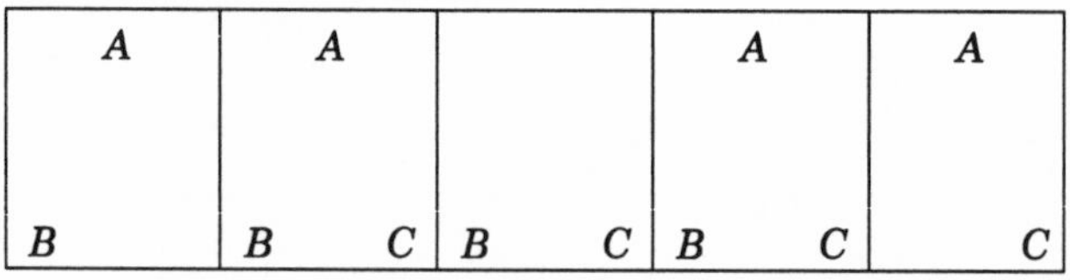

**Figure 20**

In order to achieve certainty in the matter we shall check the probabilistic counterpart,

(b*)   $(E(A/B) \,\&\, E(A/C)) \rightarrow E(A/B \,\&\, C)$.

In Figure 20 three out of the four $B$-squares are also $A$-squares, and thus $P(A/B) = 3/4$. Hence $E(A/B)$. Similarly $E(A/C)$. But only three squares are both $B$ and $C$ and of these only two are also $A$. Thus $P(A/B \& C) = 2/3$. Hence $\sim$E$(A/B \& C)$, and (b*) is not valid.

To illustrate let,

$A =$ Alf is indicted for murdering Bert,

$B =$ Two respected citizens testify to having seen Alf shooting Bert and throwing his body into the ocean on Tuesday morning,

$C =$ Two respected citizens testify to having seen Alf stabbing Bert and burning his body on Wednesday afternoon.

Surely $B$ on its own and $C$ on its own casts more than a heavy suspicion on Alf and hence O$(A/B)$ as well as O$(A/C)$, that is, it is morally necessary that Alf be indicted when $B$ and also when $C$ is given. Nevertheless $\sim$O$(A/B \& C)$, since given a set of glaringly incompatible testimonies the witnesses should be investigated for perjury or attempted judicial murder.

*Example 5*:

(d*)   E$(A \& B/C) \rightarrow$ E$(A/B \& C)$

is a theorem. We can see that this is so by observing that, according to the Conjunctive Axiom,

$$P(A \& B/C) = P(B/C) \cdot P(A/B \& C)$$

and thus

$$P(A \& B/C) \leq P(A/B \& C)$$

since $P(B/C) \leq 1$.

Thus given that E$(A \& B/C)$, i.e., given that $P(A \& B/C) \geq n$, then surely $P(A/B \& C) \geq n$, i.e., E$(A/B \& C)$. We may conclude therefore that its deontic counterpart

(d)   O$(A \& B/C) \rightarrow$ O$(A/B \& C)$

is also a theorem.

That (d) is a theorem was to be expected. It seems obvious enough that when circumstances $C$ demand the performance of two tasks, then when one of them has been accomplished we are still duty bound to perform the remaining one.

*Example 6*: In an important essay Bengt Hansson[3] lists among the theorems on deontic logic:

(e)   $[O(A \lor B/C) \,\&\, \sim O(A/C)] \rightarrow O(B/C \,\&\, \sim A)$.

Hansson's formula looks very plausible. Given that when $C$ obtains then the disjunction "either $A$ or $B$" is obligatory but $A$ is not, that does not imply $O(B/C)$, since the disjunctive obligation may be discharged if $A$ becomes true. However, given that $A$ is not true $B$ is bound to be obligatory. Thus, given the antecedent of (e), $O(B/C \,\&\, \sim A)$ seems to follow.

When however we examine (e) with our criterion ($\delta$) we find it is not a valid theorem, since its counterpart

(e*)   $(E(A \lor B/C) \,\&\, \sim E(A/C)) \rightarrow E(B/C \,\&\, \sim A)$

is not valid. Figure 21 represents a situation where $P(A \lor B/C) = 3/4$ and $P(A/C) = 1/2$ and thus the antecedent of (e*) is true, and yet the consequent is false, for $P(B/C \,\&\, \sim A) = 1/2$.

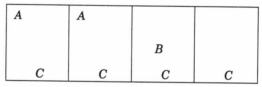

**Figure 21**

Indeed, we can imagine situations in which (e) does not apply. In certain countries, in wartime people up to the age of seventy may be called up for service but those over fifty-five are not required to do any form of combat duty. Elderly people are given a choice: those, who because of physical frailty or because of a lifelong sedentary job would find menial work too arduous, may choose to perform clerical work; others who are physically fit and would be very unhappy if they were made to sit behind a desk all day long may ask to be assigned menial tasks. We may represent all this by $O(A \lor B/C)$, meaning: Given that there is a wartime emergency all persons, in reasonable health, between the ages of fifty-five and seventy are obliged to do national service, either clerical or menial. At the same time $\sim O(A/C)$ (and of course also $\sim O(B/C)$) since nobody is forced to do specifically $A$ or specifically $B$, but each individual is given

[3] Bengt Hansson "An Analysis of Some Deontic Logics," in *Deontic Logic: Introductory and Systematic Readings*, ed. Risto Hilpinen (New York, 1971).

the opportunity of choosing between the two. Now suppose that at the moment the circumstances are such that the construction of air shelters has to come to a standstill because of a lack of material, and there is no other physical work to be done. Would an elderly recruit who is able and ready to work with his muscles, but who is horrified by the thought of office work, be forced nevertheless into clerical work in the absence of any other need? The intent of law may very well be completely clear on this matter: every elderly recruit must be given a choice between $A$ and $B$ in case $A$ is false, not because the recruit refuses to do $A$ but because circumstances make $A$ impossible, there is no obligation to do $A$. In other words $\sim O(B/C \& \sim A)$, in contradiction to (e).

*Example 7*: This paradox has recently been discussed by Ilkka Niiniluoto.[4] The following set of four sentences seems consistent:

(i)   $O(\sim p)$
(ii)   $O(\sim q)$
(iii)   $O(q/p)$
(iv)   $p$.

The first three sentences may arise from the commands:

> Don't tell Penrose the secret!
> Don't tell Sally the secret!
> If you tell Penrose, tell Sally as well!

We shall assume $p$ to be true (i.e., in violation of $O(\sim p)$, Penrose *was* told the secret). Then (iii) and (iv) together imply $O(q)$ which directly contradicts (ii).

Niiniluoto thinks that the difficulty can be removed through the realization that a system of commands may have a hierarchical structure, and when a higher command is violated it disappears from the system. Thus once the command not to tell the secret to anyone is violated by making $p$ true it is cancelled, and the conditional command $O(q/p)$ becomes effective.

The idea of a hierarchical structure exemplified by systems of command may be of significance; however, in the present context it is not needed, for there is no paradox to begin with. $O(q/p)$ and $p$ do not jointly imply $O(q)$. We realize this as soon as we become mindful of a very important point, which though fully recognized in the context of straightforward probability statements, is by no means

---

[4] I. Niiniluoto, "Hypothetical Imperatives and Conditional Obligations," *Synthese* (1986): 111–134.

universally acknowledged to apply to moral obligations. Suppose the prior probability of $A$ (= a marble drawn at random from an urn containing 1% of red marbles, is red) is $1/100$. This is compatible with the probability of $A$, conditioned on $B$ (= the marble drawn was made in Bulgaria) being $99/100$. Suppose I draw a marble from the urn without looking at it and am assured that it is a Bulgarian marble, i.e., that $B$ is true. I would then be right to assess the probability of $A$'s being red as $99/100$. This, however, as we all know, does not change the value of the *prior* probability, i.e., of $P(A)$, which is still $1/100$. Only in order to evaluate the posterior probability of $A$, that is the probability of $A$ once we are given $B$, do we have to use the equation $P(A/B) = 99/100$.

Thus, assuming it to be morally wrong to divulge a secret, that is, assuming $O(\sim p)$, we are to assume that the fraction of people among the truly upright who will keep such a secret is considerably higher than $1/2$. Should any individual violate this moral rule, that does not change the fact that a substantial majority of highly decent people do not violate it, which means that $O(\sim p)$ continues to hold. Yet the reprehensible talebearer is now required to ensure that $q$, because of the rule $O(q/p)$. The last rule is, of course, compatible with both $O(\sim p)$ and $p$; we may infer from it that the great majority of virtuous people, who on those rare occasions (because of an irresistible impulse, or a momentary attack of amnesia, etc.) when they commit an indiscretion, i.e., act so as to make $p$ true, may be relied on to follow the instruction to ensure the truth of $q$.

### 4. Disjunctive Obligations

All would agree that if, for example, I am morally obligated to donate more than $100 to a certain charity then it is also inevitably the case that I am morally obligated to donate more than $50 to that charity. It must be so, it would presumably be argued, simply because "I donate more than $100" implies "I donate more than $50."

This is just one of indefinitely many possible illustrations of the application of a theorem in deontic logic about which until recently virtually all philosophers have agreed was a valid theorem, namely:

(f)   $A - B$ implies $O(A) \rightarrow O(B)$.

In 1941 A. Ross made use of this theorem in his "Imperatives and Logic" to develop a famous paradox named after him. More recently,

Geoffrey Sayre–McCord has published an instructive, extended discussion of this paradox.[5] He points out that by the Law of Addition $A \to (A \vee B)$, and therefore on the basis of (f) we may infer that $O(A) \to O(A \vee B)$. It thus follows that if Ralph has an obligation to repay a loan, then he also has an obligation to repay the loan or to shoot his creditor. Or in general, "if there are any obligations at all, then any action satisfies some obligation," which he finds strange.

There is a considerable amount of literature dealing with Ross's paradox. Many ingenious solutions have been suggested, but I do not think it is necessary to review any of them. Given the strict parallel between deontic logic and the logic of probabilistically justified belief, we are led to the right solution by observing what happens when Ross's problem is raised in the context of the latter. Let "$JGH(A)$" denote "I am justified in believing that $A$ is good for my health." $JGH(A)$ is true if $P(GHA) \geq n$. As we know $P(A) \geq n$ implies that $P(A \vee B) \geq n$, and hence $JGH(A) \to JGH(A \vee B)$. Let

$A = $ I drink milk regularly,
$B = $ I drink methanol regularly.

Then since it has been well established that drinking milk is good for one's health, we have just shown that $JGH(A \vee B)$ holds as well. We are thus committed to asserting that drinking milk or methanol is good for our health. Yet we do not regard it beneficial or even safe to make $A \vee B$ true through drinking methanol.

We are forced therefore to say either one of two things. We may conclude that Ross's paradox is much more serious than it was hitherto believed, since it affects not merely the newfangled discipline of deontic logic but the much more firmly established probabilistic logic. Or else we may give a reason why the difficulty does not arise in the probabilistic context, in which case for a parallel reason it should not arise in the logic of moral obligations either.

Most philosophers would be inclined to choose the second option. They would admit that $JGH(A \vee B)$ holds, but that in general 'JGH' indicates only that I am justified in believing it to be beneficial for my health to make true a certain proposition, but not regardless of the manner I ensure the truth of that proposition. It is understood, for instance, that $JGH(A)$ does not support the claim that it might be good to ensure the truth of $A$ by drinking contaminated milk or milk at boiling temperature. Thus, similarly, while $JGH(A \vee B)$

---

[5] Geoffrey Sayre–McCord, "Deontic Logic and the Priority of Moral Theory," *Noûs* (1986): 179–197.

holds, only in some ways and not in others shall I derive benefit from making $A \vee B$ true: in particular, definitely not by making $B$ true. The answer to the question, "What are the ways in which $A \vee B$ is to be brought about?" is not provided by $\mathrm{JGH}(A \vee B)$; they are established separately.

## 5. Disjunctive Permissions

In 1968, George von Wright raised what he called the Paradox of Free Choice Permission. A clear and detailed treatment of the paradox was published by Erik Stenius in 1982 and suggestions for its solution are even at present still being advanced and discussed.[6] Von Wright denotes "it is permitted to make it come about that" by the letter 'M', and claims that

(a)   $\mathrm{M}(A \vee B) \to (\mathrm{M}(A) \,\&\, \mathrm{M}(B))$

is a valid theorem. There seem to be any number of examples which tend to show that (a) is indeed a theorem. For instance, when visiting a campus of another university and seeing a sign saying "Parking for visiting faculty is permitted in any area specified as 'Reserved for Faculty' or 'Reserved for Visitors '," I should be correct in inferring that I am permitted to park in any area set aside for members of the faculty *as well as* in any area designated as reserved for visitors.

In addition we are also to assume the validity of

(b)   $\mathrm{O}(A) \to \mathrm{M}(A)$,

since although not everything that is permissible is obligatory, nothing can be obligatory without being permitted. Substituting $A \vee B$ for $A$ in (b):

(b′)   $\mathrm{O}(A \vee B) \to \mathrm{M}(A \vee B)$.

And (b′) conjoined with (a) yields by Hypothetical Syllogism:

(c)   $\mathrm{O}(A \vee B) \to (\mathrm{M}(A) \,\&\, \mathrm{M}(B))$.

But as we have already seen in section 4, the Law of Addition implies:

(d)   $\mathrm{O}(A) \to \mathrm{O}(A \vee B)$.

---

[6] Erik Stenius, "Ross's Paradox and Well-Formed Codices," *Theoria* (1982): 49–77.

But (d) conjoined with (c) yields by Hypothetical Syllogism:

(e)   $O(A) - (M(A) \& M(B))$, i.e.,

(e')   $O(A) - M(B)$,

(a3)   $[O(\sim A) \lor O(\sim B)] \to O[\sim (A \lor B)]$,       (By contraposition of (a), and remembering that $M(A) - \sim O \sim(A)$)

(a4)   $[O(\sim A) \lor O(\sim B)] \to O(\sim A \& \sim B)$.   (By applying De Morgan to the consequent of (a3))

It is clear however that (a4) is wrong, for its antecedent may be true when its consequent is false, e.g., when $O(\sim A)$ holds while $O(\sim B)$ does not. By reduction, falsity of (a1), and hence the falsity of (a), follows. That this must be so becomes evident as soon as we consider the probabilistic counterpart of (a1):

$$[\sim P(\sim A \& \sim B) < n] - ([\sim P(\sim A) < n] \& [\sim P(\sim B) < n]).$$

i.e.,

$$[P(\sim A \& \sim B) \geq n] - ([P(\sim A) \geq n) \& [P(\sim B) \geq n]).$$

This expression is clearly not valid, since the probability of the conjunction which appears in the antecedent could be higher than $n$ even if the probability of one of the conjuncts was lower than $n$, so long as the other conjunct was sufficiently high to compensate for it.

To see why there is nothing strange about this result, let us remind ourselves of the point made in the previous section concerning the two separate questions that need to be raised in the context of a putative duty: the question whether a certain obligation exists, and then, if it does, how it is to be implemented, i.e., what the appropriate ways and means to satisfy that obligation are. A similar point applies to permissions as well. Walking is permitted in all public parks in this state, but that does not mean that I am allowed to walk across people sleeping on the ground. We must distinguish between a particular permission, on the one hand, and the various ways in which it may and may not be acted upon, on the other.

When $M(A \lor B)$ is issued, we know we are entitled to make $A \lor B$ into a true statement. However, $A \lor B$ may be true when $A$ is not or when $B$ is not. Thus $M(A \lor B)$ on its own, without some further information, provides no license for any action.

We should note that if we are given $M(A \lor B)$ as well as $\sim M(A)$, then we may infer $M(B)$. This looks obvious enough even to plain common sense. Given that either $A$ or $B$ is permitted and also that $A$ is forbidden, then surely $B$ cannot be forbidden. Hence to make

$A \lor B$ true is permitted as long as it is not done through making $A$ true. And as with every other statement in deontic logic, the last statement can also be verified through considering the relevant probabilistic expression:

$$[\sim P(\sim A \,\&\sim B) < n] \longrightarrow ([\sim P(\sim A) < n] \lor [\sim P(\sim B) < n]),$$

i.e.,

$$[P(\sim A \,\&\sim B) \geq n] \longrightarrow ([P(\sim A) \geq n] \lor [P(\sim B) \geq n]),$$

is true without the probability of at least one of the conjuncts being higher than $n$.

# XI

# PROBABILITY AND METAPHYSICS

## 1. Skepticism About the External World

We have applied the elementary theorems of probability theory to practical questions such as, what the chances are that a die will land in a certain way or that a lottery will have a certain outcome. Later we used these theorems in investigating the role they play in scientific confirmation as well as in our effort to gain insight into various issues in the philosophy of science. I propose to conclude this book with a relatively brief look at the way basic probability theory may be made use of in an attempt to confirm metaphysical hypotheses.

An interesting example is provided by Keith Lehrer in connection with his suggestion how to overcome Cartesian skepticism concerning the real origin of our experiences, which may be misleading in that it does not stem from an actually existing external world. Lehrer denotes by $D$ the proposition that the actual world does not exist and that our sensory experiences are forged by some powerful, deceitful demon. He denotes by $M$ the standard belief that our experiences are caused by material objects and faithfully reflect an independent, external reality. He lets $E$ designate our experiences. Lehrer begins his argument by asserting that $P(E/D) = P(E/M)$. His assertion is presumably based on the reasoning that if there exists an external world correctly described by $M$ then our experiences are bound to be $E$, that is, they are bound to be such as to testify to the truth of $M$, and if there exists a demon bent upon creating the impression that $M$ is the case then once more our experiences are bound to be $E$. On the other hand, $P(D/E) < P(M/E)$, since virtually none of us regard $M$ and $D$ as equally good accounts of our experiences; plain reason tells us that our sense impressions are far more likely to be an authentic representation of a material world than a demonically induced illusion. Lehrer argues that the common rejection of $D$ in the light of our experiences can be shown

217

to derive from a more fundamental judgment of ours, with the aid of Bayes's Theorem. By that theorem:

$$P(D/E) = \frac{P(E/D) \cdot P(D)}{P(E)} \quad \text{and} \quad P(M/E) = \frac{P(E/M) \cdot P(M)}{P(E)}.$$

Since, as he has claimed, $P(E/D) = P(E/M)$, the only reason why $P(M/E) > P(D/E)$ is that we believe that $P(M) > P(D)$. Thus, commonsense belief in the existence of an external world is based on our assigning a higher prior probability to $M$ than to $D$.

One of the more remarkable features of this argument is that probabilistic values are ascribed here in a manner we have not encountered so far. Until now we have seen two methods through which probabilistic assessments may be made:

(i) We establish the probability that a certain feature is exemplified by a given phenomenon, on the basis of past experience. This applies when we are confronted with an instance of a class of phenomena whose other instances we have encountered before. We determine the frequency at which the feature in question accompanied the past instances of the phenomenon under investigation, and if we are satisfied that the members of the class are similar in all relevant aspects to the particular phenomenon in question, then we assign the value of its frequency to its probability.

(ii) When the phenomenon we are considering has not been replicated in the past, we cannot use Method (i). We then may examine the several possible alternatives, and if we can find no significant differences among them we judge them to be equipossible and assign the same probability to each. On the other hand, if we find some reason why one particular alternative should materialize rather than any other, then we assign the greater probability to it.

It is obvious that Method (i) is ruled out in the present context, as we have absolutely no experience (prior to $E$!) that is of the remotest relevance to the question of $M$ or $D$.

Thus Lehrer must have been using Method (ii) in the reasoning that led him to assign greater probability to $M$ than to $D$. We have seen in previous chapters that there may be several ways to arrive at the conclusion that one alternative is more likely than another. Sometimes we know we must not regard certain alternatives as equiprobable lest incoherence arise. In the Introduction we claimed that this was the reason why we do not ascribe the same probability to a standard die landing face six up and to its not landing face six up. There is no scope for this approach in the present case.

In some cases we may conclude that the alternatives are distinguishable because we find that one of them accounts better for a given fact than the other. An example of this was provided in the Introduction where prisoner $C$ was ascribed a higher probability for having been pardoned than prisoner $A$: doing so we have a better account why the guard mentioned $B$ rather than $C$ as being definitely marked for execution. It is quite certain that Lehrer has not used this approach since he explicitly stated that $P(E/D) = P(E/M)$, thus holding that there is nothing in our experience that is better accounted for by $M$ than by $D$.

Finally, there are situations in which a given alternative is declared to be more probable than another because we discover that what appeared as a single alternative should actually be seen as two or more alternatives. Such was the case in the Introduction where "third coin comes down on the same side as the first two" amounted to more than a single alternative. It is hard to see that Lehrer could have made use of this approach.

Lehrer is most probably aware of all this. However, he must have reasoned that since we are admittedly confronted here with a unique situation where none of the known methods of probability assessments are applicable, the only alternative to conceding defeat is to devise some unprecedented approach. What he may have done is to convince himself that he possessed sufficient mental resources to be able to imagine himself a completely disembodied mind prior to ever having had any sense experiences of an external world and of being now able to gauge how he would feel under such unparalleled circumstances. He thus concluded that in that pristine state he would have felt inclined to judge that if $M$ or $D$ were to materialize, then the former would be more likely than the latter.

Perhaps one can offer a slightly more substantial reason for regarding the prior probability of $M$ as higher than that of $D$. Let me begin by raising the following question: Why not say that $P(E/D) < P(E/M)$, because if we were indeed the victims of a demon who conjured up for us the illusion of an external world, then surely he would have manipulated our minds so efficiently so as to prevent us from even having the ability to suspect that perhaps the external world was not real? Thus by claiming that if $D$ were true it would be unlikely that we would have our kinds of experiences which permit doubts arising in our minds with regard to their veracity, we should ascribe a relatively small probability to $P(E/D)$.

Lehrer could reply to this that we do not have much of an idea about demons and their inclinations. Given our ignorance concerning what might please a demon, we cannot say it is more likely or more unlikely that a demon should want to play a rather more complex game with us, e.g., make us on the whole believe in the existence of an external world and at the same time permit us moments of doubt as well.

It seems reasonable therefore to maintain that, regardless of what kind of world we lived in, the likelihood of $D$ would be the same. For example, if in the actual world our brains were so structured that no skeptical thought was ever permitted to enter our minds, that would not rule out $D$. Of course given our unfortunate physical disability we would not be able to entertain $D$, but "objectively" speaking the conjecture that the demon responsible for our experiences was bent upon this kind of absolute deception is as reasonable as the conjecture of a powerful demon associated with any kind of experience that takes place in the actual world.

Now by the RE,

$$P(D) = P(E) \cdot P(D/E) + P(\sim E) \cdot P(D/\sim E)$$
$$= P(E) \cdot n + P(\sim E) \cdot n \ (\text{in case } P(D/E) = P(D/\sim E) = n)$$
$$= n.$$

We have said that it is reasonable to ascribe the same probability to $D$ under any of the indefinitely many possible worlds of experience. That means that the probability we should assign to $D$ under $E$ or under any conceivable alternative to $E$ is the same. In other words, $P(D/E) = P(D/\sim E)$. This, however, entails that they both equal $P(D)$. By a similar argument, it seems to follow that $P(M/E) = P(M/\sim E) = P(M)$. Thus, if as Lehrer claimed we all take it for granted that $P(M/E) > P(D/E)$, we are committed to holding that $P(M) > P(D)$.

## 2. The Argument from Design

Unquestionably the most famous application of probability arguments to a metaphysical issue involves the argument from design for the existence of God. In the course of its long history the argument has undergone many transformations, and here we shall only be concerned with its most recent version based on the contemporary results of astrophysics. As may be known, in the last few decades an astonishing number of extremely rare coincidences, vital for producing a minimally stable universe, have been discovered. There exists, for example, an unbelievably delicate balance between the forces of gravity and of electromagnetism. If the relative magnitude of the gravitational force was ever so slightly greater than the material that makes up the stars they would be pulled together too hard, and if ever so slightly smaller then they would not be pulled together sufficiently to allow the formation of stars such as our sun, and in that case the universe could not sustain any planets and hence no living organisms. This is but one of a profusion of well-fitted, congruent conditions that seem to suggest an underlying purposeful fine tuning in nature, in consequence of which some have been driven to the conclusion that nature seems far too harmonized for it to be just a heedless hap, and thus tend to agree with Fred Hoyle that "the universe is a put up job."

Naturally, there are many who do not find such a conclusion to their taste, and they can question several of the presuppositions on which it rests. Here, however, I shall only consider some of the better-known objections that are based on a misuse of probability concepts.

Quite a number of writers have thought that the theist's reasoning is basically flawed. They claim that to impute design to the universe is to overlook the fact that each specific combination of the constants of nature is precisely as improbable as every other. If there was to be a universe, then something incredibly improbable was in any case bound to materialize. There is as much reason to be fascinated by the unparalleled special features of the actual universe as there would be if some other universe with different unparalleled special features had materialized, that is, there is no reason at all.

To quote one example, Michael Lemonick, a science writer, claims that the inference from the existence of all the infinitesimally improbable, favored conditions in the universe to the conclusion that someone is likely to have planned and willed them "isn't at all compelling":

> We can always, after the fact, find examples of highly improbable events that happened anyway. If you close your eyes and throw a dart, for instance, it will stick *somewhere* in the wall. Before the throw, chances are overwhelmingly against hitting that particular point. You hit it anyway, but so what? [1]

---

[1] Michael Lemonick, *Science Digest* (August 1986): 71.

Similar objections have been raised by philosophers. Most recently an author tells us,

> I need to cut the ace of spades from a randomly shuffled deck of cards [in order to be spared from execution]. The deck is cut, the ace shows—lucky? Yes. Mystified? In need of explanation? No. The ace is there, the mechanics of card-cutting are not magic—what is left to be understood?[2]

Without invoking any of the points dealt with at length in Chapters 4 and 5, let me just simply say that the above arguments are correct as long as all the possibilities are equally improbable, but not when one specific outcome is considerably more probable on a hypothesis which itself is not too improbable. Thus, if the condemned man is known to have paid a large amount of money to the individual who has been appointed to shuffle the cards, and the latter is known to be exceptionally dexterous with cards, then rather than assume that his drawing of the lucky card was the materialization of an event that had no more than a probability of $1/52$, we are inclined to subscribe to the explanation that the event had a considerably high prior probability: the cards were skillfully manipulated so as to save the condemned man's life. Thus, if the theist is right and his postulate of a Divine designer is not of negligible prior probability, then the actual combination of physical constants is by far less improbable on the theistic hypothesis. The existence of such a combination supports the postulate which renders it probable.

### 3. The Anthropic Principle

The favorite objection to the argument from design based on astrophysics invokes the "anthropic principle." The objection is based on the self-evidently true thesis that the universe we inhabit and observe must be such as to admit the creation of observers at some stage. There exist a vast number of universes that are inhospitable to life and hence they have no philosophers wondering why the various physical constants have the value they happen to have. It is only in that exceedingly rare universe in which the required felicitous harmony among these constants exists so as to permit sentient beings to register their surprise at this harmony, that such sentient beings are to be found. Thus there is no basis for the astonishment

---

[2] Jonathan Katz, "Why There Is Something: The Anthropic Principle and Improbable Events," *Dialogue* (1988): 118-119.

that our world is one of those very rare life supporting worlds, and hence no special explanation for it is called for or justified.

Thus Edward R. Harrison in his famous book *Cosmology* says,

> we shall now suppose that not one, but many, physical universes exist and that each is self-contained and unaffected by the rest. . . . The majority of universes in the ensemble contain little more than hydrogen and therefore lack earthlike planets and are without elements such as carbon, nitrogen, and oxygen that are essential for organic life. . . . Our universe is therefore finely tuned and we would not exist if the constants of nature had different values.

Later Harrison says that one way to interpret this is by saying,

> that the ensemble is real and only our universe or perhaps others closely similar contain living creatures. Life exists in one universe at least, and we occupy that universe. Our existence determines the design of our universe. This is the anthropic principle that has been expressed in different ways by Robert Dicke, Brandon Carter and John Wheeler. [3]

One might be wondering whether there are adequate reasons for making such a momentous assumption as that physical worlds, differing in all sorts of ways from the actual world, really existed. We shall put that question aside since an inquiry into it would not teach us much about the nature of probability. We shall, however, inquire into the way the anthropic principle and the demands of probability theory are related.

John Leslie in an often cited paper on the topic rejects the idea that the anthropic principle might be used to refute the argument for design and concludes his remarks:

> the Anthropic Principle cannot be taken as telling us that our world's laws and initial conditions must be "just right" if we are to be here to observe or discuss them *and that therefore* any semblance of a benign conspiracy between them far from excusing talk of God or World Ensemble *ought not arouse our curiosity at all.* Compare: "If the thousand men of the firing squad hadn't missed me then I should not be here to discuss the fact, so I've no reason to find it curious." [4]

The comparison however is not that compelling. After all, in the case of the firing squad there is no question that before the shooting

---

[3] Edward R. Harrison, *Cosmology* (Cambridge, 1981), p. 111.

[4] John Leslie, "The Scientific Weight of Anthropic and Teleological Principles," in *Current Issues in Teleology*, ed. N. Rescher (Lanham, Md., 1986), p. 110.

began everyone would judge the chances for the condemned man's surviving to be negligible. Inevitably, therefore, when contrary to all reasonable expectation he ends up unharmed, we are very puzzled and wonder how such a large number of riflemen all managed to bungle their assignment. On the other hand, given the existence of every sort of universe there is bound to be one which sustains life. And if someone were to wonder: But was it also inevitable that *I* should inhabit that particular universe? The answer should perhaps be: What other universe could you inhabit but the one in which humans exist?

I suggest a different line we might take to meet the challenge from the anthropic principle. According to the currently prevailing view a variety of elements heavier than helium are constantly created through the process of fusion that goes on in the interior of stars. Suppose scientist $S$ came along and suggested that in fact the laws of nature are such that the probability of the emergence of oxygen anywhere in the universe in the course of ten billion years is $10^{-100}$. Surely, even if the ideas that lie behind $S$'s theory are appealing, on a sober assessment we are bound to reject that theory. As is widely known, oxygen is superabundant throughout the observable portion of the universe. How then could one be entitled to subscribe to a hypothesis that implies that the emergence of even a single oxygen molecule is practically of an infinitesimally small probability?

$S$ may have a simple reply to his critics. "You are bound to agree that regardless of how negligible the probability for oxygen to materialize, it is logically possible for it to exist and even to exist in large quantities. Hence you are forced to admit that there exist possible worlds in which the laws of nature keep the probability of the emergence of oxygen at a very low level, nevertheless the improbable happens and there is enough of it to render life possible. It is quite natural that (in view of the anthropic principle) we should find ourselves in one of these rare worlds."

His more impartial adversaries would reject $S$'s argument. They would be willing to concede that if there were only two choices, namely either the hypothesis that our universe belongs to the vast set of worlds which do not permit the evolution of organic life for lack of oxygen or the hypothesis that it is a member of the tiny fraction of universes in which the incredibly improbable occurs and in spite of all the hostile conditions oxygen is formed, then we would have to opt for the second possibility however vanishingly small its prior probability. But there exists also a third choice, namely the universally favored theory according to which the production of oxygen from lighter elements is a common process. In view of this, it is rational to reject the suggestion that the actually prevailing circumstances are very inhospitable to living organisms, and if in spite of the low prior probability for human beings ever to evolve we nevertheless find ourselves here, that is only by the courtesy of the anthropic principle. Reason commands us to accept the standard view which permits the formation of any amount of oxygen, and according to which the emergence of human beings was fairly probable. It is after all one of the most elementary principles of empirical reasoning that when a given fact can be described as a result of extremely rare circumstances as well as the product of conditions that obtain very frequently, we prefer the latter, on the fairly compelling assumption that the probable is more likely to have happened than the improbable.

Thus the theist may be willing to concede that there exist logically possible universes where, without anybody planning it so, all the rare conditions required for life just happen to be present. But he would be reluctant to favor that hypothesis due to his adherence to the methodological principle we have used against scientist $S$: when confronted with phenomena that are essential for our existence and which may be accounted for in two different ways, according to one the initial circumstances being such as to be unlikely to produce them and according to the other the initial circumstances being bound to produce them, we are to postulate the latter. Thus the theist admits that a universe which contains sentient beings is bound to have favorable conditions for them to evolve, yet he postulates the theistic hypothesis which assigns us to a universe in which what was highly probable rather than what was exceedingly improbable has actually happened.

In sum, the anthropic principle says only that given that we *actually* exist it must be *possible* for us to exist. Whether or not such a principle can lead to any substantial result is a question I shall put aside. What is certain is that the principle is not in conflict with the rule that when there are alternative hypotheses to account for a given phenomenon, we are to adopt the hypothesis on which the phenomenon is more probable rather than the one on which it is less probable.

# INDEX

Accommodation vs. prediction, Chapter six
Adams, R., 31
Ad hoc hypotheses, 136–139
Alcohol addiction, 151

Bayes's theorem, 1, 3–5, 21, 26–27, 37–38, 49, 50, 52, 73–74, 114, 121–122, 145, 156, 218
Bernoulli, J., 5, 186, 191
Bertrand box paradox, 188–190
Biased sample classes, 199–202
Blake, W., 16

California Supreme Court, ruling on probabilities, 23
Campbell, R., 123–125
Cicero, 91
Classical interpretation of probability, 2, 181–188
Cognitive illusions, 25–29
Cohen, L. J., 25–27, 147–159
Coleridge's principle, 179–180
Condition of sustained maximum adequacy ($C_{sma}$), 127–132, 142
Condorcet, Marquis de, 95–96
Conjunctive axiom, 3, 209
Content dependence, 173–180
Cooke, R., 175–179
Cosmic coincidences, 220–225
Coulomb-Newton analogy, 82–83

Davis, M., 24
Degrees of confirmation, 58–63
Degrees of relevance, 166
Diagnostic evidence, 151, 159–162
Disconfirmation by supporting evidence, 145–147
Disjunctive axiom, 4, 20
Disjunctive properties, 177–178
Duhem, P., 117

Eells, Ellery, 51–54
Equipossible alternatives, 181
Equivalence of gravitational and inertial mass, 106–108

Evidence: non-additive, 46–50; prospective 163–171
Explanations: catchall, 170–180; deterministic, 173–175; probabilistic, 175–179

Falleta, N., 8
Feller, W., 86
Flying Doctor, Australian, 205
Foundationalism, 44–46
Four card game, 36–39
Four-color problem, 1

Galileo, G., 172
Galton, F., 7
Gardenfors, P., 164–166
Gardner, M., 129, 132–134
Geach, P., 203
Gemes, K., 79–82
Giere, R. N., 30n, 118
Gillies, D. A., 12, 58–59, 190
Good, I. J., 99–102
Goodman, N., 87–90
Graves, R., 15

Hacking, I., 46–49
Hansson, B., 210
Hari, M., 49–50
Harrison, E. R., 223
Hazards of smoking, 196–198
Hempel, C. G., 137
Hempel's paradox, 111–113
Hesse, M., 55
Hierarchical structure of commands, 211–212
Hilpinen, R., 67–69
Hit and run accidents, 22–23, 25–28
Hodge, A., 15
Hoewich, P., 57–58, 99–101, 119–121
Honesty of card-players, 145–146
Hoyle, F., 221
Hume, D., 83
Hypothetical syllogism, 66, 214–215

Jeffreys, H., 73–74, 87, 91–92
Johnson, P., 140–141
Johnson, S., 1, 179

Kahaneman, D., 25–29, 159–160
Katz, J., 222
Kepler, J., 108, 177
Keynes, J. M., 5, 11, 165
Kneale, W., 12
Kyburg, H. E., 4, 5, 11, 165, 182

Lakatos, I., 133
Laplace, S., 5, 11, 84–87, 182–184
Law of addition, 24, 213
Law of excluded middle, 36
Lehrer, K., 67–71, 217–220
Leibniz, G., 117, 196
Lemonick, M., 221
Leslie, J., 223
Lewis, C. I., 5, 39–46
Lewis, D. K., 31–34, 204–206

Martin, M., 63–65
Medical diagnoses, 149–151,
    159–161
Michelson-Morley experiment, 104–
    105, 133

Nagel, E., 175–179
Neptune, discovery of, 73–74
Newton's law of gravity, 73–74, 177
Niiniluoto, I., 95–98, 211

Oakes, M., 190–193
Ockham's razor, 198

Pagels, H. R., 129
Paradox of free choice permission,
    241–216
Parzen, E., 84–85
Peirce, C. S., 16, 41
Popper, K. R., 74–79
Principle E, 63–65
Principle of indifference, 5–15, 36,
    85, Chapter nine
Principle of insufficient reason, 196
Principle of the uniformity of
    nature, 91
Prior probability of hypotheses, 74,
    76, 82–84, 218–219

Reichenbach, H., 12, 39–46
Relevance: of evidence, 163–173; of
    explanations; 173–175; of
    probabilistic explanations,
    175–179

Rescher, N., 129
Restricted special consequence
    condition, 56
Righteous individuals, 206–207
Rosenkrantz, R., 60–61, 90–91
Ross, A., 212–213
Ross, S., 65
Rule of elimination (RE), 1, 4–6,
    Chapter two, 155, 176, 220
Russell, B., 73–74

Salmon, W. C., 82–84
Sayre-McCord, G., 213
Sequences, random and orderly,
    129–133
Shatz, D., 69–71
Skepticism, 39–46, 67–71, 79,
    217–220
Stalnaker, R. C., 31
Stenius, E., 214
Suppes, P., 130
Support measure, 76–79
Surprise events, 99–113
Susceptibility to error in
    probabilistic reasoning, 16, 41

Torricelli, E., 137–138, 180
Trial by mathematics, 22
Tversky, A., 25–29, 159–160

Van Cleve, J., 40
Vinci, T., 123–125
Von Wright, G., 214

Wartime service, 210–211
Weatherford, R., 185
Witnesses: bribed, 158–159; false,
    152–154, 165–166, 209; publicity
    seeking, 148–149; timid, 147–
    148; trustworthiness of, 95–99
World bridge championship, 64–65

Zahar, E., 133–136